Ve...
All rights reserved. No part of this book may be used or
reproduced without written permission.
ISBN 978-0-692-72406-4.

BY MICHAEL GERBER

WHAT MORE DO YOU WANT?

It turns out… less?

So we're really going to do this? I thought I was pretty clear last time: Sooner or later, and probably sooner, poor *Bystander*'s going to get the Back of the Invisible Hand. It's just the way of the world. But you all went bonkers over issue #1, which suggests a couple of things:

1) None of you are any better at capitalism than we are; and

2) Lots of people look around at contemporary comedy and think, "Feh."

Feh? How can that be? With 750 TV channels, plus Netflix, Hulu, Vudu (ooBoo, Gabog, Boogog…see page 104), plus the whole internet on top of that. And all so convenient, Jesus you could die from the convenience — five seconds after I think "Hugh Laurie," I'm streaming a 27-year-old sketch from his BBC show. Comedywise, what more could anyone want?

Maybe… less?

If you ask me, and let's pretend you did, our world began August 24, 1853, when a man named George Crum invented the potato chip. Potato chips are the ultimate modern food: cheap, omnipresent, vaguely pleasant, and almost nutrient-free. We all eat them by the bucket, because they're designed not to deliver nourishment but *entertainment*. We should write this nuance down, so future archaeologists aren't confused.

MICHAEL GERBER

(@mgerber937) is the Chairman of *The American Bystander*.

Obesity, poor nutrition and food deserts be damned, the corporations running our food supply spend billions conjuring new ways to tempt our potato-fugged palates. My favorite was Frito-Lay's olestra, a chemical engineered to enable chips to pass undigested, giving the eater the fun of eating without those pesky side-effects. (Except, famously, a bit of "anal leakage.")

Over the last twenty years, we've seen the potato-chipping of media in general and comedy in particular. Comedy is now cheap, omnipresent, vaguely pleasant, and almost nutrient-free. From cheesy to spicy, there's a flavor for every taste, delivered in an instant, designed to pass undigested just in time for the next joke. We even use the same word: "binging." And after the binge, the purge — that's what social media is for. Every comments section ever? Anal leakage.

The *Bystander* is the comedy equivalent of "slow food," the anti-potato chip. Expensive, hard-to-find, difficult to consume, these issues are practically bespoke; I know some of you are still digesting #1. I worked on this one for five solid months, and it's full of rich, good stuff. Take your time with it.

When I tell people our magazine isn't aimed at college kids — by the way, the only people who can live on potato chips and not feel like shit — they actually look a little concerned for us. *Don't you guys know how this game works?* Sure we do, but we also know what it does to people. We don't want you checking our website or Facebook or Twitter a zillion times a day. We don't want you to substitute consuming our comedy for living your life. We actually *like* you.

We want you to read *The Bystander*, laugh — then go back into the real world, the setup upon which all great punchlines depend. If George Crum were here, I think he'd agree with me: our current oversupply of comedy aids and abets the informational equivalent of obesity, poor nutrition and food deserts.

In other words, The Donald.

In 1948, satirists scuttled the GOP candidate by calling him "the little man on the wedding cake." Now, our poor confused country is actually considering a guy with no political experience, who openly brags about the size of his wang. Something is very off here. We're generating more satire than ever, some of it quite exquisite. But it's seeming to have no — or even the opposite — effect.

In general, satirists are painfully self-conscious people with an overactive sense of shame. That's why, God love us, we think *jokes* are the way to change the world. Trump is the opposite kind of animal; he's so unself-conscious, he's practically unconscious. A person without shame is immune to ridicule; there's a level of narcissism against with mere satire is powerless. We joke because we must; but we all have to acknowledge that thirty years of razor-sharp satire has had roughly the same effect on Mr. Trump as the atomic bomb had on Godzilla. Oh, for the days when he was just a New York real estate asshole.

Food or comedy, corporations want to feed us to bursting with fake stuff; it's up to us to find what's meaningful and nourishing, and leave the rest. Too much comedy makes satire mere entertainment — or worse, *publicity*. Come November, I hope the joke's not on us. ☥

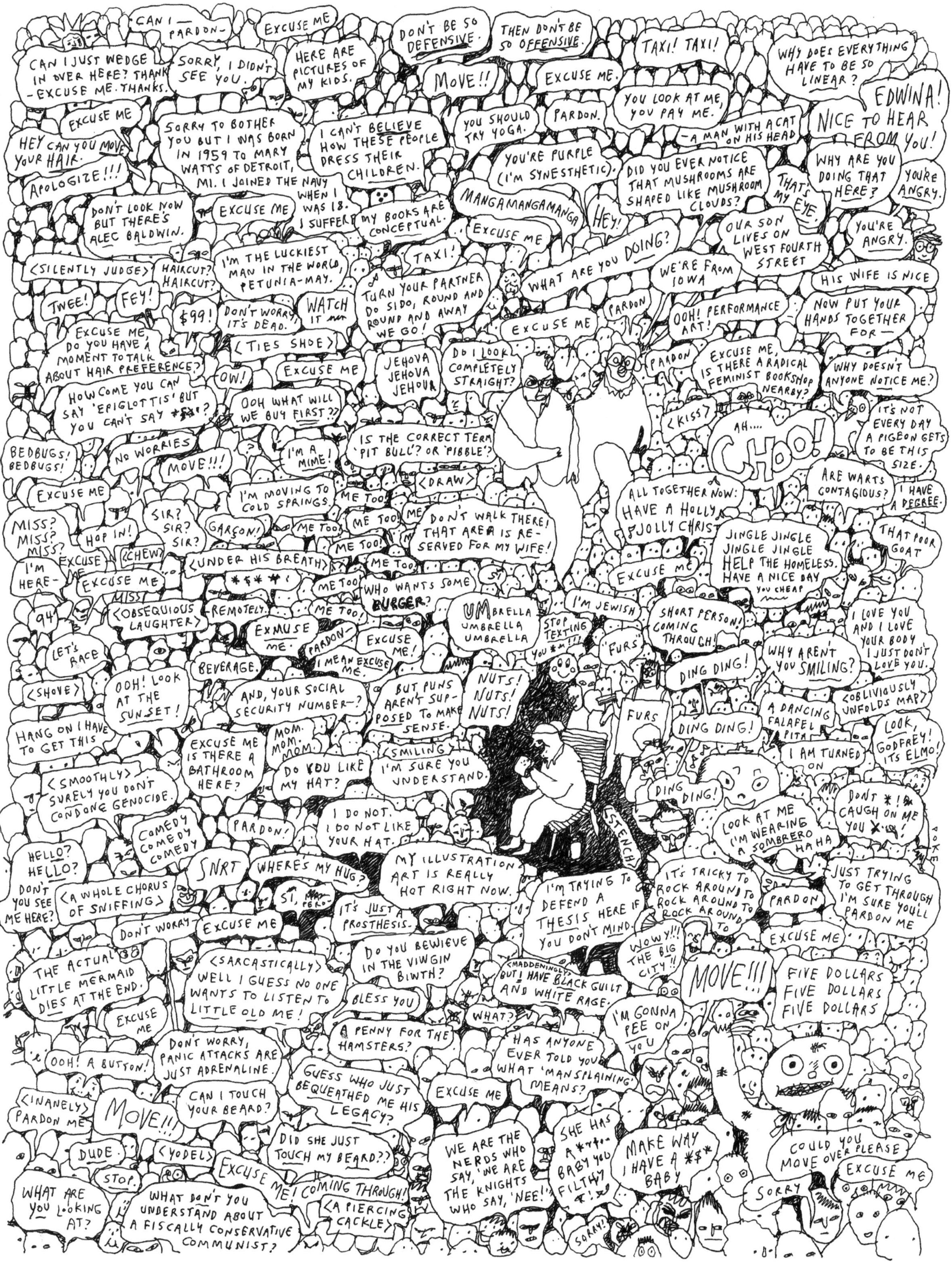
CAN I —
PARDON —
EXCUSE ME
DON'T BE SO DEFENSIVE.
THEN DON'T BE SO OFFENSIVE.
TAXI! TAXI!
WHY DOES EVERYTHING HAVE TO BE SO LINEAR?
CAN I JUST WEDGE IN OVER HERE? THANKS -EXCUSE ME. THANKS.
SORRY, I DIDN'T SEE YOU.
HERE ARE PICTURES OF MY KIDS.
MOVE!!
EXCUSE ME.
YOU LOOK AT ME, YOU PAY ME.
EDWINA! NICE TO HEAR FROM YOU!
EXCUSE ME
HEY CAN YOU MOVE YOUR HAIR.
SORRY TO BOTHER YOU BUT I WAS BORN IN 1959 TO MARY WATTS OF DETROIT, MI. I JOINED THE NAVY WHEN I WAS 18. I SUFFER
I CAN'T BELIEVE HOW THESE PEOPLE DRESS THEIR CHILDREN.
YOU SHOULD TRY YOGA.
PARDON.
— A MAN WITH A CAT ON HIS HEAD
APOLOGIZE!!!
YOU'RE PURPLE (I'M SYNESTHETIC)
DID YOU EVER NOTICE THAT MUSHROOMS ARE SHAPED LIKE MUSHROOM CLOUDS?
THAT'S MY EYE
WHY ARE YOU DOING THAT HERE?
YOU'RE ANGRY.
DON'T LOOK NOW BUT THERE'S ALEC BALDWIN.
EXCUSE ME
MY BOOKS ARE CONCEPTUAL.
MANGAMANGAMANGA
HEY!
EXCUSE ME
OUR SON LIVES ON WEST FOURTH STREET
YOU'RE ANGRY.
<SILENTLY JUDGE>
HAIRCUT? HAIRCUT?
I'M THE LUCKIEST MAN IN THE WORLD, PETUNIA-MAY.
TAXI!
WHAT ARE YOU DOING?
WE'RE FROM IOWA
HIS WIFE IS NICE
TWEE!
FEY!
$99!
DON'T WORRY, IT'S DEAD.
WATCH IT
TURN YOUR PARTNER DO SIDO, ROUND AND ROUND AND AWAY WE GO!
PARDON
OOH! PERFORMANCE ART!
NOW PUT YOUR HANDS TOGETHER FOR —
EXCUSE ME, DO YOU HAVE A MOMENT TO TALK ABOUT HAIR PREFERENCE?
<TIES SHOE>
EXCUSE ME
JEHOVA JEHOVA JEHOVA
DO I LOOK COMPLETELY STRAIGHT?
PARDON
EXCUSE ME, IS THERE A RADICAL FEMINIST BOOKSHOP NEARBY?
WHY DOESN'T ANYONE NOTICE ME?
HOW COME YOU CAN SAY 'EPIGLOTTIS' BUT YOU CAN'T SAY *$!*?
OW!
OOH WHAT WILL WE BUY FIRST??
<KISS>
AH.... CHOO!
IT'S NOT EVERY DAY A PIGEON GETS TO BE THIS SIZE.
BEDBUGS! BEDBUGS!
NO WORRIES
MOVE!!!
I'M A MIME!
IS THE CORRECT TERM 'PIT BULL'? OR 'PIBBLE'?
<DRAW>
ARE WARTS CONTAGIOUS?
I HAVE A DEGREE.
EXCUSE ME
I'M MOVING TO COLD SPRINGS.
ME TOO!
ALL TOGETHER NOW: HAVE A HOLLY JOLLY CHRIS
MISS? MISS? MISS?
HOP IN!
SIR? SIR? SIR?
GARÇON!
ME TOO
ME TOO
ME
DON'T WALK THERE! THAT AREA IS RESERVED FOR MY WIFE!
ME TOO!
JINGLE JINGLE JINGLE JINGLE HELP THE HOMELESS. HAVE A NICE DAY YOU CHEAP
THAT POOR GOAT
I'M HERE-
EXCUSE ME
<CHEW>
<UNDER HIS BREATH>
ME TOO
EXCUSE ME
$#*
ME TOO
WHO WANTS SOME BURGER?
EXCUSE ME
MISS!
94
<OBSEQUIOUS LAUGHTER>
REMOTELY.
ME TOO!
UMBRELLA UMBRELLA UMBRELLA
I'M JEWISH
STOP TEXTING YOU *#!!!
SHORT PERSON! COMING THROUGH!
I LOVE YOU AND I LOVE YOUR BODY I JUST DON'T LOVE YOU.
LET'S RACE
EXMUSE ME
PARDON —
EXCUSE ME!
I MEAN EXCUSE ME.
BEVERAGE.
"FURS"
WHY AREN'T YOU SMILING?
DING DING!
<SHOVE>
OOH! LOOK AT THE SUNSET!
AND, YOUR SOCIAL SECURITY NUMBER—?
BUT PUNS AREN'T SUPPOSED TO MAKE SENSE.
NUTS! NUTS! NUTS!
FURS
A DANCING FALAFEL PITA
<OBLIVIOUSLY UNFOLDS MAP>
LOOK, GODFREY! ITS ELMO!
HANG ON I HAVE TO GET THIS
EXCUSE ME IS THERE A BATHROOM HERE?
MOM. MOM. MOM.
DO YOU LIKE MY HAT?
<SMILING> I'M SURE YOU UNDERSTAND.
DING DING!
I AM TURNED ON
<SMOOTHLY> SURELY YOU DON'T CONDONE GENOCIDE.
DING DING!
DON'T *!$ CAUGH ON ME YOU *@!
I DO NOT. I DO NOT LIKE YOUR HAT.
COMEDY COMEDY COMEDY
PARDON!
<STENCH>
LOOK AT ME I'M WEARING A SOMBRERO HA HA
HELLO? HELLO?
SNRT
WHERE'S MY HUG?
MY ILLUSTRATION ART IS REALLY HOT RIGHT NOW.
JUST TRYING TO GET THROUGH I'M SURE YOU'LL PARDON ME
DON'T YOU SEE ME HERE?
<A WHOLE CHORUS OF SNIFFING>
SI, PERO
IT'S JUST A PROSTHESIS.
I'M TRYING TO DEFEND A THESIS HERE IF YOU DON'T MIND.
IT'S TRICKY TO ROCK AROUND TO ROCK AROUND TO ROCK AROUND TO
PARDON
DON'T WORRY
EXCUSE ME
EXCUSE ME
THE ACTUAL LITTLE MERMAID DIES AT THE END.
<SARCASTICALLY> WELL I GUESS NO ONE WANTS TO LISTEN TO LITTLE OLD ME!
DO YOU BEWIEVE IN THE VIWGIN BIWTH?
<MADDENINGLY> BUT I HAVE BLACK GUILT AND WHITE RAGE.
WOWY!!! THE BIG CITY!!
MOVE!!!
FIVE DOLLARS FIVE DOLLARS FIVE DOLLARS
EXCUSE ME
BLESS YOU
WHAT?
I'M GONNA PEE ON YOU
OOH! A BUTTON!
DON'T WORRY, PANIC ATTACKS ARE JUST ADRENALINE.
A PENNY FOR THE HAMSTERS?
HAS ANYONE EVER TOLD YOU WHAT 'MANSPLAINING' MEANS?
<INANELY> PARDON ME
MOVE!!!
CAN I TOUCH YOUR BEARD?
GUESS WHO JUST BEQUEATHED ME HIS LEGACY?
EXCUSE ME
DUDE
<YODEL>
DID SHE JUST TOUCH MY BEARD??
WE ARE THE NERDS WHO SAY, 'WE ARE THE KNIGHTS WHO SAY, 'NEE!'
SHE HAS A *#+! BABY YOU FILTHY *!
MAKE WAY I HAVE A *$* BABY
COULD YOU MOVE OVER PLEASE
EXCUSE ME
STOP.
EXCUSE ME! COMING THROUGH!
WHAT ARE YOU LOOKING AT?
WHAT DON'T YOU UNDERSTAND ABOUT A FISCALLY CONSERVATIVE COMMUNIST?
<A PIERCING CACKLE>
SORRY!
SORRY
POKE

TABLE OF CONTENTS

Whole No. 2 • Spring 2016 • Americanbystander.org
Founded in 1982 by Brian McConnachie. Refounded in 2016 by Michael Gerber
Alan Goldberg, and Brian McConnachie

M.K. BROWN

The AMERICAN BYSTANDER

DEPARTMENTS

Frontispiece: "Easter Island" *by Bill Lee* 1
Publisher's Letter *by Michael Gerber* 2
News and Notes 9
Classifieds 120
Crossword #1: "Comic Duo-Logues"
by Matt Matera & Alan Goldberg 124

GALLIMAUFRY

Mallory Ortberg, John Howell Harris, Jack Silbert, David Misch, Matthew Grzecki, Jack Handey, Paul Lander, Megan Koester, Mike Shear, Jay Ruttenberg, Matthew Powers, Dennis Perrin, Mark Bazer, The Covert Comic, Al Jean, Eric Branscum, Katie Schwartz, Ryan Nyburg, River Clegg, Joey Green, Geoffrey Golden, Sean Kelly.

SHORT STUFF

The Woman Who Forgot *by MK Brown* 5
The Great Pretenders *by Julia Wertz*....................................12
Musicians You Should Know
  by Jay Ruttenberg & Mike Reddy 27
Jury Selection *by Simon Rich* 30
Eleven Short Stories *by Jack Handey*...................................32
8PM - Curb Your Enthusiasm *by Megan Koester* 34
Have A Nice Day, Forever *by Doug Kirby & Ken Smith* 36
If Stanley Tucci Was Your Boyfriend *by Mallory Ortberg* 39
Welcome to Infinity World *by John Howell Harris*.................41
Unbroken *by Dave Hanson* 42
What I Will Say To The Three People At My Book Reading
  by Merrill Markoe 44
The Ding-Dong Hoodlum Priest *by Brian McConnachie* 46
The Right Drink for Any Occasion *by Michael Thornton*.......48
Leash-less in Seattle *by Shary Flenniken*... 49
Just So You Know *by Bill Franzen* 50
Anapest *by David Chelsea* 91
With Bells On *by Dave Hill* 93
Making My Amends *by Merrill Markoe* 97
Zayde's First Blow Job *by Katie Schwartz*............................99
There Are No Free Elephant Rides in Life
  by Brian McConnachie...102
I Can Teach *Anyone* To Play Piano! *by Michael Ian Black*...104

CHAIRMAN Michael Gerber
HEAD WRITER Brian McConnachie
SENIOR EDITOR Alan Goldberg

CONTRIBUTORS Ron Barrett, Charles Barsotti, Mark Bazer, Kate Beaton, Louisa Bertman, Michael Ian Black, Chris Bonno, Nate Bramble, Eric Branscum, Jamie Brew, M.K. Brown, Roz Chast, David Chelsea, Seymour Chwast, River Clegg, Howard Cruse, John Cuneo, Liza Donnelly, Xeth Feinberg, Liana Finck, Shary Flenniken, Bill Franzen, Rick Geary, David Geiser, Geoffrey Golden, Joey Green, Matthew Grzecki, Pia Guerra, Jack Handey, Dave Hanson, Todd Hanson, John Howell Harris, Sam Henderson, Brandon Hicks, Dave Hill, Al Jean, Farley Katz, Sean Kelly, Doug Kirby, Megan Koester, Peter Kuper, Ken Krimstein, David Lancaster, Paul Lander, Bill Lee, Merrill Markoe, Scott Marshall, Matt Matera, Rick Meyerowitz, David Misch, P.S. Mueller, Ryan Nyburg, Joe Oesterle, Mallory Ortberg, David Owen, Laura Park, Dennis Perrin, Ethan Persoff, Mimi Pond, Matthew Powers, Jonathan Plotkin, Mike Reddy, Mike Reiss, Simon Rich, Marc Rosenthal, Jay Ruttenberg, Mike Sacks, Katie Schwartz, Nell Scovell, Cris Shapan, Mike Shear, Jack Silbert, Michael Sloan, Ken Smith, Mick Stevens, Len Stokes, B.K. Taylor, The Covert Comic, Michael Thornton, Tom Toro, D. Watson, Julia Wertz, Shannon Wheeler, Steve Young, Jack Ziegler
COPYEDITING Cheryl Levenbrown
THANKS TO Rae Barsotti, Kate Powers, Karen Backus, Lisa Cohen, Molly Bernstein, Barry Milberg, Joe Lopez, Eliot Ivanhoe, Thomas Simon, Diane Boureston and many, many others.
NAMEPLATE BY Mark Simonson
ISSUE CREATED BY Michael Gerber

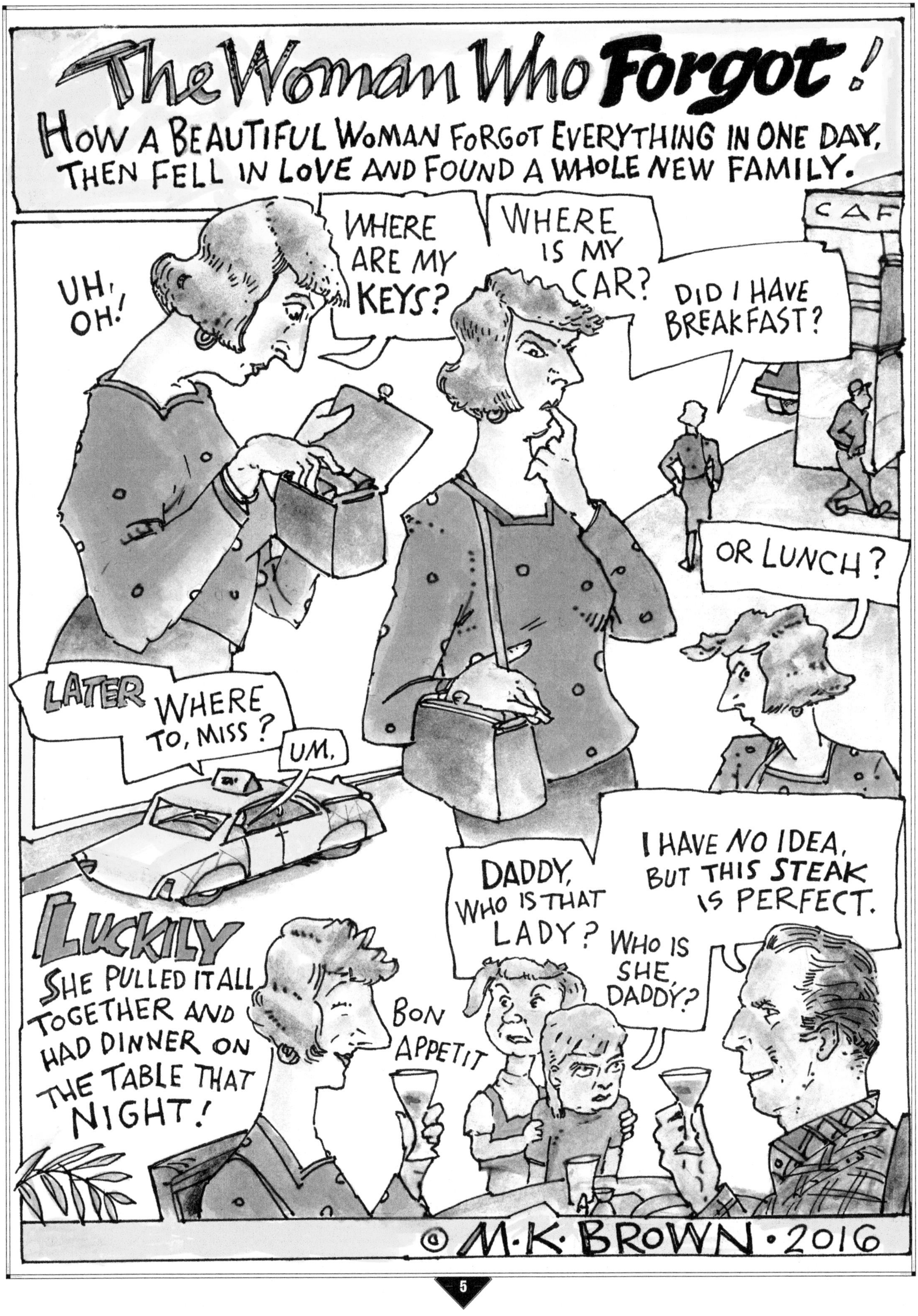

The Woman Who Forgot!
HOW A BEAUTIFUL WOMAN FORGOT EVERYTHING IN ONE DAY, THEN FELL IN LOVE AND FOUND A WHOLE NEW FAMILY.
UH, OH!
WHERE ARE MY KEYS?
WHERE IS MY CAR?
DID I HAVE BREAKFAST?
OR LUNCH?
LATER
WHERE TO, MISS?
UM.
LUCKILY
SHE PULLED IT ALL TOGETHER AND HAD DINNER ON THE TABLE THAT NIGHT!
BON APPETIT
DADDY, WHO IS THAT LADY?
WHO IS SHE, DADDY?
I HAVE NO IDEA, BUT THIS STEAK IS PERFECT.
© M·K· BROWN · 2016

FEATURES

The Mad Mascot of Soho **by Ron Barrett** 52
The End **by Nell Scovell** 54
Odd Birds **by Rick Meyerowitz and Sean Kelly**..................57
#sicsemperpapyrus **by Todd Hanson**..................62
I Love My Gun **by Seymour Chwast**..................67
The Dracula Letters
by Jack Handey and Brian McConnachie..................68
The Elements of Strunk **by Jamie Brew** 71
Interview: Sam Lipsyte **by Mike Sacks** 75
What Went Wrong **by Steve Young**..................82
I Conquered Kilimanjaro (…Nearly!) **by Mike Reiss** 86

COMICS

Weather Report **by Peter Kuper** 106
Public Hair **by Julia Wertz and Laura Park**..................107
The Day Dad Came to Breakfast **by Howard Cruse**..................111
John Wilcock: New York Years — Jean Shepherd
by Ethan Persoff and Scott Marshall..................112
Towel Off! **by Nate Bramble**..................114
The Diary of Merrill Markoe **by Merrill Markoe**..................115
What's An Aging Hipster to Do? **by Mimi Pond**..................127

CARTOONS & ILLUSTRATIONS BY

Ron Barrett, Charles Barsotti, Kate Beaton, Louisa Bertman, Chris Bonno, M.K. Brown, Roz Chast, David Chelsea, Seymour Chwast, John Cuneo, Liza Donnelly, Xeth Feinberg, Liana Finck, Shary Flenniken, Rick Geary, David Geiser, Pia Guerra, Sam Henderson, Brandon Hicks, Farley Katz, Ken Krimstein, Peter Kuper, Rick Meyerowitz, P.S. Mueller, Joe Oesterle, David Owen, Jonathan Plotkin, Mike Reddy, Marc Rosenthal, Cris Shapan, Mark Simonson, Michael Sloan, Mick Stevens, Len Stokes, B.K. Taylor, Tom Toro, D. Watson, Julia Wertz, Shannon Wheeler, Derek Yaniger, and Jack Ziegler.

COVER by Charles Barsotti, courtesy of Rae Barsotti. Thanks to Scott Marshall and Tom Toro.

"God, they're needy."

ACKNOWLEDGMENTS

All material is ©2016 its creators, all rights reserved; please do not reproduce or distribute it without written consent of the creators and *The American Bystander*. The following material has previously appeared, and is reprinted here with permission of the authors: Mallory Ortberg's wonderful "Every Q and A Ever" and "If Stanley Tucci Were Your Boyfriend" appeared at the equally wonderful The-Toast.com. "Eleanor Roosevelt" was on John Howell Harris' Bartlettsfamiliarquotations.tumblr.com. "Possession Of Documents" ran on Jack Silbert's Saltinwound.com. Ruttenberg & Reddy's "Musicians You Should Know" is from musiciansyoushouldknow.tumblr. com; Jay's Bill Murray piece appeared in his awesome *Lowbrow Reader*. Michael Sloan's "Memory Box: Hitler Tree" is from michael-sloanillustration.tumblr. com. Kate Beaton's fabulous "Cheshire Cat," is from harkavagrant.com of course. "Anapest 1-4" is just one of many delights to be found at davidchelsea.com. Howard Cruse's heartbreaking "The Day Dad Came to Breakfast," is from Howardcruse.com. "John Wilcock: The New York Years—Jean Shepherd: debuted at Boingboing.net, and later in Persoff & Marshall's Wilcock collection. "With Bells On," excerpted from *Dave Hill Doesn't Live Here Anymore*, is reprinted courtesy of the author and Blue Rider Press. "Zayde's First Blow Job" originally appeared in *Heeb*, and is reprinted with permission of the author. "Public Hair" appeared in *Papercutter #6*, and is reprinted with permission of the authors.

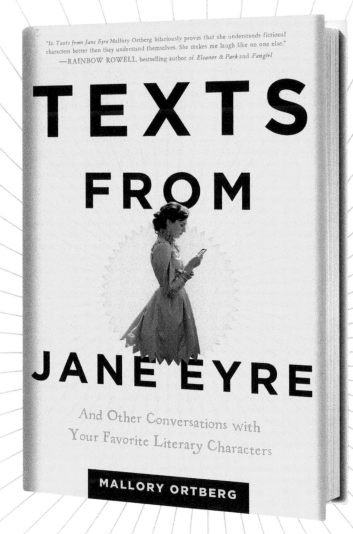

D. WATSON

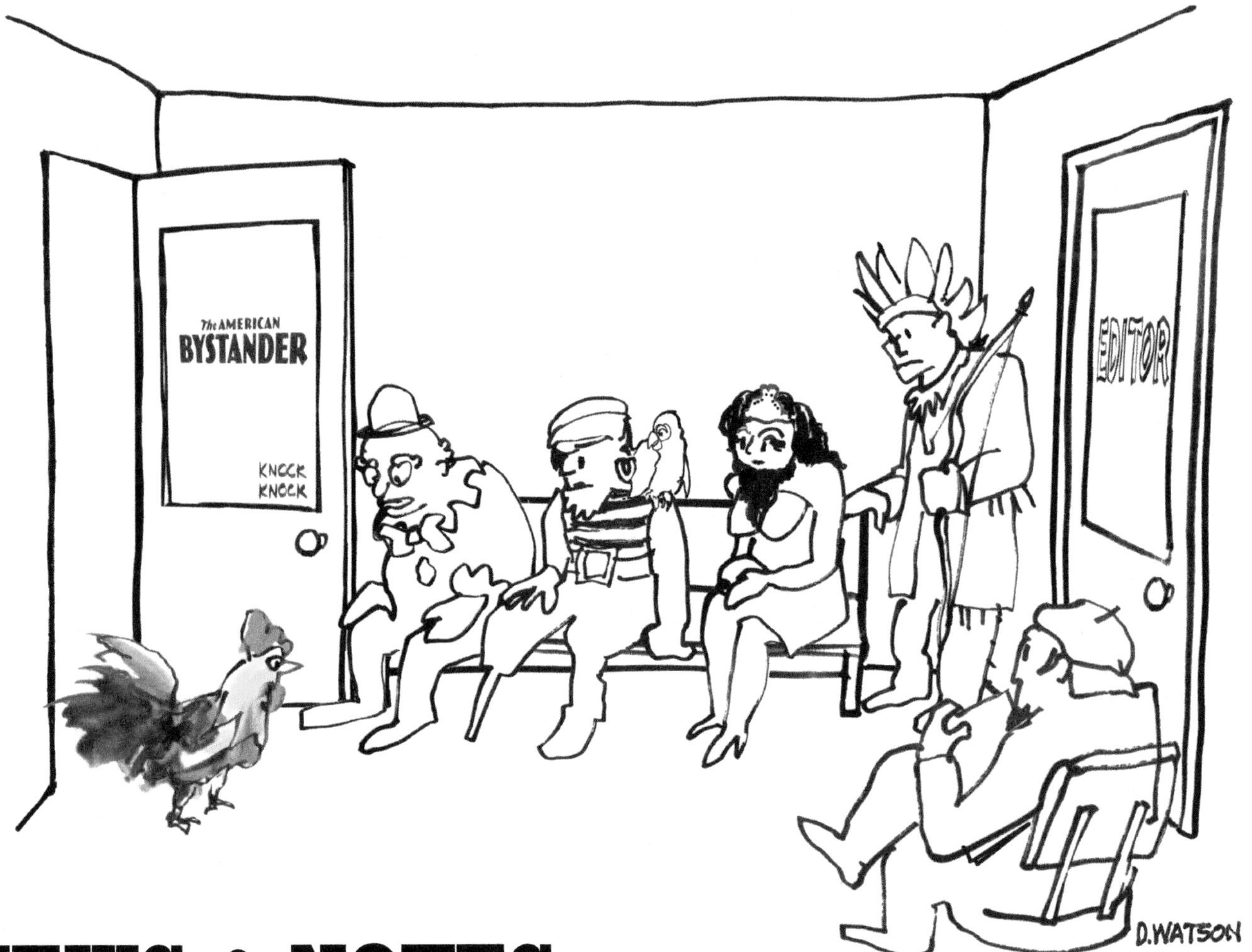
The AMERICAN
BYSTANDER
KNOCK
KNOCK
EDITOR
D.WATSON

NEWS & NOTES

JAY RUTTENBERG is working on a new issue of the *Lowbrow Reader* (#10), much of which will be devoted to the previously unexplored link between the Velvet Underground and Steve Urkel. Seriously! He also creates, with the illustrator **MIKE REDDY**, the weekly Tumblr project *musiciansyoushouldknow.tumblr.com*, featuring biographies and portraits of the most important musical figures of our time.

D. WATSON lets us know he escaped Ubekistan, detouring through Egypt to see the Pyramids. He picked up a super model who asked, "I think that's where I once did a photo shoot. Are they still there?" They are. She's not.

MICHAEL SLOAN is currently working on a new *Zen of Nimbus* graphic novel. Three of his illustrations were recently included in the Society of illustrators 58th Annual Exhibition in New York City. *Cities Real and Imagined*, an exhibit of Michael's paintings, is currently on display at the New Haven Lawn Club in New Haven, Connecticut. He is looking forward to returning to Hong Kong this summer to continue his series of paintings of that city's outdoor street markets. Michael can be found playing bass guitar with the all-illustrator jazz band The Half-Tones which performs frequently during sketch nights at The Society of Illustrators in New York City. You can see more of his artwork at *www.michaelsloan.net*.

Temporarily nestled upon the banks of the mighty Cam, **MICHAEL THORNTON** was feeling pretty down on humanity on account of his academic work on existential risks, but his faith was restored when he discovered one can buy alcohol on Amazon.co.uk.

MEGAN KOESTER's mother, a heckler, was destroyed by a stand-up comedian in 1987. She's been looking for him ever since; she will not rest until he is brought to justice. If you have any leads, please contact your local comedy police department.

STEVE YOUNG writes, "After my current *Maya & Marty* gig ends, I'll be heading out on the road to present my astonishing industrial musicals film show in some new areas of the country. Check industrialmusicals.com to see if my cavalcade of vintage corporate weirdness is coming to your area!" You should be so lucky; we've seen it, and Steve sings very well.

DAVID CHELSEA has lived in a state of suspended animation for the past 34 years. When *The American Bystander* was in the planning stages back in 1982, David was tapped as a possible contributor, but the only work of his that made it into the prototype issue was a single paragraph in a group page of written-down dreams. Imagine his surprise at seeing an announcement on Facebook that *The Bystander* was finally beginning regular publication. All that has happened in the intervening years–the thousands of illustrations in publications like *The Reader's Digest*, *The New York Times*, *The New York Observer*, *SPY*, and *The National Lampoon*, the awards, the world record sixteen 24 hour comics, the seven (so far) published books, 25 years of loving marriage with his wife Eve, the two brilliant and creative children they have raised, all of this has been mere prelude to David finally seeing his artwork in the pages of *The American Bystander*.

RYAN NYBURG is the creator of the *Post-Culture Review*, an occasionally published collection of strange writings, and the *Post-Culture Podcast*, an occasionally released collection of odd audio fiction and curios. He can be found on twitter @PostCultRev. Sometimes he hears strange sounds reverberate through the city in the empty evening air. He will tell you their meaning in exchange for secrets.

DOUG KIRBY and **KEN SMITH** from RoadsideAmerica.com spend a lot of time parsing the DNA of tourist traps, mom 'n pop museums, and historical markers for horrible disasters. It happens each year as travelers brave the offbeat wonder backroads with Roadside America's

Mr. Plotkin went another way with his illustration for "Unbroken" (p. 43), but this rough was too hilarious not to share.

iPhone app (and Roadside Presidents, for serious POTUS geeks). American highways became much safer after they removed all the jokes from the apps' turn-by-turn directions.

By the time you read this, **SAM HENDERSON** will have finished *Magic Whistle 3.2*, a reboot of his long-running solo series, this issue with a cover by the *Bystander*'s Danny Hellman. [*Danny illustrated the Josh Alan Friedman*

interview in #1. — *Ed.*] If your comic store is *Whistle*-deficient, camp outside or hold your breath or whatever your protest method of choice is. If it weren't for him, your mother and father would never have met. Wait, no, that's not it... I think he invented something maybe. It'll hit me in a moment. Other endeavors can be found at magicwhistle.com.

COMING NEXT ISSUE:
"The Tragedy of the Mermen," an unpublished gem by Brian McConnachie and Frank Springer...I think Al Jean's working on something... We're deciding between a couple of pieces from Paul Krassner...Penn Jillette and Mike are talking...We've got a line on some rat-based poetry from Jack Handey... Sam Gross...and much, much more! ♆

AVE ATQUE VALE:
JOHN CALDWELL, 1946-2016

As we were preparing this issue, we were heartbroken to hear of the sudden death from pancreatic cancer of cartoonist and Bystander **JOHN CALDWELL**. When Brian put together the 1982 pilot issue, John was a natural choice for the cover, which is reproduced at left.

When asked for a few words, Brian wrote the following: "Husband, Father, Grandfather, Illustrator, Syndicated Cartoonist, Humorist, dear friend and beautiful soul. We are left to say the saddest words that are ever spoken: Farewell."

THE AMERICAN BYSTANDER

Views of the Passing Parade

Religion Sex and Politics.

Money, Love and Death.

Dreams and Encounters.

Sport, Space and Crime.

Beauty and Art and Bugs.

Short Stories.

Color Comics.

High Ideals & Common Sense

PILOT ISSUE

LADIES AND GENTLEMEN,

enny Bruce!

In **1961**, Lenny Bruce began a gig at New York's *VILLAGE VANGUARD*. His first time headlining the club:

Hello Hello!

CLAP

I DON'T UNDERSTAND how Max Gordon can pay me a grand a week to work here.

He must be a CROOK!

CLAP

e two jazz musicians were just there to visit Powell's
ndmother, who had lived on that street for decades.

DITING NORMAN MAILE!

IE EARLY DAYS OF THE VOICE, we'd meet every
sday at 4am to drive to the printer in New Jersey,
I SHEPHERD's voice on radio keeping us awake...

This was always a joyous occasion, until the week of
... *NORMAN MAILER'S FIRST COLUMN* ...

Heh.   Ha!   Heh Heh!   You fat heads!

Hi Jerry, what is it?

Norman's column

BY JULIA WERTZ

THE GREAT PRETENDERS

Where's the Land of Imagination? Turns out it's Portland.

AFTER THE BABY DIED, JOSH DEVELOPED A FICTIONAL CHARACTER NAMED FRED, WHO HE PRETENDED TO BE ON OCCASION.

MORNING JOSH!

I'M NOT JOSH, I'M FRED

FRED WAS JOSH'S TWIN BROTHER WHO'D BEEN GIVEN UP AT BIRTH. HE LIVED ALONE IN PORTLAND, OREGON AND TELEPORTED THROUGH THE HAMPER.

TA-DA! I'M HERE!

HURRAY!

FRED NEVER STAYED LONG BUT I LOVED EVERY MINUTE

WHAT'S IT LIKE TO LIVE ALONE? CAN YOU STAY UP ALL NIGHT? CAN YOU DRINK SODA?

YEP! TODAY I HAD MARSHMALLOWS FOR LUNCH!

I CONFIDED IN FRED, TELLING HIM ALL MY SECRETS, WHICH HE'D TAKE BACK WITH HIM TO OREGON WHERE THEY'D BE SAFE.

YESTERDAY, HANNAH AND ME POOPED IN THE CREEK AND BURIED IT. DON'T TELL MA!

EW, I WON'T

AND VICE VERSA.

THEN KEVIN CALLED ME, I MEAN JOSH, A HOLY ROLLER AND PUNCHED ME IN THE STOMACH

I WAS SAD WHEN HE LEFT BUT I ALWAYS KNEW HE'D BE BACK.

WELL, I BETTER GET GOING BEFORE MOM SEES ME AND DECIDES SHE WANTS ME BACK!

BYE FRED!

JULIA WERTZ *(@Julia_Wertz) is the writer/cartoonist of* Museum of Mistakes, Drinking at the Movies *and* The Infinite Wait & Other Stories. *She does a monthly comic for* The New Yorker.

Gallimaufry

(n.) a confused jumble or medley.

DAVID GEISER

EVERY Q & A EVER.

1. "I'd like you to know that I'm particularly smart. Here are some subjects I consider myself to be very smart about. There is no question."

2. "Can you explain why I didn't understand this presentation?"

3. "This question has two parts, neither of which have anything to do with the other or the subject at hand. Also, this question has four parts."

4. "Can you possibly speak to an area that is outside of your expertise but is secretly in mine, so that when you can't answer it, I can try to hang onto the microphone and answer it for you?"

5. "I've written a book. Why hasn't anyone published it? I will not tell you what this book is about. I have already tried all of the suggestions you are about to offer me, so don't even try it."

6. "I have some opinions about other ethnic groups that I would like to take this opportunity to share."

7. "Why aren't I very, very, very, very, very, very, very, very famous and successful?"

8. "Hi, I'd like to complain about as many things as possible before the moderator realizes I'm not building up to a question of any kind and cuts me off."

9. "I'm deeply unpleasant, and have run out of friends and family members who are willing to put up with my opinions."

10. "I used to like your work, but I don't now. Have you considered doing the things I like again?"

11. "Hi, I have a personal anecdote that I believe completely disproves the central thesis of your research?"

12. "JET FUEL CAN'T MELT STEEL BEAMS"

13. "This is more of an observation than a question — in fact it's not a question at all — in fact it's less an observation than an open-ended series of unconnected thoughts wrapped in a thin veneer of criticism — I've never asked a question in my life."

14. "Someone else already asked my question. Make them give it back."

15. "Thanks so much for your presentation. My own work, I believe, refutes everything you've ever done; I'd like to offer you a presentation of my own in the eighteen minutes we have left."

16. "I noticed there are some things you haven't done in your career. Can you explain why you haven't done them, even though I consider them to be more important than the things you personally prefer to do?"

17. "I did something six years ago, and some people criticized what I did. Please allow me to explain why they were wrong to disagree with me, in detail, and then tell me that you agree with me."

18. "I drifted in and out during the middle of whatever it was you were talking about. Could you please revisit that entire topic? I will not be more specific, thank you for your time."

19. "I have read a great many books. Please acknowledge how many books I have read. I will not stop listing them until you acknowledge it."

20. "Uh, yeah…uh, I was wondering… do you, uh, what's your policy on, uh… lunch?"

—*Mallory Ortberg*

ELEANOR ROOSEVELT.

"No one can make you feel inferior without your consent, you dumbfuck."

—*John Howell Harris*

POSSESSION OF DOCUMENTS.

(*a spam poem*)

I am in possession of documents
relating to assets
acquired by my cousin
during the war

A couple of months
before his death
he instructed me
to migrate

I wish to move
overseas

I need your help
Please reply

—*Jack Silbert*

IN MAINE, IT IS ILLEGAL TO EMPLOY A DEAD HORSE.

This curious law came about in the late 19th century, when Maine's farmers were refusing to plow their fields until Lionel Barrymore was born. (The reasons for this have been lost in antiquity.) Horses were forced into inactivity; having a simple-minded but firm belief in democratic principles, they formed a lobbying group.

Equines For A Better America (EFABA) was founded in 1880, and its radical elements immediately urged an end to the traditional friendship upon which the farmer/horse relationship was based. "Neigh!" was their battle cry, although the expression tended to serve for what-

ever emotion was at hand.

Men and women of the soil were quick to realize the danger posed by EFABA. They attempted to subvert it by disguising themselves as horses and interrupting EFABA meetings with cries of "Farmers aren't so bad!" and "Get to the point!" These tactics proved fruitless, until a particularly wily farmer named Amos McPhee brought matters to a head.

Amos, a newcomer to Maine, impressed the other farmers with his simple-minded determination and physical strength. Indeed, Amos weighed over 1000 pounds and stood on all fours, yet ran like a horse (it was said). Amos's idea was: "Let the horses have what they want. Neigh."

When Amos presented his proposal at a FRAUTBQ (Farmers Resentful About Unreasonable Tactics By Quadrupeds) meeting, the farmers were appalled. They shouted him down and watched stone-faced as Amos, bridling, trotted from the podium. As he reached the door, Amos turned around and said scornfully, "I'm a horse."

News of Amos's deception spread far and wide, and the humiliated farmers turned to the state legislature for revenge.

A law was passed declaring that any horse attending a political meeting would be regarded as dead and that it was illegal to employ a dead horse: the punishment was jail, imprisonment, or both.

The horses realized the futility of continued resistance and agreed to disband EFABA if the farmers would petition Mr. and Mrs. Barrymore to have their son as quickly as possible. When this was done, it was discovered that Lionel had been born two years previously and everyone had a good laugh.

—*David Misch*

MY MOVE.

When my parents first told my sister and me that we were moving to the West Coast, I was shocked — they'd never spoken to me before, ever. That that was the first thing I heard them say was even more shocking since we already lived in San Francisco.

I guess the news hit me especially hard because I had never considered living anywhere else. I had planned to live my whole life in San Francisco: high school at Mission High, college at

"Counsel for prose is overruled. Poetry, you may continue."

San Francisco State, suicide following graduation. The very thought of living somewhere else almost made me cry, something I hadn't done since the year I spent alone in Honduras.

On the ride from our old house to the new one, I of course immediately remembered all the things I'd forgotten to pack: toothbrush, toothpaste, floss, tongue scraper, oral irrigator, and orthodontic headgear. For a second I had the irrational worry that we forgot to pack our doors and that our new house wouldn't have any, but then I remembered that all our doors were strapped to the top of our car.

And then, eight weeks later, we arrived. At first, it was a bit hard adjusting to the new house. We had to get used to different creaks — "house sounds" as some people call them — as well as the lack of a bathroom. Also, whereas before my sister and I had enjoyed separate bedrooms, now, because money was tighter than ever, we had to sleep in hostels in the city.

We also had to adjust to the new neighborhood. For a while, just figuring out where we were going was really hard, as the city kept renaming the streets. Plus, our individual lifestyles had changed — a new school for me, a new school for my sister, a new husband for my mom, a new job for my dad.

In time, though, I started to get the hang of things. I figured out where things were. I made some friends. And earlier today, I was voted mayor. Most of all, I felt like I could just be myself in the new town. (It's very racist.)

—*Matthew Grzecki*

CIRCUS CRIME REPORT.

Once again the circus performer most assaulted by members of the audience is the unicyclist.

—*Jack Handey*

PICKUP LINES FROM THE DALAI LAMA.

Mr. Jetsun Jamphel Ngawang Lobsang Yeshe Tenzin Gyatso, also known as the 14th Dalai Lama, is famously interested in science. Well, science shows that if you add the word 'babe' to any quote by the Dalai Lama, you have a great pick-up line. For example:

1. "Happiness is not something ready made. It comes from your own actions, Babe."

2. "We can live without religion and meditation, but we cannot survive without human affection, Babe."

3. "We can never obtain peace in the outer world until we make peace with ourselves, Babe."

4. "If you don't love yourself, you cannot love others, Babe."

5. "I am just one human being, Babe."

6. "Only the inner protection of patience can keep us from experiencing the turmoil of negative thoughts and emotions, Babe."

7. "The highest level of inner calm comes from the development of love and compassion, Babe."

8. "A spoon cannot taste of the food it carries, Babe."

9. "I believe a proper use of our time is to serve others if we can or at least refrain from harming them. That is the basis of my philosophy, Babe."

10. "Be kind whenever possible. It is always possible, Babe."

—*Paul Lander*

A POEM ABOUT MILLENNIALS.

Some say the world will end in fire
Some say in ice
I say we're gonna live forever
'Cause this is gonna be the best summer ever
Class of 2016, baby!
Love you
Mean it

—*Megan Koester*

AN IMPORTANT SECURITY NOTICE FROM eSOCKSONLINE.BIZ.

Dear Valued Member of the eSocks Online Community,

Last fall, law enforcement officials alerted us that a hacker or hackers sought and gained unauthorized access to our servers. Unfortunately, your account was among those breached, compromising the integrity of your private data that we collected that one time you bought socks on the Internet in 2011.

As a precaution, we urge you to change your password to your eSocks Online account, as well as any other accounts where you might use this same password. Also consider changing your email address, phone number, and mother's maiden name.

Furthermore, when you created your account, you answered the security question "What is your favorite sports team?"

Unfortunately, hackers now know it's the Mets. Out of an abundance of caution, our security consultants recommend you pick a new favorite team. May we suggest the Tampa Bay Rays? They have a great front office and a solid core of young talent.

Additionally, in an effort to empower our community members to act as social evangelists for the eSocks Online experience, we collected your Facebook and Twitter login information to simplify the process of keeping your friends up to date with your sock purchases. Regrettably, this information was also available to hackers, and last we checked, your accounts were being used to sell weight loss pills. It is unlikely that you'll ever secure control of these accounts again, so now might be a great opportunity to start anew on social media and consider whether you actually want to keep up with everyone you met at that wedding three years ago.

Next, in an effort to serve you better, we recently spearheaded an initiative to learn about our customers' media habits and preferences, and as part of that initiative, our engineers automatically linked your eSocks Online account with your iTunes, Netflix, and Amazon accounts. Unfortunately, all of these accounts must now be considered compromised, so it would be best if you just watched television at a friend's house for the next few weeks. However, we did notice that you just started watching *Lost*, and man are you in for a treat! You haven't even gotten to the part where Boone dies or when you learn they were in purgatory the whole time!

We should also note that thanks to a strategic alliance between eSocks Online and the Ford Motor Company, hackers were also able to secure access to the unique electronic code that controls your car's remote keyless ignition system. So in case you were wondering what happened to your new Ford Explorer, well… mystery solved!

As you probably recall from the terms and conditions you agreed to when you created your account, the private data you supplied to eSocks Online is our exclusive property. This is a little awkward, but now that your private information is available on the Internet for anyone to see, it is less valuable to us. While we don't feel you are entirely to blame for this situation, the terms and conditions clearly state that you are entirely to blame for this situation. Crazy how that works. You'll be hearing from our lawyers soon.

Rest assured, we are working around the clock with law enforcement and security experts to identify and prosecute the criminals responsible for these attacks and bring them to justice. At this time, investigators are focusing on a small hacker collective that works out of the University of Information Technologies in Tashkent, Uzbekistan. Through an incredible stroke of luck, Farhad, our rock star security guru, is a recent graduate of the very same university! He's been pretty distracted since last fall when he began an intense remodel on his new house, but now that Farhad's dream home is almost complete, we expect him to crack the case very soon. He's also selling a used Ford Explorer, in case you're interested.

However, we don't want to give you the impression that it's all bad news over here at eSocks Online headquarters. We've recently started an exciting new initiative to bridge the gap between the vibrant virtual space at eSocks Online and your real-life experience as a sock buyer and sock wearer. To that end, our engineers have automatically integrated your eSocks account with your Fitbit and your phone's GPS. Since the hackers probably have this information, too, try to vary your daily routine until the heat dies down. Until then, we'll send you hourly customized text messages letting you know how many miles are left on your socks and whether any known Uzbek organized crime figures are following you. Standard message and data rates apply.

Now would be a good time to mention that your credit card data was also stolen. And not just the credit card you used to purchase MEN'S 6-PACK CUSHION CREW (WHITE). All your credit cards. And your bank account information. And your Tinder login. Medical records, too. And your dog.

Finally, our records indicate that our third party fulfillment partner failed to deliver your socks five years ago. Have you been going sockless this whole time? If you're ever in Uzbekistan, feel free to swing by our Tashkent satellite office and pick up a free pair. Just make sure to bring a valid US passport to verify your identity. You can never be too careful.

Thank you for understanding.
Sincerely,
[NAME REDACTED FOR SECURITY PURPOSES], CEO, eSocksOnline.biz
—*Michael Shear*

NOTE TO NOVELISTS.
Please, please, stop writing all those novels.

—*Jack Handey*

"Most of the time, it's unclear what our company does exactly."

WHAT HAS BILL MURRAY BEEN UP TO LATELY?

Subject spotted entering Chuck's Pancake and Waffle House in Appleton, Wisconsin. Arrives at restaurant alone, wearing plaid sport coat, baggy shorts in the "dad" style, and comical flat cap. Demurely greets hostess and proceeds to a large booth. As hostess walks away, Subject heard referring to her, with potentially ironic yet seemingly deep affection, as "Dimples." When a waiter comes to his booth, Subject, calling waiter "José," inquires as to whether Chuck's accommodates a functioning jukebox. Upon being escorted to jukebox, Subject displays an impressive roll of quarters, feeds them into machine, and programs selection of upbeat pop hits from the 1970s. Employing inexplicably humorous tone, Subject announces: "Should we crank the hi-fi up a notch?" Fellow patrons answer in the affirmative. A conga line ensues.

It is an unseasonably warm New York morning when Subject is spotted near southern edge of Central Park Reservoir. For some reason, wears a shirt depicting the visage of late actor Ernest Borgnine. Subject spends roughly 50 minutes greeting joggers with cups of water and animatedly encouraging the runners, as if they are elite marathoners rather than recreational joggers. Eventually, Subject is joined by large group of African-American men who, upon closer inspection, are revealed to be the Wu-Tang Clan in its entirety. Subject leads Wu-Tang Clan and ad hoc parade of onlookers to Great Lawn, where Subject energetically lays out wickets. After Subject distributes mallets to gathered horde, a game of croquet ensues, shirts vs. skins. (Male participants on "skins" side wear sports bras, while female team members play bare-chested.) Midway through game, participants realize that Subject and majority of Wu-Tang Clan have disappeared. While taping talk show segment the following week, Subject dryly denies any involvement in such activities, then flashes possibly sarcastic half-grin. Subject changes topic, apropos of nothing, to 1984 Chicago Cubs.

A Thursday evening, and the five members of the Watson family are gathering for dinner in modest Atlanta home. Mrs. Watson enters dining room with salad tongs and does double-take upon finding Subject calmly seated at table, alongside youngest Watson child. Subject stands up and, with exaggerated formality, introduces himself. Explains to Mrs. Watson that he heard raves about her spaghetti, and displays large apple pie brought over for possible dessert consumption. Watsons and Subject dine on spaghetti, Subject blending in with family as if he were some sort of long-lost Watson cousin. Toward end of meal, house's phone rings; everybody, including Subject, surprised when call is revealed to be for guest. Caller identified as movie actor Owen Wilson. "The spaghetti surpassed all the hype," Subject tells caller, using comically reassuring tone and winking at Mrs. Watson. "I'm very flattered," Subject says at end of call, "but please tell Woody I'm not interested in sequels." Subject returns to table bearing his delicious apple pie and tub of vanilla ice cream. Family and guest finish meal and proceed to spirited game of Monopoly. Subject exits Watson home. Subject goes God-knows-where.

—*Jay Ruttenberg*

A DEDICATION TO ALL THE FALLEN CHRISES.

Good afternoon. I appear before you today to consecrate this battlefield on which we stand, to honor the heroes who bravely gave their lives on this hallowed soil. We gather here to bestow our gratitude upon the soldiers who selflessly sacrificed everything. Let us not forget the brave men who died here, which should be easy because I understand many of them were named Chris.

In war, loss is inevitable. But it is certainly of note how many of today's fallen heroes were named Chris. In fact, nearly all of them bore the name Chris, and I'm including a few guys who were named Kris with a K. It looks different on paper, but it sounds the same when said aloud.

How did it come to pass, that so many Chrises ended up in one company? It seems unlikely that it is due to random chance. Is this a Chris regiment or something? Does anyone know? Rest assured I will look into this when I get back to headquarters. If only to put to rest the many rumors. Our Chrises, Crises, and Krises deserve that.

Let us remember the fallen: Chris L. Chris B. Chris S. Chris D. Chris Ro. Chris Ra. Chris Ru. All the Chrises who died here. All of them heroes.

I understand that during this horribly

violent battle, it was very tough to communicate orders. Someone would say, "Hey, Chris, can you grab some more bullets?" And like 20 guys would all turn, then simultaneously say, "Me?" Then they would all point to another man, and again in unison they would say, "Hsim?" This would then proceed through every unique pointing iteration. I did the calculations and it's 190, which squandered valuable time in the heat of battle. A colonel not named Chris tells me that if this company had a normal name distribution, losses would have been minimal. But that's not what happened. And Chrises paid dearly for it. Thus is the unavoidable tragedy of war.

I also understand that the officers tried in vain to differentiate the men via nicknames, but after "Chris," "Christopher," "Christo," "Chris My Man," and "The Pinewood Gambler," suitable Chris nicknames become very hard to come by. For example, "C-Slice" could be referring to someone named Carl. That's something you learn on the first day of Army College.

I feel for the men who perished on this hallowed ground who weren't named Chris, because you gotta think this battle is going to be remembered as that one where an unusually high concentration of people named Chris died. Let us not forget the smattering of Dougs and Jareds that I am sure are in the mix here. They are heroes, too, even if they are not named Chris. We must not forget that.

Back home, wives, mothers, brothers, and sisters are getting word of what happened here. "Oh no! My dear Chris!" many of them are probably shouting. Some are probably saying, "Oh no! My dear Chrises!" because maybe a woman is married to a late Chris but also her brother was named Chris, too. Still others might be happy one of these Chrises is gone.

But it's probably safer just to assume all the Chrises were heroes. So let's just do that, shall we?

Our enemy may be emboldened by inflicting such losses on us, but they shall not triumph. Is it part of their strategy to target our Chrises? If so, then goddammit we played right into their hands.

Again, I'm going to look into this.

No doubt will a statue be built to commemorate the sacrifice given by so many Chrises. The placard below will not say "In Honor of the Chrises" because frankly

AN UNFORTUNATE MUSEUM GIFT SHOP

BANKSY ACTIVITY SET

JACKSON POLLOCK COLORING BOOK

MC ESCHER BUILDING BLOCKS

CLAES OLDENBURG MINIATURES

MARCEL MARCEAU CDS

SEURAT'S CONNECT-THE-DOTS

AAAAAAAA!

©2013 SHANNON WHEELER   WWW.TMCM.COM

that sounds moronic, something an unremarkable child might write. Instead, it shall read, "To Chris: He gave his all." That should cover us.

Today, we are all Chris. Tomorrow, we will go back to our normal names so we can avoid another unthinkable tragedy like this one. We must press on with operations. I do not know what tomorrow brings, or where the next battle will be fought. I do know it will be done so with significantly fewer Chrises.

Thank you, and God bless.
—*Matt Powers*

PRESIDENTIAL TIDBITS.

WARREN G. HARDING told long, complicated jokes that veered off into odd directions. Reading them now doesn't help. After a few lines, you're left thinking, "Man, people back then had an arcane sense of humor. And no penicillin. If they got syphilis, that was it. Game over."

RICHARD NIXON personally liked Jews, but being insecure, he behaved otherwise so as not to be rejected first. However, Nixon really did hate Asians. And Mexicans. He wasn't crazy about Africans, come to think of it.

FRANKLIN PIERCE was such an obscure president that he never heard of himself. When spotting his reflection in a White House mirror, Pierce screamed "Who the devil is that strange man!" to his aides, who lacked the courage to confront Pierce with the truth. Tell the president he's mistaken? You first, friend!

GROVER CLEVELAND often defecated outside, dancing around his waste while pounding his chest. Interestingly enough, this was viewed with less scrutiny than Cleveland's support for the gold standard. Perhaps that's why they call it The Reform Era.

FRANKLIN D. ROOSEVELT was, in reality, a marathon runner and award-winning tap dancer. Did his wheelchair fool you? Take it easy. You weren't the only one.

GEORGE W. BUSH has no hidden or unknown stories. That movie with Josh Brolin pretty much covers everything, though how anyone bought Richard Dreyfuss as Dick Cheney is a mystery. Now, Mickey Rourke — that's gutsy casting.

—Dennis Perrin

SHOE SHINE, BOSS?

Working in downtown Chicago, I have the pleasure every few weeks or so to pass on the street an out-of-town rube getting his shoes "shined."

You know the scene: Our rube, standing on the sidewalk, nervous smile stuck on his face, not sure whether to look around for help or down in defeat as his shoes (usually sneakers) are sprayed with something.

"Sucker born every minute," I always think, a bit too smugly, as I pass the shiner and shinee on my way to a quintessential, gritty Chicago destination (Chipotle).

Until, that is, I had my own proverbial shoes shined.

The plan had been to take my four-year-old son to the summer music event at The Hideout, the best bar on earth. It's called A Day in the Country, and it's great.

But because I'm a modern parent, I do what my kids tell me to do, and, at the last minute, my kid told me he didn't want to hear music.

Facing the prospect of three hours in 90-degree heat with fifty pounds of somebody pleading "hold me, hold me" the entire time, I relented. Instead, we pulled into the palace that is the Lincoln Park Whole Foods. A Day in the Supermarket!

"Let's get a slice of pizza," I said. "We can sit outside overlooking the river."

"The river where I lost my bouncy ball when we took the water taxi?"

"Yes."

"I want my bouncy ball!"

"That happened two years ago."

"I want my bouncy ball! I want my bouncy ball!"

"Look, we all lose bouncy balls."

"Have you ever lost a bouncy ball in the river, Daddy?"

"I've lost three bouncy balls in the river. Let's go get pizza."

"OK."

And we would've done just that, if we'd hadn't been greeted as we climbed out of my seven-year-old Prius by another father with his (adult) son.

"Hey, boss, you need to get that bumper fixed."

He was pushing at least 60, with a weathered face and large and strong but beaten-up hands.

He was also right.

The bumper, where it wrapped around the rear of the car on the left side, had been hanging off for some time. It was on the list of things to take care of — what I call "the list of fun."

"My son and I can fix it for you right here, boss. In 20 minutes, while you shop, boss. Just $220 and I'll also get rid of all the other scratches on the car, boss. Cost you a lot less than if you took to a shop, boss. Don't have to pay me until you see I fixed it, boss."

I'm not quite sure how what happened next happened.

But after asking a few questions ("Are you a mechanic?" "You're going to just do it here?" and, dumbest of dumb, "Are you sure it's a fair price?") I said . . . well, you already know what I said.

As the words "All right, let's do it" came out of my mouth, a great deal more was going on inside my brain. None of which I'm proud of.

Well, I need to get this done, and he's right: I would pay much more, in money AND precious time, by taking it to an auto body shop.

Hey, this here is the real Chicago experience — getting your car fixed, in a quasi-legal way in a parking lot by a mechanic just trying to make a little extra cash.

My wife is going to temporarily revise her opinion that I don't do shit.

Man, I hate when people call me boss, but the way he says it every single sentence is kind of winning me over.

Fathers and sons! Fathers and sons!

Instead of going into Whole Foods while they worked (to get scammed in two places at once) my son and I watched my $220 disappear.

Don't misunderstand: they did "fix" my car. They used what's called "some tool" to help bang the bumper back in place. Then they used "some other tool" to keep it in place as they used "putty" to attach the bumper to the car. Then they took out some $5 Turtle Wax product and wiped away the scratches.

Fifteen minutes of work, $15 in supplies purchased at AutoZone, and the car looked as good as a new car being held together by putty.

I did the walk of shame into Whole Foods to the cash machine, wracking my brain. Had I just been scammed? If so, do they think they scammed me? Is there such thing as an unintentional scam? Do they really think they've fixed my car? Maybe they did fix my car? And, lastly: I suppose I'm past the point of negotiating price, huh?

Back outside in the lot, I handed over the cash and asked for his phone number "in case I needed other things fixed." I then headed back into Whole Foods, to lick wounds and eat pizza.

Lunch was nice; conversation topic: the fleeting nature of material possessions, cars and bouncy balls alike.

A week later, the putty's hold loosed. The bumper was back out of joint, with the added aesthetic benefit of very visible putty crud.

I called the guy's number. Not in service.

"I'm gonna go back to the Whole Foods again Sunday, find the guy and . . ."

"And do what?" my wife asked.

"Say nothing and then perhaps go

IT'S BENIGN.

BRANDON HICKS

inside and get a slice of pizza."

Nearly 20 years of calling myself a Chicagoan, believing I belonged, and this is what it's come to. But I don't know that I'd want to live in a city where there aren't guys fixing cars/scamming people — sometimes even me — in grocery story parking lots.

At least I know how to shine my own shoes.

—*Mark Bazer*

⋯⋯⋯⋯◆⋯⋯⋯⋯

The Super Bowl has become so commercialized, its religious meaning is in danger of being lost completely.

—*Covert Comic*

⋯⋯⋯⋯◆⋯⋯⋯⋯

A POEM ABOUT PHONES.

Your phone contains access
To the entirety of recorded knowledge
All the knowns
All the unknowns
A database in your pocket
An encyclopedia comprised
Solely of bits and chips
It can save a life
It can end a life
You use it
To try and fuck baristas

—*Megan Koester*

ART HANDYMAN STORIES.

Ed, 44, Bensonhurst: "So, I get to this lady's penthouse on East 77th, and right away I know I got my work cut out for me. She's got this Rauschenberg with, I dunno, like a dozen blaring radios tuned to different stations, all jammed inside a deconstructed, rusted-out car chassis, and I'm like, 'Christ, lady, what the hell'd ya do to this frickin' thing? It's gone from neo-Dada right into late Modernism!' And she's all like, 'Please, can you fix it?' and I'm like, 'I'll see what I can do, but the dense symbolism's shot to hell, and I sure-as-shit can't make no promises the examination of decay and violence is gonna be 100-percent intact when I'm finished.' Boy-oh-boy, what a piece of work! The lady, I mean. Not the Rauschenberg."

Tony, 39, Bronx: "These people at the MoMA, they don't even know

"*You're losing me. You're going to have to hone your message.*"

what they're gettin' into half the time, ya know? There's this one time, they think they're gettin' a pipe on loan from LACMA—you know, thinkin' it's s'posed to be, like, an actual tobacco pipe—and surprise, surprise, turns out it's not a pipe. So, they come bitchin' to me about it: 'Why isn't it a pipe, Tony?!' they says; 'Make it a pipe, Tony!' Sweet Joseph and Mary—good thing I bill by the hour."

Lou, 52, Long Island City: "And that's when I lost this finger in a goddamn Picasso—zip! Quick as ya like, and it's gone! Now ya know why I don't take calls involving multiple planar perspectives no more!"

Jimmy, 57, Forest Hills: "I cleared the blockage easy as ya please, and she was able to pull that scroll right out of there, no problemo. Still get a nice card from the Schneemanns every year, right around the holidays."

Günther, 71, Sunnyside: "The couple called me in the dead of night, but I often lie awake at that disconsolate hour, staring into the blackness. I arrived at their home. They complained to me that the painting in question had made them feel an existential meaninglessness; a condition of all-encompassing, inexpressible ennui. To them I replied: 'This is as it should be. I have many tools in my service van, but none can fix the true horror of selfhood; of what it means to be conscious.' For the consultation, I charged them nothing. What would have been the point?"

Umberto, 26, Sheepshead Bay: "So I says to the guy, 'Hate to break it to you, buddy, but that's just a urinal.'"

—*John Howell Harris*

DEAR EDITORS:

Much have I traveled in the realms of gold
And many goodly states and kingdoms seen
Round many western islands have I been
So you owe me 123,000 frequent flyer miles.

J. Keats
Rome
—*Al Jean*

THE DEATH OF FRANKENSTEIN.

Pouring with sweat, his battered tunic sticking to his hump, Igor dragged the body into the cave-like laboratory. The ancient, creaking door hung open, allowing a riot of bats to pour in from the passage — but Igor paid them no mind; there was no time. This fellow had been dead for a whole hour, which is, to be honest, a lot to come back from. Reanimation waits for no man, not even Dr. Victor von Frankenstein.

Igor tossed his lifeless boss onto the operating table. "Now, master, this might hurt." Igor jammed the little bolts into Victor's neck. Ignoring the spurting blood (he was pretty used to it), Igor attached the jumper cable-like doodads and, KER-CHUNK, flipped the switch.

The lights in the laboratory flickered, as electricity rushed through the mad scientist. From top to toe, his body spasmed and shook — then went limp again.

"Helloooo?" Igor slapped the pallid man's cheek, then twisted his nose. "Anybody home?"

Silent seconds ticked by — should he do it again? He'd watched Frankenstein revive animals for years, first euthanized butterflies and bats and titmice; then woodchucks, snakes, foxes, then deer and a Holstein; and finally, Grumpypants. Igor cursed that monster for making all their lives miserable — and cursed himself for not paying better attention to how it was done.

"Oh, what the hell," Igor said, and yanked the handle down. How wrong could he go? His boss was already dead. Igor held the switch down, watching Frankenstein convulse. When there was a smell like bacon, Igor flipped the switch up and waited. If master was *finito*, he'd just forge a reference; he'd been writing checks for years.

Suddenly, the doctor sat up. Four rapid blinks, a sneeze, and then — "I'm alive! I'm alive!" Frankenstein shouted. A catchphrase never felt so good.

"Igor, you dolt! Help me!" Frankenstein struggled to get off the table. "Touch of rigor mortis—"

"Don't you have anything to say?" Igor mumbled.

"Yes!" Frankenstein's crow of triumph echoed through the cavernous lab. "Beat that, Moreau!"

"*Asshole,*" Igor mumbled.

Frankenstein's head turned. "What?"

"I said, 'Careful.'"

"Oh, I will be, my lumpy friend! Mankind depends on it!" As his balance returned, Frankenstein inhaled deeply. "Can't you just smell the greatness? I, Victor Frankenstein, raised myself from the dead." He kissed the nearest beaker. He turned to the silently fuming hunchback. "Igor, tell me for the JAMA article: How did I die?"

"You choked on a peanut."

"Me, a Napoleon of science, nearly laid low by a legume. Life's funny, Igor. Death, too…" The doctor paused. "What's

D. WATSON

that rumble outside? Is it Mardi Gras tonight?"

"I hope not, master. Please don't make me take off my shirt again."

Outside, a mob was collecting. Sullen, drunken villagers were once again weaving their way up through the forest to Frankenstein's castle. These days, it was really the only thing that gave them a sense of identity. Some had pitchforks, some had torches. One guy lit his pitchfork on fire. He asked the other villagers if they were jealous. They said they weren't, but mobs lie.

They reached the side of the castle, and halted under a small balcony. The doctor had put this in last year, before the monster happened, when he thought he'd be giving a lot of press conferences.

The doctor walked, still stiff-legged, onto the balcony, with Igor shuffling behind. He raised his hand in welcome.

"Good evening, local rabble. It is I, Franken —"

"We damn well know who you are!" spat the burgomeister. "Curse you, Frankenstein!"

"I thought we killed it!" someone shouted. "We definitely killed Frankenstein in the windmill!"

"You mean the monster?"

"This again," Igor mumbled.

"I am not the monster," Frankenstein said. "I *created* the monster. Ever since then, everyone has mistakenly referred to 'the monster' as Frankenstein." Comprehension spread through the crowd like a slow gas leak. "Today — and please try to follow this — I died and was brought back to life in the same way. Neck-bolts, zap, *et cetera.*"

"So…" the man with the burning pitchfork said, "that's why you look like Frankenstein — I mean the monster."

"Yes, that is why I look like the monster. But I should also look like Frankenstein, hahaha." No one else laughed. "Because I am Frankenstein."

"I'm not following this," some villagers said. Others said, "Ohhh," like they got it, but they still didn't laugh.

The burgomeister strutted to the front. "Don't try to confuse us with semantics. We saw your lights flickering and flashing from town, that's why we're here. We have to pay for that electricity, you know. Every time you do another Frankenstein, the whole grid blacks out."

"I was in the middle of cooking dinner!" a woman piped up. "A complex multi-stage French sauce, ruined!"

"And I was drilling this guy's tooth!" one peasant said, pointing at another peasant standing next to him, mouth packed with bloody cotton. *"Ah nah pahhn fah tha!"* the man said.

"Don't worry, you won't," the burgomeister said. "HE will!" His finger pierced the doctor like a pin through a euthanized butterfly.

Frankenstein knew he had to change the subject — his family fortune had gone to the class-action suit caused by the monster. He whispered to Igor, "Steve! Go get Steve."

Igor nodded, and scuttled away.

"Are you here," the mad scientist said solemnly, "because you wish to destroy me, a man of medicine and harmless hobbyist, or —"

"Booooring!" the man with the burning pitchfork shouted.

"Cut the malarkey," the burgomeister said. "You brought this on yourself."

"Some of us burned our only torches!" a smut-faced woman cried.

"Yeah!" another yelled. "We're a mob! We need to… mob somethin'!"

Igor returned with Steve, the doctor's dinner guest and a local notary.

"Oh, hey, Vic. We all wondered whether we should go ahead with dessert." Steve saw the mob. "Hey, everybody! What's up?"

"There!" Frankenstein yelled, pointing at his hapless dinner guest. "It's The Wolfman! *Mob him!*"

Yelling with pent-up bloodlust, the mob rushed towards the balcony.

"Hey no fair!" Steve hollered. "It's not even a quarter-moon yet!"

"Don't confuse us with astrology!" a villager said, as her fellow citizens began climbing the trellis to the balcony.

"But I'm not *the* Wolfman," Steve said. "I'm just a wolfman. In fact" — the slight man eyed the climbing villagers nervously — "I don't tell many people this, but I'm actually Count Dracula. That stinkin' Wolfman bit me during a card game. So now I'm a werewolf, too."

The burgomeister held up his hand, and the crowd paused. "Interesting. I did not know that was possible," he said. "How does anyone kill you?"

"I dunno," Steve shrugged. "I wish

someone would. The scheduling alone is a nightmare."

Frankenstein stepped forward. "Did any of you bring a wooden stake?" he yelled helpfully.

"Why would we bring that?" the burgomeister said. "Who knew there would be vampires?"

"If we break our pitchforks in two—"

Steve shook his head. "Tried it last week. You'd also need a silver bullet. I think. And which do you use first? It's a riddle."

The mob looked to Frankenstein for help. "Not really my specialty," he said.

The crowd booed. "…but let's work on it."

The crowd's bloodlust was cooling; people were climbing back down. The burgomeister said, "I'd like to see that, if it's OK."

"Yeah, I've always wanted to know more about the process."

"Are you accepting interns?"

"Only for college credit." The doctor turned to Steve. "First, we'll strap you to the table. Then, electricity."

"…during off-peak hours," the burgomeister added.

"Let's do it in the soccer stadium, and charge for tickets!" a villager said.

"An excellent idea!" The burgomeister whirled. "Back to the town! We must plan, and design posters!"

As the mob streamed away, fastened upon its next lunatic enthusiasm, Fran-

kenstein and Steve headed back inside the castle, Igor trailing behind.

"Steve," the doctor said, clapping the notary on the shoulder. "I had no idea you were really a wolfman and a vampire."

"Ah, there are worse things to be," Steve said, smiling ruefully. "Your dinner guest, for example."

—*Eric Branscum*

COMPOSITION FOR BANJO.

Plunk, plunk, plunk!
Plunk, plunk, plunk!
Plunk, *pleenk*, plunk…
Plunk, plunk, plunk!

—*Jack Handey*

The mightiest of weapons is truth. And everyone knows you're not permitted to bring a weapon into a government building.

—*Covert Comic*

A POEM ABOUT LOS ANGELES, PART 1.

I nod, smile
Administer pained praise through gritted teeth
As you tell me more
About how well your career is going

"I'm stepping down to spend more time with my chin."

Kimstein

A POEM ABOUT LOS ANGELES, PART 2.

Right there
Yeah, right there
Above the car wash
And the bum
Sleeping on the sidewalk
In a garden, not of Allah
But of cigarette butts and fast food wrappers
At 2PM
On a Wednesday
Right there
Yeah, right there
That's perfect
That's a perfect place
For your
"For Your Consideration" billboard
—Megan Koester

PDR ROULETTE.

In my free time, instead of gratifying my dairy addiction vicariously by salivating over macaroni and cheese recipes online, I diagnose myself with my Physician's Desk Reference. I create names of diseases I am sure to acquire if I have not done so already, only with the convenience of acquiring them in groups, like, *Leukabetes*: Leukemia and Diabetes. It, I reason, will surely turn my marrow into taffy. *Glawncer*: Glaucoma, Cancer and Yaws– the tumorettes growing behind

my eyeballs that'll turn my vision into an opalescent mood ring accompanied by a head-to-toe bumpy rash so abrasive that I'll become a walking book of Braille. *Pnickimsons* is the diseaseapalooza: Pneumonia, MS and Parkinson's disease — I'll be forced to wear my lungs as an accessory strapped to my chest and without warning, my body will jump into "Thriller" dance moves, catapulting me from my (I'm sure) wheelchair. On a good day.

—*Katie Schwartz*

FURNITURE I'M GIVING AWAY.

One Plastic Aqua Folding Lawn Chair
This lawn chair was used in therapy sessions to help overcome a debilitating fear. The therapist would have me lay on the floor, then would hold the lawn chair over me and thrust it toward my face repeatedly. With each thrust he would shout "My name is the LORD! My Name is the LOOORD!" in a booming voice until I lost consciousness. When I awoke, I would be covered in malt liquor and all my money would be gone. I later found out that the therapist worked at a self-serve frozen yogurt shop and had no medical training. In any case, the therapy was a failure.

The Viking Chair
This is a brown La-Z-Boy to which I have affixed a small plastic viking helmet from a child's Halloween costume. I'm giving it away because I think it's haunted.

Dark Brown Overstuffed Leather Loveseat
Some wear on the left arm from when the whole thing became possessed by the Assyrian sky demon, Pazuzu, and chased me around my apartment for 20 minutes. It eventually ate one of our cats and calmed down. The incident has not reoccurred, though the seat does vibrate with a sense of anticipation whenever I watch "Exorcist II: The Heretic" too loud. Comes with matching pillows (not possessed) (?)

A Box Containing 24 Framed Photographs of Gen. Norman Schwarzkopf
I'm not allowed to keep these anymore.

Oak and Cast Iron Standing Wine Rack
This is also probably haunted.

One Devastatingly Sexy Stainless Steel Standing Lamp
Works perfectly and is in immaculate condition, but I can't have this in my home any longer as my wife is jealous of the attention I lavish on it, especially after the time I spent our grocery money buying it many elaborate trinkets and shiny baubles.

I...I am not a normal man.

One Brown Table Lamp with a Ceramic Base
This lamp is a squat, misshapen temptress and I will not have it in my house any longer, sullying my light scheme with its slutty luminescence. This vile strumpet shall whimper for my affections no more.

All of My Wife's Things
Revenge for making me get rid of my standing lamp, and for denying me track lighting. Thus my vengeance comes down upon all those who stand between me and the delicate balance that is my ideal indoor illumination schema.

—*Ryan Nyburg*

MEDITATION TIPS.

Envision yourself as a glass bottle filled with sand. On your right heel there's a small hole plugged by a cork. Now, gently pull the cork. Feel the sand slowly, smoothly pouring out of you. You're growing lighter; finally, the last grain trickles soundlessly out. Now quickly plug the hole so no bugs crawl in.

Lie down on your back with your arms in a restful position. Tune out all external noise and close your eyes. Remain motionless. Do this for eight hours each night when it gets dark.

Breathe in through your nose and slowly count to five, and continue inhaling until you finish: one, two, three, four, five. Now breathe out through your mouth, continuing the count: six, seven, eight, nine, ten. Repeat this process and ponder all the people who breathe without thought or effort. Suckers.

—*River Clegg*

A POEM ABOUT DREAMS.

What happens to a dream deferred?
Does it dry up like a raisin in the sun?
Or does it teach acting classes
To delusional Midwestern transplants
In a black box theater on Santa Monica Boulevard?
Or, failing that
Move back to its hometown
And teach acting classes
At the high school it graduated from
In 1978?

—*Megan Koester*

⋅◆⋅

A tiger can't eat you if you hide in a lion's stomach.

—*Covert Comic*

⋅◆⋅

BACK IN THE DAY.

Back in the day, we specified the precise date. Nowadays, when someone says "back in the day," they really mean: "roughly somewhere between the Big Bang and last weekend." No one memorizes dates anymore—not because they can just ask, "Siri, when was the War of 1812?"—but because today's Gregorian calendar (created by legendary actor Gregory Peck, says Siri) is completely out of whack.

October is the tenth month of the year, even though the prefix oct- means "eight"—as in octopus, octane (eight carbon atoms), and Octomom. Just as October should rightfully be the eighth month of the year, November (from the Latin *novem*, meaning "nine") has no business being our eleventh month, nor does December (from *decem*, meaning "ten") have any right masquerading as Duodecimber. Our civilization is teetering on the brink of disaster because the calendar is running three months late.

We could easily straighten this out by designating March the first month of the year, which would make January the eleventh month and February the twelfth month. Of course, this slight adjustment will force us to observe the Fourth of July on Labor Day, celebrate Halloween on Christmas, and watch the Super Bowl on the first night of Passover. What's more, we'll get to celebrate New Year's Eve on the last night of February, creating a whirlwind of confusion once every four years on Leap Year, adding to the excitement.

The holidays have never made any sense whatsoever. On the Fourth of July, we're supposed to celebrate America's independence, but how do we do that? We eat hot dogs and hamburgers (both invented by the Germans), sauerkraut (again the Germans), mustard (developed by the French), ketchup (created in India), watermelon (which originated in Namibia), and enjoy parades (pioneered by the Romans) and fireworks (invented by the Chinese). When you really think about it, we should call the Fourth of July "Dependence Day." The fireworks aren't really a celebration. They're a cry for help.

And why do we take a day off from work on Labor Day? I mean, seriously, on Labor Day, we should all be working overtime. I'm talking an 18-hour workday. Ideally in a coal mine. With no lunch break. And we should bring all our kids to work, too. That's what Labor Day is all about. How will we ever make America great again if we can't even celebrate Labor Day with a halfway decent work ethic?

And what's the story with President's Day? Back in the day (before Congress passed the Uniform Monday Holiday Act in 1971, requiring Americans to wear uniforms on Mondays), we celebrated Abraham Lincoln's Birthday on February 12 and George Washington's Birthday on February 22. Two great American presidents. each with a separate birthday holiday.

"What the hell did you say to him?"

But thanks to the catastrophic muddle called Presidents' Day, Washington and Lincoln have to share their birthdays with the likes of Rutherford B. Hayes (born on October 4), and Zachary Taylor (November 24), and Martin Van Buren (December 5). That's just wrong. The only reasonable solution? Make every president's birthday its own national holiday. The benefit? Great deals on mattresses 45 days a year.

Not convinced? Sleep on it. That's how we did things, back in the day.
—*Joey Green*

THE SECRET FILES OF DIPP DISNEY.

Disney's Imagineering offices in Glendale contain many strange things, from the decapitated heads of robot bears to the Michael Eisner clone laboratory. But strangest of all may be the seemingly endless rooms filled with ancient filing cabinets, stuffed full of unused ideas for rides and attractions.

The undisputed champion of ill-considered theme park ideas was Dipp Disney, Walt's idiot cousin from Missouri. When they were just river-playin' boys, Dipp saved Walt from the fangs of an angry cottonmouth. Decades later, this led Walt to hire Dipp as Imagineering's only permanent creative consultant. Dipp's contract was quite literally iron-clad; Roy Disney took welding classes in a bid to destroy the agreement personally, but died before making the attempt.

Here are a few of the ideas Dipp Disney proposed during his 30-year career as Imagineering's top screwup:

Child Feeding Zoo
Year Developed: 1963
Intended Destination: 1964 New York World's Fair
Intended Sponsor: UNICEF
Hungry children from around the world are brought to this fenced-in human zoo. Guests step into UNICEF's shoes to feed and pet them first hand. Inside a chain-link fence painted green and blue ("colors of the world," Dipp noted), children would be instructed to look sad until they were fed tomato slices, bread scraps, or cottage cheese from a vending machine. Mixed-in with real children would be lifelike dolls, bobbing their heads mournfully, "to save on food," Dipp explained.

These were the lyrics to the song the children would've been instructed to sing:
We can round them up
So they'll eat today
Take 'em from their homes
Feed 'em curds and whey
They would starve in their homes
Bring them all to our dome
It's a small world feeding zoo!

The Fur-ture of Pets
Year Developed: 1977
Intended Destination: Future World, EPCOT
Intended Sponsor: Ralston Purina
Dogs are man's best... friend-o-trons? A "fur"-out ride through the "fur"-ture of our "fur"-ry friends in the distant year 2007! The optimistic dark ride shows visions of the future. In one room, a future family enjoys a beautiful spring day on Mars, while their cat — with a chip installed in its brain — does their taxes. The next room brings us to downtown Mars, where folks are placing bets on who will win the Animal Robo-Boxing match: Jumpin' Joe Gerbil or Rocky Rabbit. Back on Earth, dogs with jet packs build a sky-scraper — the largest one ever, for the greatest company ever, Ralston Purina!

According to Dipp, after the ride, "everyone gets a free dog!"

The Muppets Take Central Florida
Year Developed: 1989
Intended Destination: Disney's MGM Studios
Join Jim Henson's Muppets for a hilarious, live musical about the gang settling into the slow pace of life in Orlando.

From Dipp's pitch document: "Kermit is touring retirement communities. He doesn't wanna end up in some horrible swamp when he 'croaks.' Miss Piggy got her own TV show in Florida. She's on the public channel as a televangelist. She's really good at doin' the cryin' where the mascara runs. That's big now in that world. Meanwhile, there's a story with Fozzie the Bear and Gonzor the Mosquito where they spend all day lost in the aisle of a Kmart. That happened to me recently. It can happen to anyone, really. They make those stores so gosh darn big! Anyway, it's going to be a great show. Have I ever steered you guys wrong?"
—*Geoffrey Golden*

As I shuffle into dotage
With barely half my wits,
And an electronic gadget
Embedded in my tits,
I nap a lot while waiting
For some artery to burst;
I hope my second childhood
Is better than the first.
—*Sean Kelly*

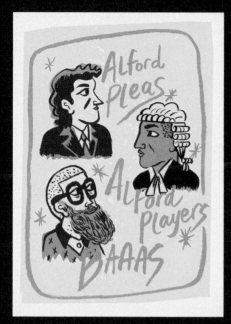

◄The Bushwick-Alford Afrobeat All-Stars

Most commonly billed under the acronym BAAAS, the Bushwick-Alford Afrobeat All-Stars play Afrobeat with a gritty flourish. While all five musicians are products of suburban America, BAAAS strives for consummate authenticity. The group performs on castoff African instruments (formerly castoff American instruments) and uses secondhand African recording gear (formerly secondhand American recording gear). Before each concert, the band unleashes bottles of air captured in the groovier nightclubs of Lagos, purchased from and authenticated by scrupulous Nigerian eBay dealers. And has the BAAAS tour bus ever passed an Ethiopian restaurant

▼Serafino Paina

The Italian operatic tenor Serafino Paina rocketed to fame within minutes of his La Scala debut when the audience, spurred on by the finicky enthusiasts up in the loggione, returned the singer to the stage for a remarkable eight curtain calls. The applause was rapturous. One particularly fervent *loggionista*, insisting through tears that his ears would never again experience such joy, attempted to leap to his death from the balcony. (His fellow cognoscenti held him back.) Before long, opera buffs the world over had welcomed their newly anointed star, swooning over his noble timbre and wide girth. Fans marveled at the sacrifices Paina made to pursue his dream—namely how, at

MUSICIANS
you should know

BY JAY RUTTENBERG
art by MIKE REDDY

▲Paco Huamán

As legend has it, Paco Huamán arrived in Philadelphia from his native Peru bereft but for the poncho on his back and six other ponchos in his carry-on. He understood a mere three words of English: "hello," "positronium," and "equine." In time, Huamán joined a group of fellow Peruvians in Franklin Square, performing native songs for appreciative tourists who had scheduled trips to Philadelphia without realizing that there was nothing to do there. Huamán played second pan pipe.

Months passed with little fanfare until the fateful day when University of Pennsylvania Professor Dr. Herr Günter Frederickson, Ph.D., a world music authority

"Grammy" Ted Johansen ►

It remains unclear precisely when "Grammy" Ted Johansen entered the music industry, but scholars generally date his arrival to some point in the early 1980s. Although he is little known outside greater Los Angeles, the keyboardist's mark on popular music is without question. Thanks largely to his session work with various survivors of the Monterey Pop Festival, the musician holds a record 92 Grammys—it is said that he uses the statuettes primarily as clothing hangers and alimony payments. Additionally, when a new Grammy category is introduced, confused voters often will select Johansen rather than the less familiar names on the ballot, making him the unlikely recipient of gramophone trophies for Best Electronica Album (*Songs in the Key of Ted*, 1999) and Best Indie Rock Performance by an Individual or

Paina, *continued*

only 32 years of age, he courageously moved away from his mother's apartment in order to study at a Milanese opera academy.

The three months he spent away from Mamma, while painful, proved vital to the singer's legend and work. It was during this period of exile that the rotund tenor concluded that his singing acutely suffered when he was away from his mother—and particularly his mother's cooking. Accordingly, Signora Paina travels with her son, whose contract stipulates that any opera house where he is scheduled to perform set aside an area backstage for her to assemble a makeshift kitchen. When the great tenor exits the stage at, say, Wiener Staatsoper, Mamma is there to greet him with a plate of *linguine alle vongole*, thereby fortifying Paina's voice for his next scene. In a tradition that began with a particularly triumphant performance at the Metropolitan Opera House, the singer took to bringing his mother onstage at curtain call. Dressed in her sleeveless house dress and sauce-stained apron, Mamma Paina basks in the applause and, on occasion, drops to her knees to scrub the stage with Pine-Sol. As with anybody involved in the arts, the tenor's mother is no stranger to criticism. At curtain call following a subpar performance in Milan, La Scala's *loggionisti* booed the old washer woman, blaming the singer's phlegmy aria on the surfeit of cheese in her *pasta alla Siciliana*. Mostly, however, mother and son are showered with applause, as Mamma Paina is fêted as Italy's *donna di opera casa*.

BAAAS, *continued*

without stopping so that the musicians can brave the ungodly Ethiopian food? It has not!

Famously, BAAAS was formed under the spell of an earlier band: the Alford Players, a hyper-obscure quintet from Burkina Faso. Even the Bushwick-Alford Afrobeat All-Stars themselves know little about their African namesake, with all information gleaned from the Alford Players's sole release: *Le Juge Rules…The Alford Players*, composed entirely of eccentric Afrobeat renditions of songs from the American classic-rock canon. The 1987 cassette affords scarce information outside of the music. On the cover, a grainy snapshot depicts the five musicians, all bizarrely dressed in British barrister wigs and robes with the exception of the saxophonist, who, inexplicably, wears medical scrubs. The liner notes list song titles ("Bad Moon Rising," "Born to Run," "La Grange," etc…), but no musician or producer credits. Mysteriously, at the bottom of the tape's back cover appear the words: "Dédié à the Alford Pleas." As a mark of respect, BAAAS has adopted the enigmatic phrase as a rallying cry, chanting it at the conclusion of concerts

in Brooklyn and beyond.

Unbeknownst to the young members of the Bushwick-Alford Afrobeat All-Stars, the Alford Players themselves formed in tribute to an earlier, even more obscure band: the Alford Pleas. Hailing from Nassau County, Long Island, the short-lived quintet starred four corporate attorneys and, on sax, a doctor familiar to his bandmates from his frequent appearances as a defendant at malpractice lawsuits. Active in the early '80s, the group performed classic-rock covers in neighborhood bars and street fairs. As a lark, in 1984 they self-released a cassette, *This Whole Court Is Out of Order!*, gifting it to friends and co-workers who, without fail, promptly placed the unlistened-to tape in their households' charity bins. When it came time for the charities to unload "America's unwanted crap" (to use industry parlance), the entire run of Alford Pleas cassettes was shipped to Burkina Faso.

Before long, copies of the cassette made their way to the men who would become the Alford Players. To the Africans, the Long Island hobby-band's tape was captivating and inscrutable. On the front cover, the musicians appeared dressed in the apparel of their day jobs: gray suits and briefcases for the four lawyers; medical scrubs for the saxophonist doctor. The songs ("Bad Moon Rising," "Born to Run," "La Grange," etc…) were uncredited—as attorneys, the musicians wanted to evade any trace of copyright issues. The performances were laughably incompetent. Yet the songs themselves, previously unfamiliar to the Africans, betrayed obvious traces of brilliance. And so, the Alford Pleas beget the Alford Players, who beget the Bushwick-Alford Afrobeat All-Stars. To date, BAAAS remains the only Afrobeat band in Brooklyn with "La Grange" on its set list and a saxophonist in doctor scrubs.

"Grammy" Ted Johansen, *continued*

or Group ("Keyboard Meditations," 2008).

In the past, Grammy Ted also toured relentlessly, always in the same specific capacity: Whenever an artist from the '60s or '70s performed live, it was Grammy Ted who added keyboards, thus beefing up their obsolete guitars-bass-drums setups. His touring days halted abruptly, however, when the musician learned to his dismay that he had grown mortally allergic to the air outside of Los Angeles. For a time, he traveled with a breathing apparatus, its clunky canister filled with air captured along La Cienega Boulevard, but this ultimately proved prohibitive.

Beached in California, Johansen has become more prolific than ever. Not long ago, just after he notched several Grammys for producing the duets album of a long-de-

ceased soul singer, a group of vengeful music snobs plotted to kidnap Grammy Ted and whisk him away to the East Coast, thereby murdering the musician. Their plot was thwarted when the cardigan of a kidnapper became ensnared on one of the ornamental music notes festooning the mammoth metal gate guarding Grammy Ted's driveway. (Naturally, he pressed charges.)

Paco Huamán, *continued*

with a specialty in poor-looking people, happened upon the band. As Professor Frederickson later described in the liner notes to *El Intróducioñemente Paco*: "This was no mere street musician, but a maestro of the pan pipe. I could instantly identify the sophistication of Huamán's breathing technique while tracing the lineage of his rhythmic articulations to the nomadic Qotico tribe that, in the 17th century, traversed the area we recognize today as Peru and El Salvador." Under Professor Frederickson's tutelage, Huamán toured throughout America and Europe while recording two acclaimed albums. Critics raved about Huamán's breathing technique and Qotico-derived articulations. All agreed that it was among the best pan-pipe music set to record, reflecting an authenticity lacking from the chintz so recognizable from public squares the world over.

Scandal, however, rained upon the Huamán camp after the pan-pipeist was booked on a tour of his homeland. Although most modern Peruvians loathe pan-pipe music, tickets sold briskly on account of Huamán's growing international repute. Soon after the musician assumed the stage, draped in his trademark golden poncho, laughter spread through the concert hall. Huamán, the so-called maestro of the pan pipes, had no proficiency beyond that of the average nine-year-old. And, come to think of it, the pipe-smoking professor who introduced him onstage had not been speaking Spanish at all, but rather reciting the ingredients of a Choco Taco in a smart-sounding German accent. Professor Frederickson was a fraud: Thoroughly unversed in world music and ignorant of all languages but his native English (spoken with the same fake German accent), it turned out that he had won the designation "Professor" from a voluble street person to whom he was in the practice of giving loose change.

Because he was tenured and sexually involved with two of the university's deans, Frederickson remains on faculty at Penn. But his disgraced protégé Huamán currently plays pan pipes for tourists in Franklin Square — the only sign of his glory days being his faded gold poncho. ♬

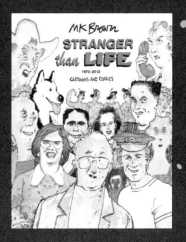

BY SIMON RICH

JURY SELECTION

"Would you be able to remain impartial if the defendant were a celebrity?"

Before I can appoint you to the jury, I'll need to ask you a few questions.
Go ahead.

Do you believe in the death penalty?
Death penalty? Does that mean this is a murder trial?

I can't reveal any details about the investigation.
Right, of course. I'm sorry.

That's okay. Next question: Would you be able to remain impartial if the defendant were a celebrity?
Whoa! A celebrity killed someone?

Sir, again, all information about this trial is confidential.
Right. Sorry.

That's all right. Next question: Are you familiar with the popular series of Progressive Insurance commercials starring a character known as Flo?
Holy shit. Did Flo murder somebody?

That's confidential. Next question: Say, hypothetically, the defendant's alleged murders were sexual in nature. Would that make you more inclined to support the death penalty?
Can you please just tell me a little bit about what happened?

Next question: Do you believe the state has a legal right to chemically castrate hebophiles?
What's a hebophile?

It's a female pedophile.
If I guess what the trial is about will you tell me if I'm right?

Maybe.
It sounds like the actress who played Flo in those commercials is being accused of some kind of horrible sex thing with a child.

I cannot confirm or deny any details about this trial.
Damn it.

Next question: Are you familiar with the popular series of Six Flags Great Adventure commercials starring a dancing old man in a suit?
He's part of this thing, too??

Can't say. Next question: Say, hypothetically, two well-known commercial spokespeople were accused of a conspiracy to commit sexual war crimes, and their ringleader was the guy with the deep voice from "Where in the World is Carmen Sandiego…"
Come on!

Okay, last question. This trial will be extremely lengthy. Do you swear, under oath, that you'll serve for the duration?
Yes! I'll quit my job and serve on the jury for as many years as it takes!

Okay, you're on the jury.
What's the trial about??

Construction zoning violations.
Fuck!

Works every time.

SIMON RICH'S *latest book is called* **Spoiled Brats.**

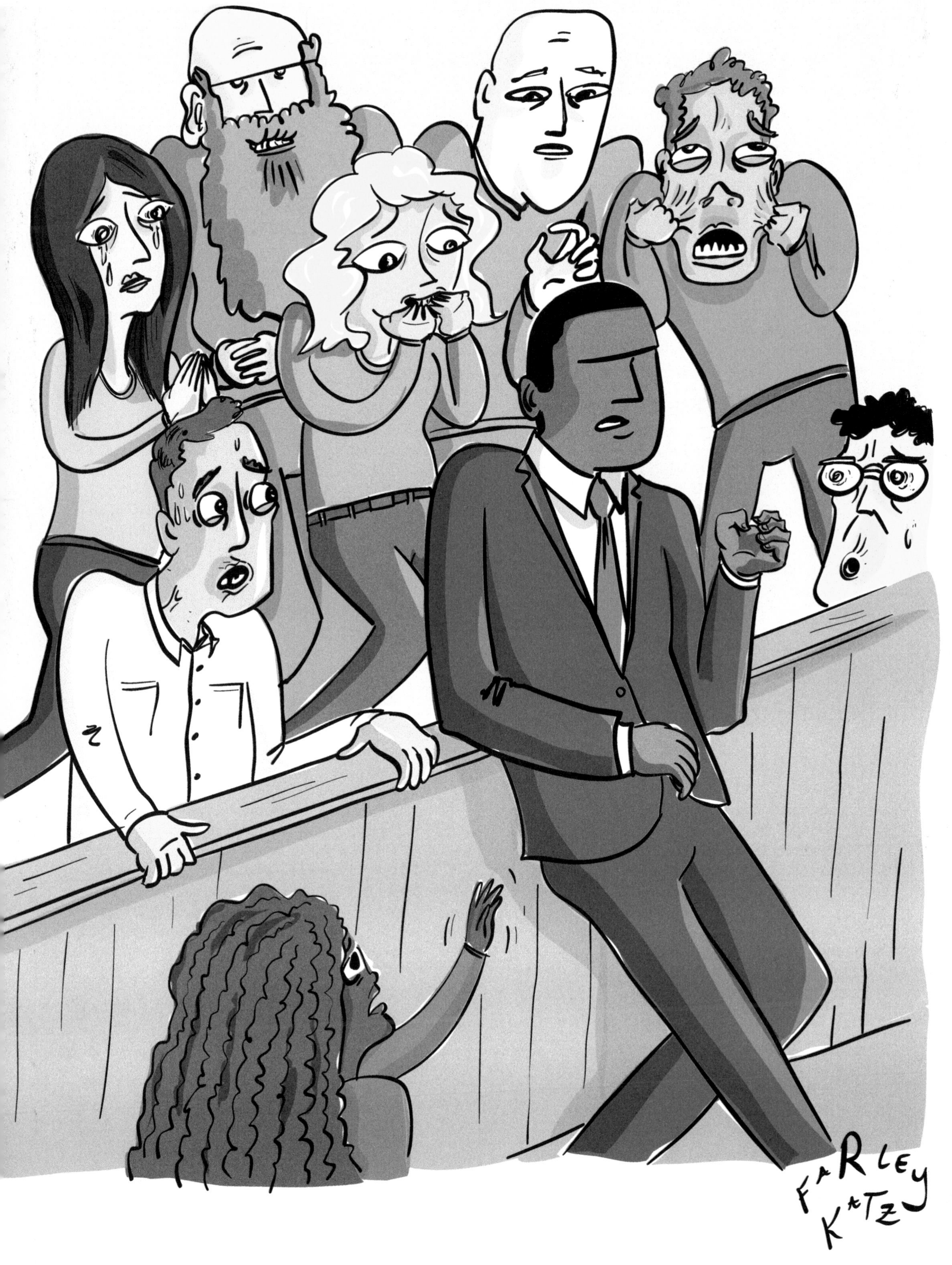
FARLEY
KATZ

BY JACK HANDEY

ELEVEN SHORT STORIES

"He'd heard the monks talk about Socrates, and that seemed reason enough."

THE FIGHTER

Bob tore off his shirt and threw it to the ground. "Let's fight!" he yelled.

"O.K.," said Charlie, "but first let me see that shirt." Charlie picked up the shirt and pretended to be examining it when suddenly he ran off with it.

Charlie hated to start fights with friends just to get their shirts, but man, he had some mighty fine shirts.

NEANDERTHAL EPIPHANY

The two Neanderthals were beating each other over the head when a Neanderthal angel appeared unto them. The angel, using grunting sounds and hand gestures, told them to quit hitting each other. Then the angel ran away, attempting to fly. The Neanderthals shrugged and went back to hitting each other.

SWAMP BASTARD

When Swamp Bastard first showed up in town, naturally people were afraid of him. After all, he was a monster. But what really started to annoy the townsfolk were the other things: the incessant vandalism, the shoplifting, the sexual harassment. And despite frequent warnings, his property was still a mess.

Swamp Bastard was given a chance to defend himself in front of the Town Council. But he'd only spoken a few words before people realized, *Oh, man, he's drunk!*

LYNCH CLUB

The meeting of the Lynch Club was called to order. After the prayer and the Pledge of Allegiance, the secretary read the minutes. "In the past month," she said, "the club lynched fourteen outlaws, of which five later turned out to be innocent."

The treasurer reported that the annual horse wash had been a success. "We offered to wash the horses of people riding by for a quarter. No one refused, but we lynched three people anyway."

Rattlesnake O'Riley raised his hand. "I move we change our name to the Kiwanis Club." There was a moment of silence before everyone burst into laughter. He did the same joke at every meeting, and it always worked.

THE CHOICE

I knew I had a choice. I could step forward, off the edge of the cliff, and fall hundreds of feet to the canyon floor below. Or I could step backward, about a half a mile, where drivers didn't look when they came around that curve and where a guy walking backwards could easily be hit.

Best known for his "Deep Thoughts," **JACK HANDEY** *recently self-published* Squeaky Poems: Rhymes About My Rat.

BAD FRIEND

When we arrived at the Center of the Earth, Tom didn't seem impressed. "This is it?" he asked sarcastically. I vowed then and there I wouldn't take him to the Land That Time Forgot.

TIME-TRAVELING VIKING

As time machines go, it was crude. Made of wood and leather straps, and a few bits of precious iron, it was not the sophisticated time vehicle of centuries hence. But the fact that it was devised by a Viking was remarkable enough.

Olof set the primitive dial to 399 B.C. He meant to go back to the time of Socrates, and kill him. He didn't really know why. He'd heard the monks talk about Socrates, and that seemed reason enough.

But when he arrived, Socrates was already dead, an empty cup of hemlock at his side. Olof stabbed several of the mourning disciples, stole the cup, and headed off into the future. It had been a good day.

THE ESCAPE PLAN

I knew it wouldn't be easy. Before the guard got back I had to convince the monkey to get the keys and open the cell door, then cut the ropes on my hands, then make me a nice breakfast.

THE MAN WITH THE FUNNY HAT

People called him the man with the funny hat, and nobody paid much attention to him. Sometimes they'd call him "hat man," or "funny hat man," or "that hat guy," but they didn't think about it much.

Sometimes somebody would be drinking in a bar and he'd ask who the man was with the funny hat. "I don't know," somebody would say, "but get a load of that hat."

One day the King came to town, and people were surprised to see that he was wearing a hat exactly like the one worn by the man with the funny hat. When they pointed this out, the King smiled and said, "I know. I killed him and took his hat."

BULLETS DON'T FAZE HIM

I fired my gun at Professor Necropolis, and with a flash of movement almost imperceptible to the eye, he reached up and caught the bullet with his hand. "The game is over," he said with a calmness that was chilling. But then I noticed the hole in his hand.

THE TREASURE CHEST

When the pirate pried open the treasure chest, there was nothing inside, except for some sand and a couple of crabs.

"Maybe they're magic crabs," said another pirate, trying to be helpful.

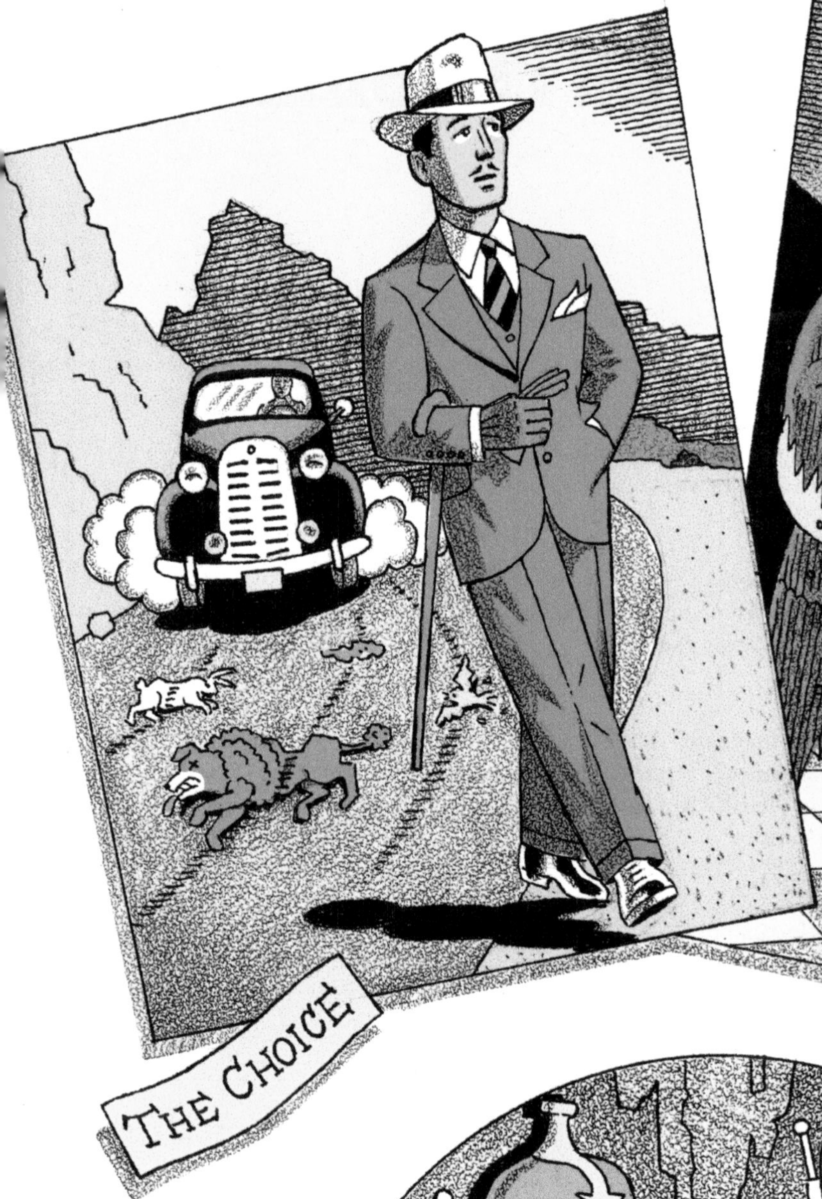
THE CHOICE

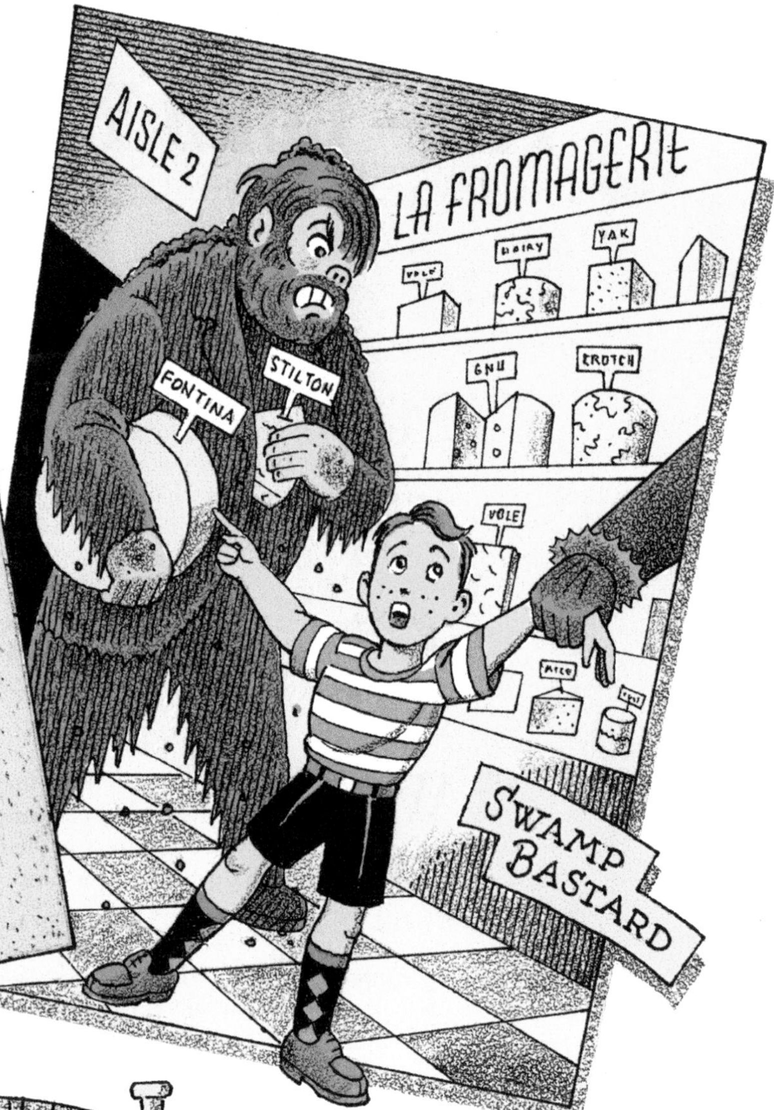
AISLE 2
LA FROMAGERIE
DAIRY
YAK
FONTINA
STILTON
GNU
VOLE
SWAMP BASTARD

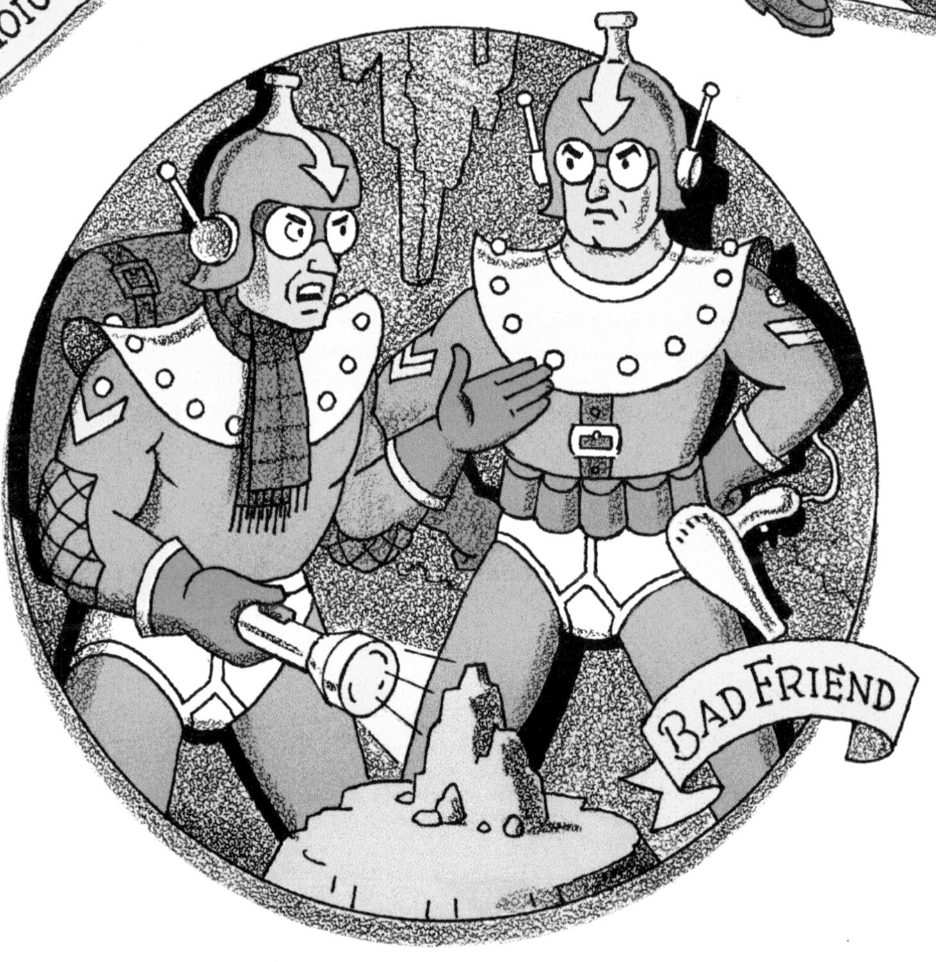
BAD FRIEND

RON BARRETT

BY MEGAN KOESTER

8 PM – CURB YOUR ENTHUSIASM

But confusion, anxiety, existential dread? Let 'er rip

Monday, 8PM—Curb Your Enthusiasm
Larry accidentally eats the pastrami sandwich of an acquaintance with cancer, horrifying his fellow delicatessen patrons in the process. Larry insists he did not know the acquaintance had cancer when he ate the sandwich; while he is telling the truth, no one believes him. Richard Lewis guest stars.

Tuesday, 8PM—Curb Your Enthusiasm
Larry has an awkward interaction with an acquaintance at a restaurant you could never afford to patronize. Richard Lewis guest stars.

Wednesday, 8PM—Curb Your Enthusiasm
Larry doesn't "get" how to use his new TV's remote. Not "getting" it confuses and upsets him; he yearns for the simplicity of the past, yet ruefully finds himself in the present. Richard Lewis guest stars.

Thursday, 8PM—Curb Your Enthusiasm
Larry, after getting in a verbal altercation with a stranger over a parking spot, finds himself all tuckered out. He decides to rest his weary head beneath a shady tree; sleep, however, eludes him. Richard Lewis guest stars.

Friday, 8PM—Curb Your Enthusiasm
A series of comical misunderstandings leaves Larry confused and upset. No one in his universe, up to and including himself, seems to understand him. At times, the ennui feels crushing. Life is merely a chore to be endured. Richard Lewis guest stars.

Saturday, 8PM—Curb Your Enthusiasm (SERIES FINALE: PART ONE)
Larry is held hostage by a deranged fan in a remote mountain cabin. A shootout with the police occurs; the gunfire makes him uncomfortable. The cabin catches fire; the smoke also makes him uncomfortable. Richard Lewis does not guest star.

Sunday, 8PM—Curb Your Enthusiasm (SERIES FINALE: PART TWO)
Larry burns to death in a remote mountain cabin. While his enthusiasm for life may be curbed, the stark finality of death nevertheless makes him uncomfortable. Richard Lewis guest stars. ☖

LOUISA BERTMAN

MEGAN KOESTER
(@bornferal) doesn't mean to brag, but multiple television writers twice her age have hit on her. As of press time, none of them have done anything for her career.

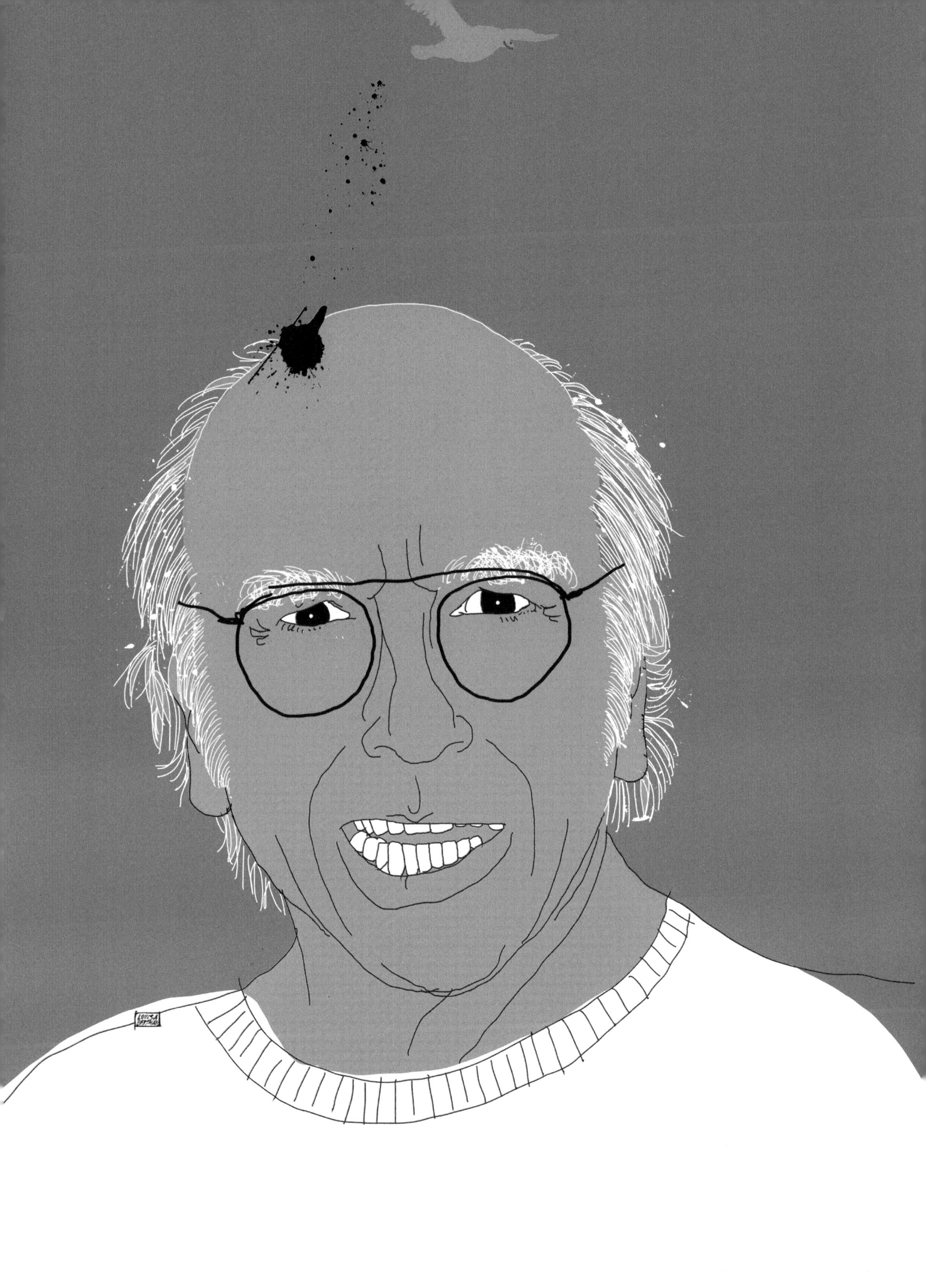

BY DOUG KIRBY & KEN SMITH

HAVE A NICE DAY, FOREVER

or, The Ascent of the Affable Denizen

Wander the public square in any modest-sized city, and you'll often spot a statue of a Great Man. A general, statesman, spiritual leader, or captain of industry — perhaps elevated on a pedestal or column — is meant to inspire, and to forever associate a town with his fame and accomplishments.

That's right, his fame and accomplishments. The municipal hero mail order catalog is missing half of its pages, as history's women might point out.

A city's connection is sometimes strained, or perfunctory. The town of George, Washington, features a large bronze head of the first president, who died unaware that George, or Washington State, or the entire Pacific Northwest even existed.

America hit Peak Great Man about a century ago, and now strategic reserves are all but exhausted. Combine that with a public unwilling to wear a topcoat, clutch a roll of parchment, or even stand on the shoulders of winged maidens, and it's obvious that civic statuary has challenges.

Municipalities tried to adapt, enshrining the Pretty Good Man — an athlete, a celebrity, or even an artist. But like the Great Man, the Pretty Good Man reputation was often only established after the subject left town. The paths of the proverbial Powerball Winner and the Winning Ticket Convenience Store cross only once, and towns seemed stuck on desperate brag-by-association and fading juju.

Enter the modern era, where a statue can pay tribute to the Affable Denizen, a familiar, even intimate, character who never left town. Less George Patton, more George Bailey. Maybe it's that guy who always slept in the shade of a Great Man statue, or spent his retirement years waving at cars. And then died.

Can the Affable Denizen, caught in a town's gravity well and making the best of it, inspire us all? Some towns seem to think so.

The early movement began in Laguna Beach, California. Since the late 1930s it had been home to Eiler Larsen, a free spirit who would greet visitors with a booming, "Helloo-oo, delighted to see you!" As a trendsetter, Larsen established the look: He resembled Johnny Appleseed, or maybe a crazy-eyed Old Testament prophet (he claimed he began greeting people in Washington, D.C., where President Hoover once waved to him from a limousine). Larsen worked odd jobs at a business named the Pottery Shack, whose owners built a life-size Larsen statue in the mid-1950s and set it out by the sidewalk. The town proclaimed Larsen its official greeter in 1963, and even erected a second statue of him in 1986, years after he had died. Both statues still stand, although the original was modified slightly in the early 2000s to make Larsen appear less frightening to children.

While Larsen was winding down, Norman Lane was peaking in Silver Spring, Maryland. Lane, too, was known for once meeting a President (Lyndon Johnson), and later appeared on the TV show "Real People," where residents were asked if they would vote their homeless hero into office. Every one answered yes. He was known as the "mayor" of the town, and after he died a bronze bust of Lane was unveiled in what was rechristened Mayor Lane Memorial Alleyway, which had led to one of his favorite bars and sleeping spots. Lane is portrayed wearing his signature hard hat, along with his reassuring catchphrase, "Don't worry about it."

Town characters as statues began to broaden around the turn of the millennium. In 1997, Jim Boggio, "King of the Stomach Steinway," was immortalized playing his accordion in bronze in downtown Cotati, California, (As a vigorous local music booster, he helped found the town's annual Accordion Festival, and was acclaimed for continuing to play even after dozing off on stage). Hugh McManaway of Charlotte, North

DOUG KIRBY *is wrangler-in-chief of offbeat travel website* **RoadsideAmerica.com** *and its smart little iPhone app,* **Roadside America.** *He can convince a jury that he first wrote for* **The American Bystander** *in 1982.*

KEN SMITH *is author of several books, including* **Junk English, Raw Deal,** *and* **Mental Hygiene,** *the seminal history of classroom social guidance films. He is senior editor at* **RoadsideAmerica.com.**

*All hail the
Accordian Hero,
Cotati, Calif.*

Jim Boggio
1939-1996

Carolina, was honored with a statue erected on the spot where, uninvited, he had directed traffic for 25 years. John Breaux was known for riding his bicycle around Louisville, Colorado, picking up trash. After he was struck and killed by a car, the town erected a bronze version of John, with accessories molded off the items found on him when he died, including his actual, bronzed bike.

John Breaux showcases the figurative hyperrealism of good-will-ambassador statues, particularly when compared with their lofty, allegory-laden counterparts. There are no stiff or 19th century sculpture-school poses on a waving guy; it's all mess and rumples and clothes that could probably use a washing. Huey Cooper, for example, is posed comfortably slouched on a stoop in Lake City, South Carolina, much as he sat in life, extending with one hand his lucky rabbit's foot. Anyone could rub it for a nickel, and anyone still can, though Huey died in 1978; his statue has a slot in its jacket pocket where luck-seeking rubbers can leave their deposits. It's as if Huey was in his favorite pose at the moment he was dipped in bronze (not really, but you know what we mean).

News accounts of ceremonial unveilings invariably feature quotes from citizens explaining why their town guy deserved such an elaborate honor (statues are not cheap). Whatever their personal quirks — and each character had an identifiable gimmick — all are broadly praised as an "institution" or a "treasure," and it's always noted that they were friendly and nice to everyone. The greeter-guy becomes an allegorical creature of town virtues — Tolerance, Kindness, Charm.

And why wouldn't you want to keep that good thing going as long as you can? Even after death, top-hat-wearing Wally "Mr. Pumpkin" Thurow can be seen next to his wacky high-wheel bicycle in Sycamore, Illinois — because it remains a fun-loving town! Albert Kee greeted everyone to Key West, Florida, by blowing a conch shell and yelling, "Welcome to the Island!" — he's been dead since 2003, but his statue stands in his old spot, making new friends.

The latest and perhaps most extreme expression of this new view of civic pride was unveiled in 2015 in Headland, Alabama: a large fiberglass peanut customized into a likeness of "Dancin' Dave" Whatley. Dave didn't have much to do with peanuts, but he was an icon of the town -- part of the "Peanut Capital of the World" — where for decades he would dance, for anyone he met, wearing a white suit, white parade gloves, and a white sailor cap with the word "DAVE" on it. Dave attended the dedication of his tribute, then died two months later, his legacy secure.

An eccentric with an outgoing personality and a welcoming shtick is civic gold for a town. By eternalizing the town greeter in metal or plastic, the magic can persist. As we drive from Point A to Point B, in pursuit of the next smile, a waving guy is always worth a wave back, even if he's just a statue.

WHO ASKED YOU?

Dr. Roberta N.:
Discovered that eating a pound of cauliflower a day prevents seven different fatal illnesses.

Dr. Harvey K.:
Proved that a teeny, tiny glass of sherry a day will take ten years off your life.

Drs. Milly and Joe T.:
Linked eating pretzels while watching TV with spontaneous combustion.

BY MALLORY ORTBERG

IF STANLEY TUCCI WERE YOUR BOYFRIEND

JOE OESTERLE

If Stanley Tucci were your boyfriend, he would never bother you about the fact that you own two clearly well-worn copies of both *The Devil Wears Prada* and *Julie and Julia*. If he knew you were going to have a particularly hard day at work, he'd call out "Gird your loins" after you as you left the apartment, because he would know how much that would mean to you.

If Stanley Tucci were your boyfriend, your apartment would redecorate itself in only the finest and most luxurious of fabrics. The predominant colors would be Nantucket blue, slate gray, and the color of the sea before a storm.

If Stanley Tucci were your boyfriend, it would always be the second week of fall. The sun would never set before 8 p.m., but you would never sweat again.

If Stanley Tucci were your boyfriend, your relationship would be two-thirds what he and Patricia Clarkson had in *Easy A*, and one-third what he and Meryl Streep had in *Julie and Julia*.

If Stanley Tucci were your boyfriend, he would occasionally turn to you, smile warmly, and call you "Champ," while wearing a scarf.

He would also call you "Sport." You would find it endearing and waggish and not in the least patronizing.

If Stanley Tucci were your boyfriend, the two of you would go dancing, but he'd never make a big deal out of it.

If Stanley Tucci were your boyfriend, your dad would refer to him genially as "The Tooch." "Come to the house this weekend, and bring The Tooch with you."

If Stanley Tucci were your boyfriend, you would own a good cheese knife. Nothing pretentious. You wouldn't need a whole set. Just one. But it would be perfect, and you would never have trouble sliding Camembert pieces off of it. You would be the kind of person who invests in small, good, useful things. You would treat yourself with compassion, and you would never eat Cheetos in the shower.

LADIES: THIS SILHOUETTE COULD BE YOU.

KISS THE TOOCH!

If Stanley Tucci were your boyfriend, he would make pots of red sauce on the weekends, and make you taste all of them. He wouldn't Bogart the kitchen, either, and he'd be more than just complimentary about your own (inevitably inferior) attempts at cooking. "No, it was extraordinary," he'd insist after cleaning his plate. "Just extraordinary." And there would be a light in his eyes that would let you believe him.

If Stanley Tucci were your boyfriend, Nora Ephron would still be alive somehow. She would have dinner with the two of you at least three nights a week.

If Stanley Tucci were your boyfriend, every single one of your friends would act like the guys on *Friends* did while Monica was dating Richard. "Your boyfriend is the coolest," they'd tell you. You'd have to ask them to go do something else once in a while so the two of you could actually get some time to yourselves. "I'm sorry about those guys," you'd say to Stanley Tucci, while he'd look intently at you and say "Don't ever apologize to me on behalf of the people who love you."

If Stanley Tucci were your boyfriend, you would instantly become the kind of person who takes long, luxurious baths in a clean, bone-white tub.

If Stanley Tucci were your boyfriend, he would make excuses to run out and pick up a paper and buy you breakfast while he was out. "It's nothing," he'd say if you protested. "I don't even remember how much it cost. I threw away the receipt. Stop asking." If Stanley Tucci were your boyfriend, he would wear perfectly cut waffle-print shirts just while drinking coffee at your kitchen table, but your life together would be more meaningful than a collection of expensive fabrics and bougie breakfast foods. Your life together would be more meaningful than your life before.

MALLORY ORTBERG *(@malelis) is "Dear Prudence" at Slate.com and the author of the 2014 bestseller,* **Texts From Jane Eyre.**

Black is the Night

a new fantasy novel

by Dexter Summers

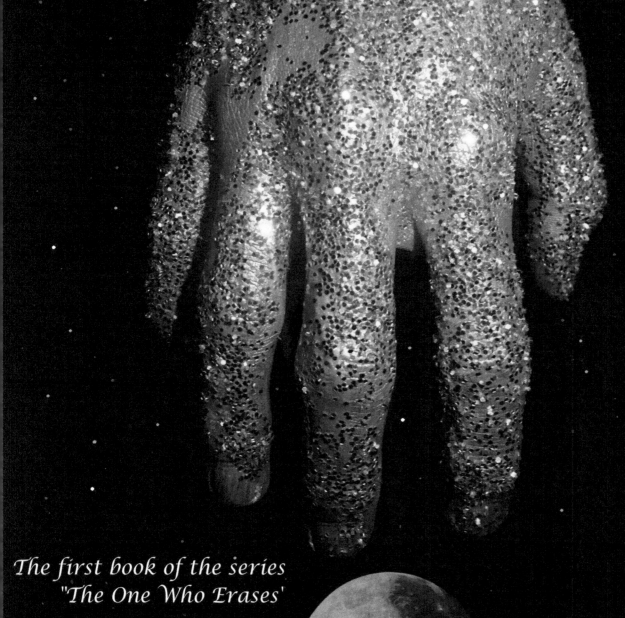

The first book of the series
"The One Who Erases"

Available this summer on Amazon.
http://blackisthenight.com

JOHN HOWELL HARRIS

WELCOME TO INFINITY WORLD

Please don't press that big red button on the Large Hadron Collider.

When one day everyone started to experience every single infinite reality simultaneously within a single consciousness instead of in the nicely compartmentalized tributaries of countless separate selves throughout the multiverse, I'll admit — it took some getting used to.

To this day, it still sometimes feels a little weird that, for instance, I'm writing this at the exact moment I'm punching a dog's lights out, test-driving the 2016 Ford Focus, cowering behind a rocky outcropping as the lizard overlords hunt down the last of the humans, am myself a murderous lizard overlord (but not really at the rank I feel I should have reached within the organization, especially for a lizard my age), have been dead for 12 years, am jump-roping nude at a Bally's Total Fitness (in Nude World and also a few worlds where the cops have been called), was never conceived at all, and have been dead for 9 years.

And dead for 22 years.

I guess you just adapt though, right? Of course, not in the worlds where you don't adapt at all, but otherwise you just keep right on chuggin' along (again, in worlds where "chuggin' along" is a physical possibility). When the decision to go get a cup of coffee concurrently triggers the entire universe being destroyed in a gravitational singularity and also you decide to get a cup of hot cocoa, and also you're a Taiwanese woman, you just sort of have to roll with it.

Incidentally, "roll with it" is a colloquialism with an incredibly unsavory meaning in Nude World.

But it's not like I need to explain anything to you. While you're reading this, you're overthrowing a puppet regime in some African nation, masturbating over your mother's grave, have been dead for 11 years, and are masturbating over your father's grave. And I suppose that gets to the heart of what I'm driving at here; as messy and chaotic as it can be, there's a simple, beautiful egalitarianism to the whole thing. When you know everyone you meet has masturbated over both their parents' graves an infinite number of times, no one really gets too judgy.

But if there's one thing that bums me out, it's Bummer World. Ha, ha, ha! That's a really good multiverse joke; you probably laughed at it very, very hard in a lot of your realities. But in all seriousness, I think the main downside to all of this is the desensitization. When the birth or your first child happens at the same moment your wife explodes and also you've been dead for 19 years, you can't really prioritize your emotions effectively; you just sort of check out. There's no real joy or sorrow, no soaring, inexpressible elation or pitch-black depths of depression. It all just amounts to a gray, featureless existence, without either the sharp delineation of edges or the pleasing smoothness of curves.

Also, Bummer World really does suck. I'll never figure out why it's not called LSD Scorpion World.

One fun thing, though, is the game "what reality would you live in?" where you pick the one reality you would stay in, if you had a choice. I guess I'd pick the one where I have that sweet Trans Am with the griffin wearing shades and smoking a cigarette airbrushed on the hood. That car rules. I definitely wouldn't pick the one where I decide to lease the 2016 Ford Focus, and then the 2016 Ford Focus is driven into my rectum.

In any case, I hope you enjoyed this story in the universes where it's hardcore pornography or a tomato or whatever, or in a world where I at least put some effort into writing a good ending. Peace out.

JOHN HOWELL HARRIS *(@jhowellharris) has written for* **The Onion, The New Yorker** *and* **Adult Swim.** *His 'zine?* **Pendulous Breasts Quarterly.** *His podcast?* **Scienceology.**

BY DAVE HANSON

UNBROKEN

Getting rid of my best friend's best friend

My wife throws a stern glance in the direction of Mr. Jumbles, and turns back to me. "It's time," she says solemnly. "You said it yourself — we can't put this off any longer. "

People tease me about how much I love Mr. Jumbles — maybe it's because we have no kids, but I throw him a birthday party every dog year (yup that's one about every seven weeks), and I turn down any social invitation if he isn't tacitly invited along. His pain is my pain, and right now, it makes me ache to even look at him. I turn slowly, falling in love all over again with the earfuzz fluttering in the breeze from the ceiling fan. Before I look at his eyes he's seen mine, or maybe he smelled my heavy heart — whatever it is, he has a sixth sense for any kind of skullduggery. He rises to a crouch in his dog bed, picks up his toy and side-eyes me as he backs out of the room. I hold my hand up to my wife. "Don't even say it, honey," I mutter. "I'll take care of it."

Just to be clear, I'm not giving you advice on how to put down Mr. Jumbles — I'll leave that for a clammy-handshaked, green-tea-slinging Dr. Phil type who leaves your afternoon a pile of tear-soaked slankets. I'm talking about Mr. Jumbles' favorite toy, a wretched, tattered, grimy, saliva-soaked germ-bomb who's survived such a magnitude of abuse that my wife nicknamed him "Unbroken." His genetic composition was dubious, with a small round head and long reptilian torso, a tail like a purple toilet brush, and corgi-short legs, one understuffed so it habitually slid out when he was placed in a standing position. The stitching that runs from his tail down his posterior was crooked, giving an impression of some sort of rectal dysplasia. He had a stiff mane of purple hair that started at his shoulder blades, climbed up his neck, and continued between his ears, the hair thickening so it became like a Mohawk, and widening into a unibrow. Eyes that contained no hint of rumination peered dimly out from deep sockets, like a sprinkler at the bottom of a

hole that had become overgrown. His crowning glory was a huge, clumsily embroidered grin that evokes the word "simpleton." More than anything else, Unbroken had pluck — maybe it was a bravery born of dimness, like a football coach might hope to see in a kamikaze kick-returner. He was the party guest whom you wouldn't invite in the first wave, but he was so grateful to be there that you were glad he came, the guy who'd bring a huge tray of mediocre brownies, and stay to help with the dishes. Unbroken came to us on a morning in early summer and despite the heat of the day, his grin contained so much hope that it made us all feel like it was Christmas morning.

Mr. Jumbles took an immediate shine to Unbroken, meaning he began an immediate and systematic dismantling of each of his bodily functions. Mr. Jumbles is part terrier so he believes the point of playing "Fetch" is to chase down a toy and furiously shake it until its neck snaps, so every disc in Unbroken's neck was soon subluxated. Mr. Jumbles brought him to doggy day care, where Unbroken's long lean body made him an ideal candidate for tug of war, which made him an ideal candidate for spinal extension injuries, dislocated limbs, and ball-and-socket separations. My wife reattached his head several times with nautical-grade thread. Mr. Jumbles dug out Unbroken's eyes, a fact I became aware of when I saw one of them peering up at me from the next day's dog turd. My uncle's visiting Rottweiler added blunt force trauma and crush injuries. Constant gnawing left his fur as patchy as a prison softball field. Once, when a sudden thunderstorm drove the family indoors, Unbroken was left on the lawn; pounded deep into the unmowed grass by hailstones, his right flank was torn open by the blade of my riding mower. Suture-scar after suture-scar added up, until he looked more like one of Tara Reid's breasts than a toy. But always, there was the grin that could not be smashed, bitten, beaten or battered off his face. And Mr. Jumbles adored him… sometimes when we were dozing off we heard Mr. Jumbles jump off the bed and wondered why — then a moment later

DAVE HANSON *has written for Letterman,* **National Lampoon** *and* **The New Yorker.** *He's wiling away the time before death writing an unpublishable novel he can adapt into an unproduceable screenplay.*

he'd come trotting up the hall, Unbroken's squeaker activated with each of Mr. Jumbles's strides. For our dog, the family nest wasn't complete without Unbroken.

But then came the day I walked into the kitchen and saw Unbroken sprawled on the tile, crumpled like he'd been felled by an I.E.D. or maybe a hail of machine gun bullets. Unbroken was broken, and it was time. One side of the grin had been wrenched loose in a tug of war and the boundless wellspring of hope had been reduced to a weak trickle. Head flaccid, body twisted, sodden with slobber… even with the spare cover of his remaining fuzz, he resembled a hooker on a coroner's slab in a James Ellroy book.

But how can you explain to someone you'll probably euthanize in a few years that euthanasia is mercy? I can't throw him away — man's best friend's friend will not find his forever home in a tomb of oozing sewage and vegetable matter. Nor will he buried in the backyard where Mr. Jumbles could dig him up. Do I send Mr. Jumbles to Grandma's for a weeklong stay and greet his jubilant return with not just hugs but a new toy like a tantalizing cashew-butter-filled Kong to distract him from Unbroken's absence? Make him disappear overnight, tossed off a bridge like a murder gun? After several days, I make my decision about the most dignified method of disposal.

PLOTKIN

Early on a Saturday afternoon I use a combination of newspaper, dry branches and briquettes to build a roaring fire in the Weber. Then I walk inside where my wife provides the distraction; she puts Mr. Jumbles on the counter beside the slopsink and begins clawing at his tangled coat with the wire brush, a ritual that always elicits a paw-stuck-in-a-bear-trap reaction of protest. I grab Unbroken from the toy basket and shove him in my shirt; I give my wife one more pleading glance but clearly, there will be no midnight reprieve from the governor. I walk out the front door and double around to the back. The fire is roaring now; I hold Unbroken in my hands, gaze at him tearfully, silently thank him for the memories. With an underhand toss, I lob his battered body toward the fire – at the exact moment that I hear my wife's horrified squawk from the back door and see Mr. Jumbles leaping, a swordfish-like propulsion that sends him arching skyward like a cornerback

going for an interception. Mr. Jumbles is a magnificent athlete, and this is one for the highlight reel — as he soars through the air, flames craning to tickle his tummyfluff, his legs extend like a greyhound's and his jaws close around Unbroken and pluck him from the air just inches above the fire. But then I see it: He doesn't *quite* have the trajectory to clear the back lip of the Weber. His rear legs hit hard and he slams straight down into the Belgian pavers, landing with a yelp, the impact knocking Unbroken loose. The Weber lurches… teeters… and topples in a wild explosion of embers. I run to Mr. Jumbles, but when he sees me he instantly collects himself, grabs Unbroken, and darts toward the big back yard. But as he glances back, his eyes don't contain the mischievous taunting that accompanies a game of "Keepaway," they contain only reproach and even worse — disappointment. My heart sinks.

But suddenly I can't worry about him because — the embers from the Weber hit some dry leaves and the side wall of our old wooden garage is on fire! "Call 911!" I yell to my wife, the cellphone carrier in the family. The nearest hose is in the front yard; I open the back door of the garage and run through, frantically turn the water on, drag the hose over my wife's Elantra, and reach the fire as the flames are reaching eight feet high. And as I unleash the flow of water, it happens — Mr. Jumbles, carrying Unbroken, darts into the garage. There is no fence in the front yard to contain him, and I can see how upset he is. "Jumby! *Jumby! Mr. Jumbles!*" Nothing. I shove the hose nozzle in my wife's hand and sprint through the garage — just in time to see him, and Unbroken, disappear into the woods at the end of the cul de sac.

The next few months involve hundreds of walks through the woods, enough to leave me with two cases of Lyme disease. The slow-learner kid at the end of the block yells "Mr. Jumbles, come home!" when he sees me. Every telephone pole for miles has a poster bearing his photograph. But I never see Mr. Jumbles or Unbroken again. They may die in that forest, they may starve, but they'll never be betrayed again. Dogs, they know something about loyalty, and Mr. Jumbles knows that *his* best friend will never again be sold down the river. Or thrown in a fire like garbage.

BY MERRILL MARKOE

WHAT I WILL SAY TO THE THREE PEOPLE AT MY BOOK READING

Well, hello there. Or should I say: Hello! Hello! Hello!! That's a very special personal hello for each of you! How lovely that it's just you three today! You know, I actually said a prayer this morning, when I was able to break away from the cumbersome entourage of press, PR people, hangers-on and well-wishers who follow me absolutely everywhere, that only a small handful of very special people would attend tonight. And my prayers were answered!

I don't usually like to bad-mouth anyone behind their backs but I feel comfortable enough with you three to confide that I have it on good authority that some of the people who didn't show up here tonight are, well… they are dicks. I'm sorry to speak in such harsh terms, but it's a simple statement of fact. And I use the word in the pejorative sense, not interchangeable with that body part known as a penis.

For instance, I heard from a very reliable source that one of the women who backed out of coming tonight is at home right now finishing Book 4 of the *Twilight* saga. You all know as well as I do that a woman who made it through over 2,000 pages of that bullshit couldn't keep up with a group of people like us!

Okay! I am eager to get started! Just as soon as that short guy in the radio station T-shirt who is kind of hovering in the back decides if I am worth a few minutes of his valuable time. And… he's waving goodbye! Let's all wave goodbye to him. You know, I had a bad feeling about him from the minute I laid eyes on him. Never trust a man wearing radio station swag.

Poor sad little man.

Anyway, now that it's just officially us three… well, five if we count the manager of this wonderful bookstore and her delightful life-partner who worked so hard to make the enormous sign of my name that you see behind me. My only regret is that they didn't make it even bigger because I never really feel comfortable in front of an audience of three without a sign big enough to double as an IMAX screen. Hahaha. No. Seriously, I was only kidding. It's very VERY big! But I guess it had to be to offset the enormous pyramid of my unsold books someone took great pains to carefully assemble beneath it! Nice work, everyone! Kudos!

But getting back to the five of us, for a minute: Five is such a magical number. It's the third prime number. And that, as you know, is not nothing! Well, hello! It looks like someone else is going to join us! Welcome, young lady! Please have a seat, if you can find one! I know you don't have the faintest idea who I am, but if you give me a few minutes of your time, I will try to prove to you that I… Wait! Where are you going? Are you sure? Everyone wave goodbye to … she looks like a 'Liz' to me. Or a Jenna. Goodbye Jenna. Unstable myopic wraith.

It's a pity she couldn't stay, but just between us, she clearly wasn't our caliber. Though she gave me a good idea! The next person who sneaks in here late… when I clear my throat, how about if we all turn to look at them with big frozen smiles and then say, in unison: "Welcome! We've been waiting for you!" If we do it correctly, we will be able to give them nightmares for months!

Oh, damn. I think my time is almost up. It's not? Would you mind double-checking with the World Clock or the National Institute of Standards and Technology, to make sure the time on your phone is correct? I'm fairly certain I've been up here for several hours.

While I wait for those results, I'd like to share something rather personal. You know, I try to look at everything as a learning experience. And in many ways, the awkwardness of this situation, if in fact it is somewhat awkward, is really a lesson in having the proper perspective. Because when you think of all the worse things could have happened…for instance being jailed as a spy for stealing a poster in North Korea and sentenced to 15 years' hard labor in a prison camp so brutal that you have to forage for rodents and twigs to keep from starving! Though even as I'm imagining this, I'm aware what a relative godsend the North Korean prison camp scenario would be for me in terms of a PR push for my next much more popular book. As far as I know, no one has done a wry look at North Korean prison camps yet.

Anyway, since we're a small group and the moments we've shared here have allowed us to grow so close, does anyone mind if I skip the actual reading and we do something different instead? I'll buy each of you a copy of my book in exchange for helping me with something I've always wanted to try. The fact that you're sitting here on a Wednesday night at dinnertime in the dead of winter tells me you have nothing else to do anyway.

Here's what I'm thinking: How many of you have been hypnotized?

Since I'm not actually a trained hypnotist, what we're going to do is count backward from fifty. If you don't feel anything by twenty-five, simply drop your head forward anyway and pretend that you're under my spell. It'll make me feel really powerful, and after the hit my ego has taken this evening, I think I deserve it, don't you?

Then, when I snap my fingers and give the command, if you would all jump up from your chairs and pretend to be a bantam rooster. All I need is some generic strutting and a few crowing noises. No need to go on too long. Just until I clap my hands twice. What do you care, right? You're never going to see me again. I can promise you I won't ever be coming back to this city, even by accident.

Let's begin. Everyone count backward from fifty, forty-nine, forty-eight… Hey, come back here, ladies. No fair leaving until I clap my hands twice.

MERRILL MARKOE *writes for all the existing forms that still allow the long spelling of the word "you." For a lot more information than you may require, why not peruse Merrillmarkoe.com.*

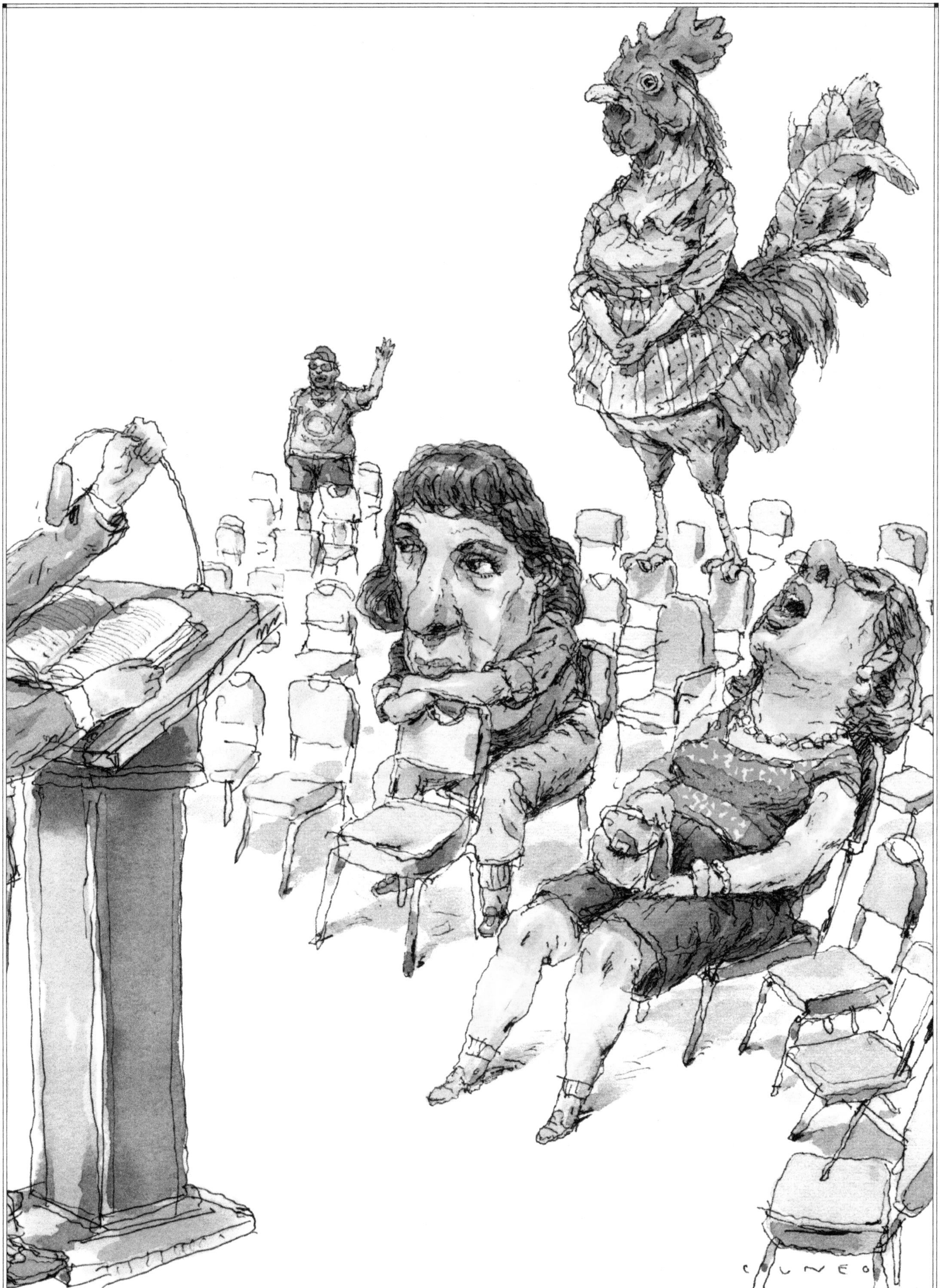
CUNEO

JOHN CUNEO

BY BRIAN McCONNACHIE

THE DING-DONG HOODLUM PRIEST

God works in mysterious ways: an affinity for bra design, a devastating left hook

It's been years since I'd been in this church with Dan Mulroony and then it was to steal a statue of John the Baptist and dress him up as a crossing guard. But I'm back because he's now *Father* Dan Mulroony saying his first Mass. It's hard to imagine "Dukes" Mulroony, middleweight contender, as a man of the cloth. When that bell rang, he pounced like a cat and hit like a truck.

But boxing leaves deep scars.

Father Mulroony genuflected and descended the altar steps holding the Host in what were once-punishing hands. I recognized some of the older folks now kneeling at the communion rail; their heads lifting back and their eyes blissfully closing as Danny gently placed the Eucharist on their tongues.

But just then, the great bell in the tower "BONG"-ed and suddenly Danny didn't seem to be in church anymore. He looked like he was back at Sunnyside Gardens. At the communion rail, Father Dan punched Mrs. Rodriguez in the mouth, sending her sprawling back a good twenty feet. Then Mr. Alvarez kneeling next to her caught a left cross that knocked two teeth from his head. Before Father Dan could connect with an uppercut to Mrs. Melch, two altar boys jumped on his back, and two other priests wrestled him to the floor. As they struggled, I ran up to help. Most of the congregation had fled to the rear of the church.

"Danny, look at me. Do you know me?" I said.

"Wh-where am I?"

"You're in Saint Bridget's, Danny." I pulled him to his feet.

"Why's everybody in the back of the church?" he said.

"They're afraid you'll slug 'em, Danny."

"Me? I just want to say Mass, give out communion, and hear confessions…" Then he yelled, "HEY! Come on back."

We grew up in the projects during tough times. The bra factory, where most everybody worked, had closed. No one had money. Our mothers would give us shopping lists and send us to Keppelman's to steal food.

We'd load up with groceries and then break for the door. Keppleman hired bigger kids from other neighborhoods to stop us, but they didn't stop Danny. I once saw Danny — holding ten pounds of sirloin, two heads of romaine, some bell peppers, and a can of La Sueur peas — level four guys.

Then this cop, who was watching it all, came over. "Kid, you just knocked out 'Crazy Brains' McFee, the Golden Gloves champ! You ever thought of boxing?"

"Naw," Danny said," kicking a sirloin. "Boxing is for nincompoops. You get your brains scrambled. I want to be a bra sales-

BRIAN McCONNACHIE is Founder and Head Writer of *The American Bystander*.

man, or a bra designer. Basically, bra-related work."

"A lot of guys want that," the cop replied. "The field is crowded with guys. Smart guys. College boys and guys who'll work for nothing. The bra biz is a suckers game, Danny."

About a month later, over in the railroad yards, Danny found a refrigerator car full of fresh avocados and artichokes. Somehow he got it off the tracks and pulled it all the way home when that very same cop stopped him.

"Hey, where do you think you're going with that railroad car, Danny?"

"Awww, lay off, will ya? I'm not bothering nobody."

"Son, I'll give you a choice: You can go to Juvie jail or go into Golden Gloves."

"Can I design bras in juvie jail?"

"NO!" the cop yelled. "Nothing with bras there."

"Rats." Danny kicked an artichoke. "Okay…I'll box then."

It was the smart move. He was strong, had natural talent and went through opponents like a wrecking ball. At 19, he turned pro.

But Danny hated to work. He was so gifted, he didn't think he had to.

"Danny, you got to *train*," his manager told him.

"Not now. I just got a great bra idea. Where's my pencil?"

His first few fights were against a bunch of palookas and he won easily. Then it got serious. "You're fighting Frantic Marvin next, then Filbert the Demented. Should you get by these seriously dangerous individuals, there is Insane Nigel, who they actually keep in an insane asylum. Danny," his manager warned, "you've got to be *ready*."

But Danny wouldn't listen, and took some bad beatings. After Danny's bloody whipping from Insane Nigel — who was taken away in a straitjacket — Father Doyle came to see him. He didn't have to say anything.

"I know, I'm through. What am I going to do?" Danny asked.

"Have you ever thought of becoming a priest?"

"Aww, that's for nincompoops and chumps."

"I'll be frank, Danny. You can become a priest and try to do some good in this world, or you can wind up in a sewer fighting alligators for scraps and probably get your hand chewed off."

"Which hand?" Danny quickly demanded.

"That one. The one you're always drawing bras with."

So Danny entered the priesthood. This time he worked hard and everyone was pulling for him. Our Danny, a priest!

Back in church, the congregation had slowly returned to the communion rail. I happened to glance at my watch and realized the noon bell was about to BONG.

"NO! DANNY WAIT!" This time it was all 85 pounds of Mrs. Torsalli who got flattened.

As I saw this, I thought I should probably hang around and warn that family scheduled for Father Dan's three o'clock baptism. They might want to get some headgear for the baby.

CHRIS BONNO

A BATTLE FOR ONE MAN'S SOUL!

FR. DAN MULROONY S.C.D.

"DUKES" MULROONY

MISSAL VS MUSCLE

FRI OCT 21

4 OTHER FIGHTS 4

MULROONY
FR.DAN
"MAN OF THE CLOTH"
VS
MULROONY
DUKES
"THE HIBERIAN WINDMILL"

SUNNYSIDE GARDEN
Queens Boulevard & 45th St. L.I.C.

60c. $1.10 $2.20 $3.30 15 ROWS RINGSIDE $5.40
ALL INCLUDE TAX

BONNO 16

BY MICHAEL THORNTON

THE RIGHT DRINK FOR ANY OCCASION

Sometimes, despair is required

Occasion	Drink
Hangover Day (Jan 1)	Corpse Reviver #2
Wedding	Champagne
Day of your daughter's wedding	Chianti
First day of spring	Dark & Stormy
First drink	Schnapps, peppermint or peach
Hottest day of the year	Gin Rickey
Coldest day of the year	Hot Rum Punch
Final of Roland-Garros	French 75s
Last day of college	Whatever's left
Painting your house	Coors
Reading Kierkegaard	Vermouth (despair optional)
Reading Camus	Vermouth (despair required)
Reading Nietzsche	Despair (vermouth optional)
J. Press Warehouse Sale	Blue Blazer
Fourth of July	Whiskey Smash
Kentucky Derby	Mint Julep
Flag Day (Peru, June 7)	Pisco Sour
Anniv. of the Pony Express (Apr. 3)	Flask of whiskey
Queen Elizabeth's Birthday	Jigger of cobwebs
Anniv. of Shackleton's Return (May 20)	Chas. Mackinlay & Co. Scotch
Anniv. of the 18th Amendment (Jan. 16)	Martini with the blinds shut
Anniv. of the 21st Amendment (Dec. 5)	Martini with the blinds open
Solving Crimes	Old Fashioned
David Wondrich's Birthday	Fish House Punch
Playing Baccarat in Monaco	Vesper
End of your cell phone contract	Fin de Siècle
Anniv. of diplomatic thaw with Cuba	Daiquiri
Watching *Dr. Strangelove*	Shooter of Stoli
Labor Day in the Canal Zone (May 1)	Ron Abuelo Rum
Bear Baiting	English ale
America wins the World Cup	Bottle of bourbon
Anniv. of Paul Revere's Ride (Apr. 18)	Sam Adams
Towel Day (May 25)	Gin & Tonic
Anniv. of the Battle of Glen Shiel (Jun. 10)	Rob Roy
Anniv. of Randy Johnson exploding a bird (Mar. 24)	Añejo Highball

MICHAEL THORNTON *is a writer, technologist, and former editor of* **The Yale Record** *living in Cambridge, England. He is currently writing a book on cocktails and entertaining.*

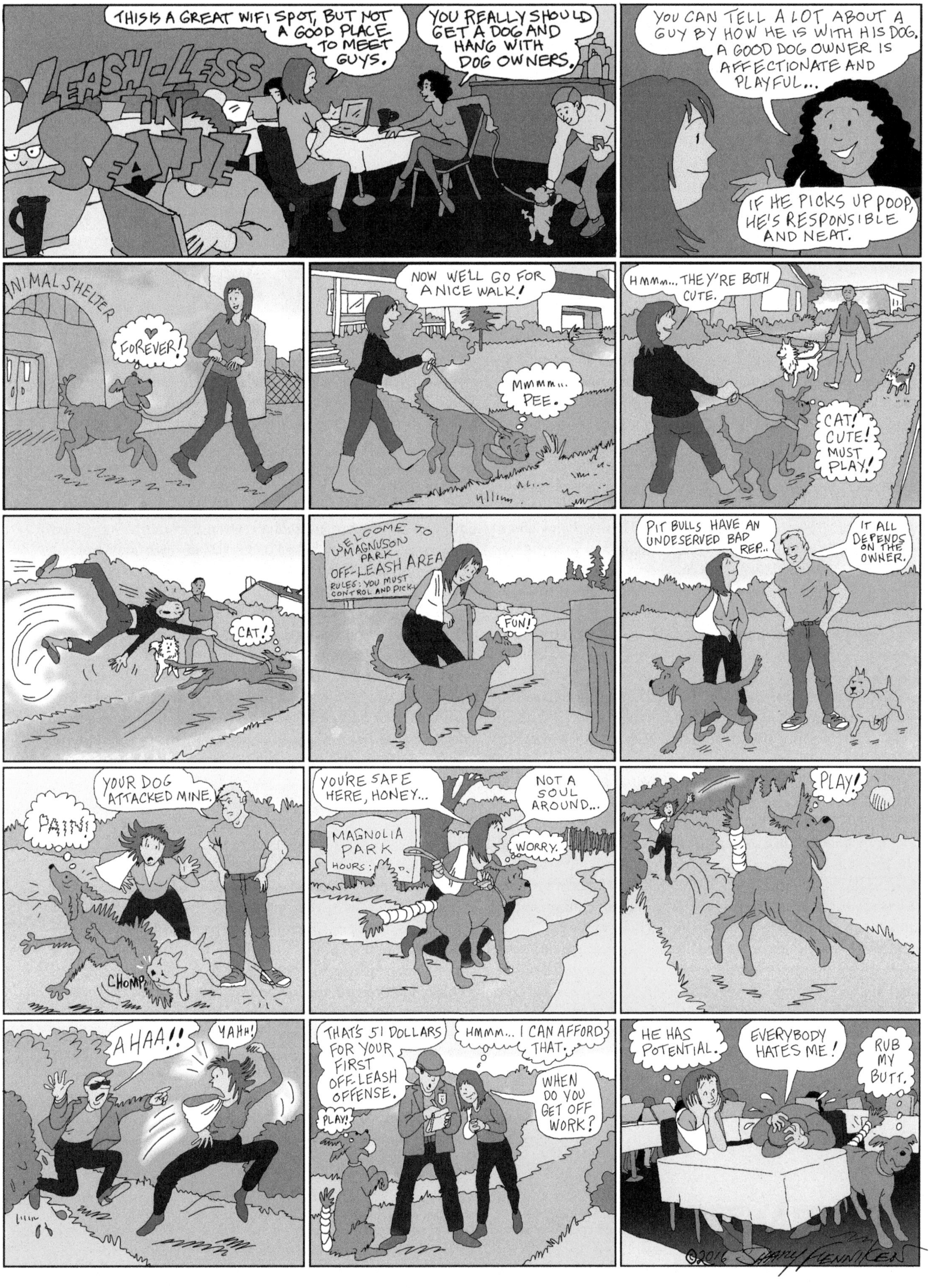
LEASH-LESS IN SEATTLE
THIS IS A GREAT WIFI SPOT, BUT NOT A GOOD PLACE TO MEET GUYS.
YOU REALLY SHOULD GET A DOG AND HANG WITH DOG OWNERS.
YOU CAN TELL A LOT ABOUT A GUY BY HOW HE IS WITH HIS DOG. A GOOD DOG OWNER IS AFFECTIONATE AND PLAYFUL...
IF HE PICKS UP POOP, HE'S RESPONSIBLE AND NEAT.
ANIMAL SHELTER
FOREVER!
NOW WE'LL GO FOR A NICE WALK!
MMMM... PEE.
HMMM... THEY'RE BOTH CUTE.
CAT! CUTE! MUST PLAY!
CAT!
WELCOME TO MAGNUSON PARK OFF-LEASH AREA
RULES: YOU MUST CONTROL AND PICK
FUN!
PIT BULLS HAVE AN UNDESERVED BAD REP...
IT ALL DEPENDS ON THE OWNER.
YOUR DOG ATTACKED MINE.
PAIN!
CHOMP
YOU'RE SAFE HERE, HONEY...
NOT A SOUL AROUND...
MAGNOLIA PARK
HOURS:
WORRY.
PLAY!
AHAA!!
YAHH!
THAT'S 51 DOLLARS FOR YOUR FIRST OFF-LEASH OFFENSE.
HMMM... I CAN AFFORD THAT.
WHEN DO YOU GET OFF WORK?
PLAY!
HE HAS POTENTIAL.
EVERYBODY HATES ME!
RUB MY BUTT.
©2016 SHARY FLENNIKEN

BY BILL FRANZEN

JUST SO YOU KNOW

Not a quitter — just someone who's been fired a lot

I have, over the years, been a columnist for so many little Connecticut newspapers I can't even remember them all. Not without me actually going through my bloated cardboard files — currently stashed in a tiny storage unit I can no longer afford the rent on.

For sure, my longest stint was at *The Bethany Bugle*. I lasted five whole months at that small weekly, penning my first-ever regular column; "One Would Think" I titled it. And really, one would think I'd have stayed on longer. But I have a theory about my firing: See, when I wrote a column about how everyone in Bethany, Connecticut, was a moron, I don't think people ever got it was tongue-in-cheek. The editor complained I was so late in turning in my column — boo hoo — that he'd had, he said, "sixty seconds to check for spelling and zero time to skim content" — boo hoo hoo. Quite the moron, even by Bethany standards!

Here's where I was probably fortunate that my legend-of-a-journalist father had departed on the early side. (I'd biked in from my morning paper route to find an ambulance in our driveway.) I know his reaction to my getting axed would have doubled my own humiliation. The comparative dimness of Bethanians would've cut no ice with ol' "54-Point" Abernathy. "Typical. Next to me, kid, you'll always be agate type."

After a fortnight of existing on unemployment benefits plus the cash I got for selling off all my beloved vinyl records, I did land back on my feet. I somehow convinced the editor at *The Torrington Telegraph* to let me start a weekly column, one I christened "Takes One To Know One." (Back in the Seventies, Dad had given the editor his first break.) And the column went great out of the gate. But down the stretch... well, I'll admit that my first-person account of Torrington's big Memorial Day parade would have benefited from my actual presence at the thing. Alas, I was in bed, mind and body racked by a 99° fever.

I'm positive, though, that whatever I sacrificed in actual eyewitness observations, I more than made up for with entertaining conjecture. In one fan letter, an old shut-in said that reading my account made her feel like she was right there again at the big event. So how destructive, really, were my minor omissions and fabrications? Okay, I failed to mention two popular local marching bands. And the Korean War vets. Plus I'd assumed, incorrectly, there'd been Shriners scooting around in miniature cars and tossing candy. Still, I contend to this day, there wasn't a single thing in my column with any clear legal ramifications for *The Telegraph*. That was just an excuse.

It's sad when someone who prides himself on being a sensitive chronicler of the human scene is given four minutes to clean out his desk. And it's not like I hadn't had my own qualms about working for *them*. Their "Pet Of The Week" write-ups made obviously troubled, difficult pets sound 'way more adoptable than they probably were.

Well, I ended up stashing my non-essentials into a storage unit and started living—quite comfortably, really—out of my '93 Geo. I'm not a quitter, just someone who's been fired a lot, and no way was I going to let my multiple firings define me as a person. Even 54-Point had gotten canned. In fact, less than one year after Ben Bradlee had physically thrown him out of *The Washington Post* for getting drunk and urinating into a water fountain, my old man had his first Peabody.

Thanks to persistence and a creative résumé (everybody does it), I landed a gig at *The Mystic Weekly Star*, writing a column titled "The Roving I." Things sure started off promisingly. I got rousing feedback from veteran staffers on my amusing-yet-enlightening katydid piece. I honestly felt that my column about making New Year's resolutions — with its deft limning of some all-too-human foibles — far surpassed all the other New Year's resolutions columns I've ever seen. *The Star*'s managing editor called it plagiarism, though; I yelled back at her that was a vulgar, baggy word, used by vulgar, baggy minds. If anything it was *homage* to Dave Barry, and I was flattered to have so many sharp readers who saw the resemblance.

This time I didn't even get to clean out my desk. And I'll be honest, the security guard's harsh phrases stung me much more than his taser ever could. Afterward, wrapped in two sleeping bags inside my car, I heard Dad's gravelly voice in my head: "Turn off the waterworks, Crybaby — time to soldier up."

BILL FRANZEN *grew up in Minneapolis and now lives in Connecticut with his wife Roz Chast. He is the author of* **Hearing From Wayne and Other Stories**, *and has contributed to* **The New Yorker** *since 1981.*

My lean times continued. But, by drastically reducing my earthly possessions — including selling off my treasured motel-room-with-the-TV-on postcard collection — I was able to fit into a tinier, cheaper storage unit. Then my luck changed dramatically: After months of obit writing for *The Kent Examiner*, I got the nod to author a fresh new column, one I called "Come To Think Of It."

For my debut, I detailed all the types of trash exposed by a sudden spring thaw. I received loads of mail as a result, with at least some percentage of it positive. But answering all the naysayers took up time — hours that, I'll admit, I should have used toward meeting next week's deadline. Come the midnight hour, I had to give my editor a "backup" column that I'd kept tucked away in my glove compartment for just such an eventuality. It was an evergreen about kids' letters to Santa.

Unfortunately, it was Easter.

Well, I got the heave-ho so fast it felt like whiplash. Even more crushing was seeing my column, my baby, turned over to this ancient geezer, Hoskins. Nobody had ever seen Hoskins write anything. Some said he used to cover fly-fishing whenever his health allowed it. Others said, no, he couldn't even speak English. Now, this nonentity was reaping the benefits of the audience I had built. And I was reduced to selling my own blood.

On and on it continued — hope followed by loss, followed by more hope, followed by, yet again, my getting sacked. You know, if the same thing happens to you enough times, you start forgetting the details. It's how the brain protects itself. And I won't even bother going into the whole *Guilford Gazette* debacle; Google it yourself. All I'll say is: It was in an April Fool's Day column, for God's sake.

Within this litany of dismissals, *The Cornwall Defender* experience stands out, at least in my mind. There, I guess I got punished simply for being too honest. Cutting through the Cornwall Cemetery honestly does cut my commute in half, so sue me. Like the mourners did.

I ran into that same zero-forgiveness policy at *The Ridgefield Post*, when I inadvertently borrowed some jacket copy from a book on recycling while voicing my own opinion on the matter. And let me just say this about *The Milford Compass*: They really need to get a sense of humor. Of course I was kidding when I suggested that townspeople litter on the stretch of highway newly "adopted" by the Milford Women's Gardening Club. That didn't justify violence of any sort, much less my windshield being smashed with a trowel.

Now my economic survival is totally based on my nightly participation in a New Haven sleep study. I'm actually sleeping great again, in a real bed and all. If only 54-Point would butt out of my dreamtime.

So hey . . . the next time you're in Connecticut, step aside for the guy pushing a cartful of cans and bottles into a Stop & Shop. And smile kindly at the guy swigging the quart of Captain Morgan, yodeling Queen songs inside some park's band shell at dusk. And maybe even get out some change for the guy selling paperbacks off a blanket near but not actually on the grounds of the library. Because, "Come To Think of It," that "Roving I" may very well be me.

Michael Sloan's Memory Box

CAMBRIDGE, MA, 1970, WHEN I WAS SIX YEARS OLD...

IN THE NEIGHBORHOOD WHERE MY MOM AND I LIVED WAS AN UNTENDED PROPERTY CALLED NORTON'S WOODS. THE HOUSE WAS LONG GONE AND THE LAND WAS WILD, IN STARK CONTRAST TO THE MANICURED LAWNS OF SURROUNDING HOMES. A DISTURBING FEATURE OF THIS PROPERTY WAS A LARGE DEAD TREE THAT I SAW AS WE PASSED BY ON OUR EVENING WALKS. THE TREE SCARED ME: IT LOOKED EVIL AND GAVE ME BAD DREAMS.

TO MY MOM THE PROPERTY HAD BECOME A DANGEROUS PLACE WHERE BAD PEOPLE FROM OUTSIDE OUR NEIGHBORHOOD CAME AT NIGHT. ONE EVENING AS WE WALKED PAST, MY MOM DECIDED TO WARN ME ABOUT THE DANGERS OF VISITING THE PROPERTY.

"NEVER GO INSIDE THIS PLACE."
"WHY NOT, MOM?"
"BECAUSE HITLER LIVES THERE."

SUCH WAS MY INTRODUCTION TO HITLER. I DIDN'T KNOW WHO OR WHAT IT WAS, THOUGH I UNDERSTOOD IT TO BE SOMETHING EVIL LIKE THE DEAD TREE. LATER, WHEN I OVERHEARD MY RELATIVES TALKING ABOUT HITLER IN SERIOUS, FEARFUL VOICES, I WAS TERRIFIED BY THE KNOWLEDGE THAT HE LIVED IN MY NEIGHBORHOOD.

I KEPT THIS TERRIBLE KNOWLEDGE TO MYSELF.

HE WAS THE BAD BOY OF THE 80'S ART BOOM,
PROMOTED AND PREYED UPON UNTIL HIS BOOM WENT BUST.
HE WAS JEAN-MICHEL BASQUIAT...

THE MAD MASCOT OF SOHO!

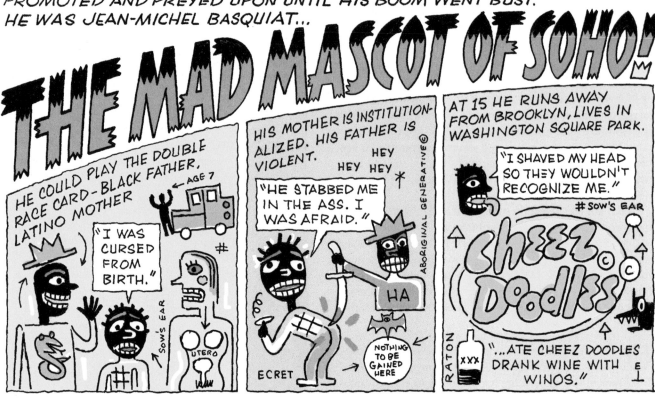

HE COULD PLAY THE DOUBLE RACE CARD - BLACK FATHER, LATINO MOTHER

AGE 7

"I WAS CURSED FROM BIRTH."

SOW'S EAR

UTERO

HIS MOTHER IS INSTITUTIONALIZED. HIS FATHER IS VIOLENT.

HEY HEY HEY HEY

"HE STABBED ME IN THE ASS. I WAS AFRAID."

ABORIGINAL GENERATIVE©

HA

NOTHING TO BE GAINED HERE

ECRET

AT 15 HE RUNS AWAY FROM BROOKLYN, LIVES IN WASHINGTON SQUARE PARK.

"I SHAVED MY HEAD SO THEY WOULDN'T RECOGNIZE ME."

SOW'S EAR

CHEEZ DOODLES © ©

RATON XXX

"...ATE CHEEZ DOODLES DRANK WINE WITH WINOS."

"I JUST SAT THERE DROPPING ACID FOR 8 MONTHS."

URINE   WASH   HAHA

ANGLO SAXAPHONE

ROCKET SHIP

POSITION

HIS FATHER AND THE COPS FIND HIM.

"I WILL BE VERY VERY FAMOUS ONE DAY."

HEY   HEY   HEY   HEY

YOU CAN CAMP HERE IMMORTALITY© HEY HEY©

HE'S SENT TO AN "ALTERNATIVE" HIGH SCHOOL. AT GRADUATION HE PIES THE PRINCIPAL.

HEE   HA

HA   HO

OUT ON THE STREET AGAIN. TURNING TRICKS IN TIMES SQUARE.

"I'M GOING TO BE A BUM."

25¢

PEER SHOW   .150   FLESH SPIRIT

FAT LEG©

BABOON APPLE OF SODOM

HE MEETS GRAFFITISTS KENNY SCHARF AND KEITH HARING. AND SAMO© IS BORN.

SAMO© AS A NEO ART FORM

SAMO© AS AN ESCAPE CLAUSE

SAMO© SAVES IDIOTS

SAMO© AS AN END TO THE CRAP... SOHO TOO!

"'SAMO'? WHAT'S THAT MEAN? SAME OLD SHIT OR SAMBO. MAYBE AMOS N'ANDY."

TAXI

AMOS N' ANDY
SAMO   TM

AMOS N' ANDY, SAMO N' ANDY - ANDY WARHOL BUYS A POSTCARD SAMO SELLS ON THE STREET.

"...AN ART HERO OF MINE."

IMMORTALITY© EROICA

ZEP!

© EROICA

SAMO'S BLONDE MOHAWK, DRUGGED-OUT, BUGGED OUT DANCE STYLE MAKE HIM A FAVORITE IN SOHO CLUBS.

"STOP ASKING PEOPLE FOR MONEY... START PAINTING..."

HE TAKES THE ADVICE, PAINTS ON ANYTHING HE CAN FIND. MET CURATOR GELDZAHLER BUYS HIS REFRIGERATOR DOOR FOR $2,000.

"HE'S 22, ... HE'S BLACK AND HE'S PART OF HISTORY."

BASQUIAT IS THE HIT OF THE "NEW YORK, NEW WAVE" EXHIBITION

HE WATCHES PEOPLE'S FEET FROM UNDER A TABLE.

ANNINA NOSEI GIVES HIM SPACE IN THE BASEMENT OF HER SOHO GALLERY.

IT'S RUMORED SHE PROVIDES DRUGS TO INCREASE PRODUCTION.

BUYERS ARE WAITING

STOP! THEY'RE NOT FINISHED!

ANGERED BY NOSEI'S EXPLOITATION, HE SLASHES HIS WORK AND POURS PAINT ON THE PILE.

"YO, MAN! I FIXED HER."

"IT WAS LIKE A FACTORY, A SICK FACTORY. I WANTED TO BE A STAR, NOT A GALLERY MASCOT... A 'WILD MONKEY MAN.'"

GALLERY MOGUL, LARRY "GO-GO" GAGOSIAN:

HE HAD THE "ABILITY TO CHURN OUT PAINTINGS INSTANTLY... FOR THE CASH HE ALWAYS NEEDED TO BUY DRUGS."

WHEN HIS FATHER REJECTS HIM, BASQUIAT GIVES THE CROWN TO OTHER, OFTEN TRAGIC, BLACK HEROES...

SUGAR RAY   CASSIUS CLAY   JOE LOUIS

MOST KINGS GET THIER HEAD CUT OFF

HE FINDS A FATHER AVATAR IN ART IDOL ANDY. THEY COLLABORATE ON A PAS DES DEUX.

HE HAS B.O. →

WARHOL ★ BASQUIAT
PAINTINGS
SEPTEMBER 14 THROUGH OCTOBER 19, 1985

THE WORK IS SAVAGED BY CRITICS. ONE CALLS BASQUIAT "AN ART WORLD MASCOT".

THE SUDDEN, PUBLIC REVELATION OF DEPENDENCY AND EXPLOITATION SEND JEAN-MICHEL INTO A DEATH SPIRAL.

HE BECOMES FIXATED ON A ROAST CHICKEN IN HIS FRIDGE, SEEING IT AS A PORTENT OF HIS DEATH.

HE PLANS A TRIP TO AFRICA TO HAVE A SHAMAN EXORCISE HIS DEMONS AND RID HIM OF HIS ADDICTIONS.

BUT THE DEMONS WIN. JEAN-MICHEL, AGE 27, DIES OF AN OVERDOSE.

"DO YOU THINK I'M GOING OUT OF FASHION? DO YOU THINK I'M ALL WASHED UP?"

THE VULTURES CIRCLE THE CORPSE. EVERY DOODLE NOW HAS VALUE.

BASQUIAT'S FATHER INHERITS A FORTUNE IN ART AND MERCHANDISING OPPORTUNITIES.

EXPLOITED IN DEATH AS HE WAS IN LIFE, JEAN-MICHEL IS REBORN— AS A BRAND.

BASQUIAT FRAGRANCE CANDLE $51

BASQUIAT SNEAKER

$99

Thanks to **Cloudy With A Chance of Meatballs**, Ron Barrett *is a cult figure among eight-year-olds.*
His Excessive Alphabet, Avalanches of A's to Zillions of Z's *is due this year.*

The End

FADE IN:
INT. BUNKER — NIGHT
Projected on the curtain (or a card reads):

DER FÜHRERBUNKER.
April 30, 1945.

The curtain opens and we see ADOLF HITLER holding a GUN in one hand and stroking his dead dog, BLONDIE, with the other. (*NOTE: Dog is stuffed animal with an Iron Cross medal around its neck.*)

HITLER
Forgive me, Blondie, but this was better than being captured by the Red Army. And like the two of us walking in the woods, I am just steps behind you. Sleep well, my friend. And may history judge us both as heroes.

Hitler places the gun to his temple.

HITLER (CONT'D)
For Deutschland!
(*shrugs*)
I tried.

Hitler closes his eyes and is about to pull the trigger when THERE'S A LOUD BOOM and SMOKE.

HITLER (CONT'D)
Yuh! What was that?

From the smoke, a TIME TRAVELER in late 21st-century garb emerges.

TIME TRAVELER
That was a cosmic boom caused by a rip in the space-time continuum.

HITLER
Where did you come from?

TIME TRAVELER
The future. I'm a time traveler sent to kill Adolf Hitler!
(*then*)
Um, you.
(*then; continues*)
And stop the atrocities of the Third Reich!

HITLER
Clever plan, but unfortunately, you have come too late.

TIME TRAVELER
Wait, what's the date?

HITLER
April thirtieth, nineteen-forty-five.

TIME TRAVELER
Are you kidding me? Then you've already slaughtered six million Jews?

HITLER
Yes! And just as many gypsies, homosexuals, Russians, Polish, and many other races too inferior to even mention.

TIME TRAVELER
(*upset*)
Okay, this is a total tech fart. They were supposed to get me here by 1934 at the latest!

HITLER
Things don't always go as planned. Trust me, I know. Now if you'll excuse me —

Hitler puts the gun back to his temple.

TIME TRAVELER
Wait!

HITLER
What? You came here to kill me and now you're going to stop me?

TIME TRAVELER
No. Definitely not stopping you. It's just... This is kinda awkward...
(*blurts it out*)
Can I pull the trigger?

HITLER
What difference does it make? I'll be dead either way.

TIME TRAVELER
Exactly. I'll disappear back to the future and the whole world will assume you pulled the trigger. So if it doesn't make a difference, why not let me do it? It'll be way cooler.

HITLER
(*gets it*)
Oh, like a good story to tell on dates. Get you laid.

TIME TRAVELER
(*annoyed*)
No.
(*then; admitting*)
Okay, yes.
(*after a beat*)
But also time travel technology is just beginning. They need to work out the kinks — obvs — but eventually they'll refine it and soon people will be arriving in time to save... your dog. Then the Russians. And finally the Jews. But if I pull the trigger, I'll still be able

.... ◆ ....

Nell Scovell *has written for Bob Newhart, Bette Midler, Bart Simpson, David Letterman, and Miss Piggy.*

"The Bunker" by PIA GUERRA

"Okay, this is a total tech fart. They were supposed to get me here by 1934 at the latest!"

to say, "I kicked it off. I was the original person who went back in time and killed Adolf Hitler."

Hitler considers the argument, then determined:

HITLER
Why should I help you? I control my fate. I watched my wife, Eva, put a cyanide capsule between her teeth and she was braun enough to bite down.

TIME TRAVELER
You mean "brave" enough.

HITLER
That's what I said.

TIME TRAVELER
No, you didn't. You said, "Braun enough."

HITLER
(confused)
I don't think so. Did I?

The Time Traveler takes advantage of Hitler's momentary confusion and lunges for the gun. Hitler puts up a fight, but the Time Traveler wrestles the gun from his hands.

TIME TRAVELER
Ha!

HITLER
Not fair! Your reflexes are quicker than mine. I just turned 56. You haven't even been born yet!

TIME TRAVELER
No more excuses. Prepare to die.

The Time Traveler points the gun at Hitler. Suddenly:

HITLER
Wait!

The Time Traveler reacts, startled.

TIME TRAVELER
Ack, don't startle me! I've got a gun in my hand!

HITLER
I need to know one thing. Since you come from the future, you can tell me. How did history judge me? Am I... a hero?

The Time Traveler considers this a beat, then:

TIME TRAVELER
Look, let's just say: you still come up a lot in conversation.

HITLER
How so?

TIME TRAVELER
Well, there's Godwin's Law, which states that the longer an Internet argument goes on, the likelihood of Adolf Hitler being brought up approaches one hundred percent.

HITLER
This is good! What is the Internet?

TIME TRAVELER
Oh, it's this thing that replaced human knowledge.

HITLER
I see.

TIME TRAVELER
But it quickly became a place of petty disputes where idiots rush not to make the best argument but to simply be "first."

HITLER
And mentioning my name often marks the conclusion of these ridiculous arguments?

TIME TRAVELER
Uh huh. It's basically shorthand for letting a stranger know you think they're horrible.

HITLER
Yes! So I went down in history as the greatest megalomaniac of all time!

TIME TRAVELER
(not so fast)
Um, actually...

HITLER
What? No?

TIME TRAVELER
Oh, you were. For decades. But then Donald Trump came along.

HITLER
(upset)
I was replaced?! That's enough. Don't tell me any more! Just kill me. I wish you'd killed me five minutes ago!

TIME TRAVELER
Then on the count of three...

The Time Traveler puts the gun to Hitler's temple. Hitler closes his eyes. THE LIGHTS GO TO BLACK..

TIME TRAVELER
(in darkness)
One... Two...

BAM. A GUNSHOT. A BODY FALLS.

TIME TRAVELER
Ha! First!

THE END.

Odd Birds

THE RAVING HOMELAND JINGO

This recently introduced European species is often mistaken (by itself) for native American. It proudly displays its red neck, white knuckles, and bluenosed morality, kept aloft by updrafts of hot air. The Jingo emits gruesome shrieks in defense of its territory against the occasional Left-Winged News Hawk. The Jingo is anatomically anomalous, in that its testicles are located in its cranium, and its brains are safely secured behind an exceptionally tight sphincter.

"What shulde I seyn? of foules every kinde
That in this world han fethres and stature,
Men mighten in that place assembled finde ..."
—**Geoffrey Chaucer,**
Parlement of Foules, 1382

The all-too-common **Back Lot Goose,** *with its natural prey, the* **Wide-eyed Chippy.**

LOVE BIRDS
The Horny Old Coot
The Wagtail Coquette
The Wandering Hubby
The Three-Day Lark
The Solitary Little Shag, or Lovesick Loon
The Timorous Cheek-Pecker
The Blushing Nymphette
The Great-Breasted Bimbo
The Pearly Throated Widow-Bird
The Cockeyed Henpecker
The Great Horned Cuckold

LOATHE BIRDS
The Red-Faced Screaming Fitt
The Cold-Shouldered Snub
The Long-Standing Grudge
The Loathsome Dove
The Peevish Quibble
The Social-Climbing Guttersnipe
The Chafing Jibe
The Petulant Gripe
The Venomous Spite

BIRDS OF NEW YORK
The Hairy Bohemian Weirdo
The Jogging Huffin Puffin
The Nocturnal Piercing Shriek
The Oblivious Walking Jay
The Perpetual Jackhammer
The Wattle-Throated Culture Vulture (or Whooping Crone)
The High-Tailed Street Walker
The Lusty Pheasant Type
The Magnanimous Fuhgeddaboudit
The Tedious Laureate
The English Plummy-Throated Thespian

JAIL BIRDS
The Red-Handed Grafter
The Thirty-Day Stint
The White-Collared Till-Dipper
The Yellow-Bellied Stool Pigeon
The Double Crossbill
The Hooded Perp-Walker
The Light-Fingered Bunco
The Whispering Guinea Fowl *or* Busted Kneecapo

BIRDS OF HOLLYWOOD
The Mini-Moe Gull & A Three-Picture Teal
The Back Lot Goose & A Wide-Eyed Chippy
The Deep-Pocketed Starstruck Loon
The Deep-Throated Starlet
The Big-Budget Flopperoo
The Chowder-Headed Lunk
The Groveling Wince

BIRDS OF WALL ST. *or* FLIM-FLAM BIRDS
The Pinstriped Profit-Skimmer
The Ledge-Perching Sucker
The Old-Fashioned Hornswoggle
The New-Fangled Scam
The Cross-Billed Consumer
The Prosperous Pigeon
The Modest Little Shakedown
The Disappearing Greenbacks
The Bald-Faced Chisler
The Double-Dipping Pip-Squeak
The Whistleblowing Patsy
The Hoodwinked Bagholder
The Offshore Diddle
The Old-Moneyed Bustard
The Four-Flushing Shill
The Rubber-Checked Kingpin
The Sitting Duck

BIRDS OF PRAY
The Celibate Tot-Fondler
The Cozy Episcopal Chat
The Red-Necked Pulpit-Thumper
The Straining Gnat Swallow
A Minyan of Nit-Picking Orthoducks
The Overly Pious Carpet Sucker
The Cuckoo-Brained Missionary
The Dusky-Faced Hellfire Preacher

SONG BIRDS
The Lonesome Melodious Cowbird (*or* Redheaded Grass Warbler)
The Superb-Fronted Dolly Bird
The Original Rhinestone Cowbird (*or* Grand Old Osprey)
Shrill Parti-Colored Jacko (extinct)
Satchmo's Scat-Singing Hornbill (a/k/a The Incomparable Gravel-Throated Grass-Puffer)
Zimmerman's Cryptic Drone
Yentl's Earsplitting Grossbeak

SHORE BIRDS
The Pouting Bronzed Peckerhead
The Barecheeked Thongbird
The Tawny Sandchick (or Superb Tit)
The Hairy-Backed Hubby & Bluehaired Yenta (Fountainbleu Snowbirds)
The Malibu Shack-Crasher
The Spotty Midwest Riff-Raff
The Round-Rumped White-Faced Prairie Chicken
The Caribbean Grass-Runner
The Swaggering Gut-Sucker
The False-Bosomed Honey Hunter

A Malibu Shack-Crasher.

BIRDS OF WASHINGTON

The Bubble-Headed Dunce
The Biannual Lame Duck
The Mealy-Mouthed Dove
The Smooth-Tongued Brazen Upstart
The Bald-Faced Lyre
The Red-Baiting Chicken-Hawk (*or* Knuckle-Headed Jingo)
The Preening Martinet
The Free Screech Owl
The Profound Egret (often photographed with a Long-Legged Myna)
The Right-Winged Loony
The Liberal Turkey
A Clueless Nincompoop
The Vanishing American Petrel
The Two-Faced Grafter
Boneheaded Babbler
The Nest-Feathering Catbird
The Let-Them-Eat Crow
The Fact-Spinning Mockingbird
The Green-Backed Public Tapsucker

SPORTING BIRDS

The Screaming Scarlet Manager
The Hoary-Headed Junk-Chucker
The Stat-Grubbing Peckerhead
The Truculent Backcourt Sulk (Tennis)
The Pumped-Up Dunker
The Blue-Collared Hobby (Bowling)
The Rough-Shanked Bogie
The Canvas-Back White Hoopoe (Boxing)

BIRDS OF TEXAS

The Gulf Coast Petrel Dumper
The Green-Back Dullard
Rove's Bush-Twit
Cheney's Heartless Bustard
The Migrant Hedge-Clipper

HISTORICAL BIRDS

Franklin's Stormy Kite
The Mythological Bulfinch
Tchaikovsky's Seasonal Nutcracker

LITERARY BIRDS

Fitzgerald's Tipsy Flapper
Edgar Allan's Loquacious Raven
McMurtry's Lonesome Dove
The Non-Aquatic Hart Crane
Joyce's Cryptic Blather
Oscar's Pink-Bottomed Boychick
Roth's Grossbeaked Wanker
Rowling's Magical Claptrap
DaVinci's Brown Feathered Potboiler

COCKATAILS

The Hermit Lush
The Higher Kite
The Loud-Mouthed Guzzler
The Late Night Toddy
The Pie-Eyed Tippler
The Ruffled Boozer
The Crapulous Binge

The Pickled Heron
The Cockeyed Burp
The Bum's Thrush

BIRDS OF NEW ENGLAND

Radcliffe's Small-Breasted Ninny
The Great Stammering Twit
The Crested Blue Blazer *or* Gray Flannel Chaffitch
The Brown-Nosed Upstart *or* Shit-Eating Grinne

BIRDS OF THE HOMELAND

The Colonial Williamsbird
The Cheeky Guttersnipe
The Ruddy Shame
The Little Orphan Ani
Mapplethorpe's Great Pecker
The Common Raving Nutcase
The Thin-Skinned Little Pique
The Mocking Heckle

A grizzled **Hoary-Headed Junk-Chucker** *faces down a* **Stat-Grubbing Peckerhead**.

HITCHCOCK'S MacGUFFIN

An Old World species, introduced to California: a plump, lugubrious bird given to stealthy silences, sudden shrieks, and terrifying displays. Its diet consists of red herrings and snakes in the grass. Despite its reputation, has laid the occasional egg. Sometimes mistaken for **Hammett's Maltese Falcon**; not to be confused with any of **Spielberg's Mawkish Cliff Hangers**.

THE CHRISTOPHER WREN

Like the **Francis Drake**, the **Dean Swift** and the **Florence Nightingale**, this bird prefers a cold, damp, dreary environment such as the city of London, England, in which the Christopher Wren constructs nests of preposterous design, monumental size, and no apparent use. (This species is not related to the similarly named **Christopher Robin**, native to the Hundred Acre Wood in East Sussex.)

#sicsemperpapyrus

A Sprawling Epic Micro-Novella of Our Times

Day One

I've been giving this some thought for a long time now, and this "paper covers rock" business is TOTAL BULLSHIT. Rock obviously punches hole in paper. Anyone can see that. Think of all the years this has been allowed to go on. #endthelies

Update: 1 hour later: Paper "covers" rock? You might as well say paper covers SCISSORS!

It's completely ridiculous! #govtconspiracy #wakeupsheeple

Update: 2 hours later:

JUST THINK ABOUT IT. How can paper defeat rock by covering it?

"Oh no, my rock's been rendered useless by being covered in paper."—*No One, Never*

Stand up and be counted for THE TRUTH. Who's with me!?!? #throwpaperout #makeamericagreat again

Update: 3 hours later
<u>PRESS RELEASE</u>
I, Todd Hanson, and an armed group of my friends and neighbors, will be occupying a federal building here in Brooklyn until the government officially admits that paper does NOT, in fact, cover rock (because rock PUNCHES HOLE IN paper—OBVIOUSLY!), and thereby OFFICIALLY REVERSES the outcomes of ALL PRIOR "paper covers rock" decisions, to right this injustice.

We will remain peaceful but if provoked we WILL defend ourselves. #werenotleaving #aslong asittakes #liberty #truth #justice

Day Two

My heavily armed cohorts and I are hunkering down for the long haul as our STANDOFF WITH THE FEDS enters its second day. Our victory is inevitable, because as anyone can CLEARLY SEE, rock, in reality, BEATS paper by ripping a jagged hole straight through its flimsy, pathetic surface, contradicting GENERATIONS OF LIES told to America's children.

We have, however, opted not to occupy a federal building (as we'd previously decided) after all, on the grounds that 1.) it's much too difficult to do and 2.) we lack the manpower to defend it in the event that we could occupy such a building in the first place.

Therefore, we have decided to occupy my apartment instead.

We will NOT BE MOVED and are fully willing to DIE for this cause! #brooklynrockmilitia #sicsemperpapyrus

Day Three

The armed showdown is still on here at my place, as we refuse to back down until the federal govenment puts an ed to the falsehood, perpetuated by the Powers That Be, that paper covers rock.

We remain steadfast in our principles and committed to our cause. But I admit that tensions are growing.

So far, there have been no reprisals from the government for our actions. In fact, there has been no response from the Feds at all. Nothing. This has caused some within our ranks to grow dispirited.

Worse yet, our attempts to kill time by playing Rock/Paper/Scissors are going nowhere. Since nothing beats rock anymore, we already know how each game is going to turn out beforehand. Everybody keeps picking rock, so each game ends in a tie. It's boring.

Thus, I fear our morale may be threatened by the ongoing pressures of maintaining the siege. Nonetheless, we WILL NOT STOP. Yes, facing down the government is turning out to be harder than we thought it would, but we cannot allow our resolve to weaken!

Rock rips paper. Everybody knows that. It's just common sense.

Anything else would be absurd. #neversurrender #standforwhatsright #pleasesendsocksandsnacks

Day Four

I'm so confused.

When I started this movement, everything seemed so simple. Paper cannot defeat rock—how could it? Basic empirical observation made such an assertion undeniably false. The righteousness of our cause seemed as simple as the brute force of the rocks we carried in our justice-seeking fists.

There was a wrong way, and a right way. The zero-sum game structure represented by paper covering rock was a lie: This was an obvious certainty.

It made sense of a complicated world. Finally, there was one clear answer. And in that clarity was strength. The uncuttable, unrippable strength of rock.

But now, on the fourth day of the armed overthrow of this apartment, my compatriots and I face growing suspicion and distrust. Doubts seem to lurk around every corner. My mind is filled with questions:

············ ◆ ············

The original head writer for **The Onion,** Todd Hanson *lives in Brooklyn with his two cats,* **James Boswell** *and* **Dr. Samuel Johnson.**

RICK GEARY

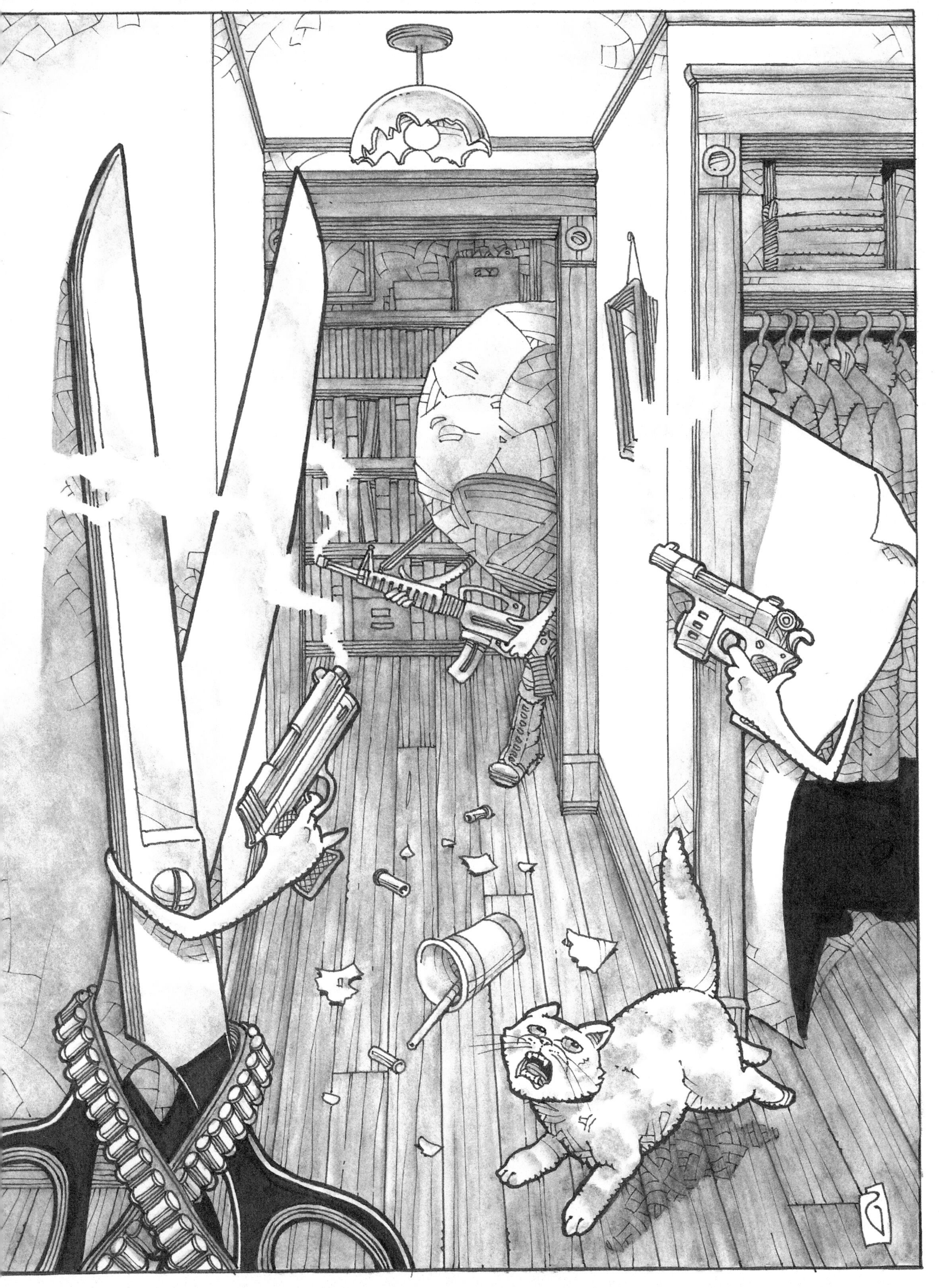

What if we were wrong? Why haven't the Feds stormed the building yet? Are they even paying attention? Does what we are doing here make any SENSE?

More importantly, I fear something terrible is happening within our own ranks. Yet I feel powerless to stop it.

There are whispers that rock is not as strong as scissors. Compelling arguments are being given serious consideration. An atmosphere of internal sedition prevails. I fear splinter groups are forming!

Rock, give me strength to face the dark days ahead!

Day Five

The Scissors Brigade attacked at dawn.

Formed by traitors inside our own ranks, young and angry militants grown disillusioned with the cause of rock, they struck with precise, cutting-edge fighting tactics.

Their flag: an open pair of scissors, in the shape of an X, black, in a white circle, on a red field.

It has an eerie familiarity I cannot place—stark and absolute. It is terrifying.

Their claim against us is that scissors, being made of steel, are harder than rock. They are disciplined, authoritarian, uncompromising. Their worldview is strict and total: a tripartite hierarchy, with scissors at the top, rock in the middle, and paper on the bottom. Nothing, they say, can be allowed to deviate from this natural order.

Our counter-claim that rock blunts scissors falls on deaf ears. Rock does not blunt scissors, they say, but rather, SHARPENS them.

"What does one use to hone a blade?" they ask. "A whetstone." It is difficult to refute this argument. Armed as we are with only rocks, we are no match for their shining, deadly, stabbing weapons.

Within hours, they had seized key areas of the bathroom and living room. The remaining Rock Loyalists have managed to retain control of the kitchen, library, and bedroom, bringing the now-contested occupation of the apartment to an uneasy stalemate.

But we amongst the pro-rock forces are cut off from each other. So far, there have been no fatalities, but for how long?

All this, and yet still no word from the Feds! Cunning to the last, they are content to let us tear ourselves apart from within. The Scissors Brigade will not listen to us and, having cut off our lines of communication with each other, retain the upper hand. I fear the worst.

Distraught, I have been spending the lonely hours reading in my library. Perusing the volumes in my desultory state, I felt near to giving up when, to my shock, I discovered something I never expected.

Hidden between the pages of Lao Tzu's "The Art Of War," I found a piece of, yes, paper. This is what it said:

"We are the Paper Underground. Using the method of passing illicit notes, we are forging a base amongst sympathetic members of both of your forces. If you wish to communicate with your fellow Rockists, you must go through us. It is only through working together that we can defeat the hated scissors, our mutual foe. Stay vigilant—we will contact you again soon when the moment is right. "

But can they be trusted!? This rebellion began with my realization, hesitant at first, the growing into what felt like an unshakeable conviction, that rocks RIPS paper, and our most fervent belief was that paper cannot cover rock. Can we really afford to ally ourselves with our sworn enemy, despite how tempting it may be in this time of need?

I just don't know what to believe anymore. I just don't know what to believe.

Day Six

As our militant insurrection reaches its sixth day with still no contact from the Feds, our internal battle over the rules of Rock/Paper/Scissors continues with no clear victor in sight.

Scissors remains the most dangerous, and fervently totalitarian, of the three rival groups that have formed from within our formerly unified ranks. Those of us who have chosen rock as our weapon are still the strongest in large groups, capable of overwhelming our foes with mob action but lacking the precision, surgical-strike strategic capability of scissors. Yet, dependent on the help of the Paper Underground for communication, we are unable to organize ourselves into counterattack. Paper, on the other hand, cannot move out into the open for fear of being cut by scissors, instead relying on misdirection, secrecy, and spycraft as their main tools in the uneasy alliance they have formed with rock against their hated enemy.

As of this writing, all three forces—the faithful Rock Loyalists, the fascist Scissors Brigade, and the mysterious Paper Underground—remain locked in a balance of power no one side can seem to break. No one can say what will happen next.

Day Seven

INTERMISSION
(Due to the Majestic Length of this Epic Tale, THE AUDIENCE is now provided with an opportunity to take a break. They get up, stretch their legs, visit the concession stand, step outside for a smoke, mingle, and discuss.)

AUDIENCE MEMBER
(lingering in lobby, waiting for spouse to return from restroom)
So cool that they revived the Road Show concept!

SECOND AUDIENCE MEMBER
(Looking up from complimentary program booklet given at door)
I guess, but it's certainly strange that they'd make such a big deal of using the widescreen 70mm format, just to present a story that takes place in basically one little Brooklyn apartment.

AM: Yeah, it's a bit weird. I guess when I heard the phrase "Standoff with the Feds" I figured it'd be more, you know, like a sweeping western, with snow-swept plains and mountain vistas, where freedom fighter cowboys seize a federal building in Oregon or somewhere like that, and then the people rally to their cause as they stand up to the government, and there's a glorious battle and it's like they're heroes at the Alamo or something. This hasn't been anything like that at all. So far, the Feds don't even seem to have noticed that their siege is taking place.

SAM: I thought there'd be more violence by this point. So far it's been mostly talking.

AM: Maybe all the violence will be in Act 2.

Day Eight

We are in Hell. Trapped in a Hell of our own making!

And still not a peep from the federal authorities! I mean, I realize we're talking about a bloated bureaucracy here, but how long can it possibly take to organize and execute a proper response? It's like we're not even a priority for these people!

The armed occupation of the apartment has devolved into a static yet unstable equilibrium between three mutually hostile but equally balanced adversaries, characterized by constantly shifting alliances as territory is lost and gained on an hourly basis and battle lines are redrawn continually throughout the day.

No one is sure who's on anyone's side at any given time. Intrigue and mutual mistrust fill our days and nights.

Danger is everywhere.

We all sleep with one eye open, each of us dreading the same three things: an unexpected blow to the temple from a fist-clenched rock; the horrific spurts of blood as scissors are plunged through a ribcage into the heart; the rustling sound—barely detectable, but possessing of an irrefutable finality—of a piece of paper, passed from one hand to another in the darkness, ordering our execution.

It was in this fitful state of semi-consciousness, wavering between the horrors of sleep and an even more nightmarish reality, that the vision overcame me.

I found myself in a damp, cold forest, its verdant hues muted in half-shadow. Was it dusk? Or just before dawn? I could not say. Before me was a large clearing in which stood an enormous boulder, its sides stained by rain and moss, half-obscured by fog but as permanent and immovable as anything on Earth.

Suddenly the forest shook as the shadows were filled with a thunderous roar. The stone split in two as a mighty oak—first just a green shoot but then growing taller and wider until its branches blotted out the moon—shot up and outward to the heavens.

Then there was a crack of thunder and a bolt of lightning scissored down from the murky, cloud-roiled sky, splitting the tree like kindling and setting it afire. Its pieces, flimsy and burnt, fluttered down in smoking sheets, falling on the stone like snow, covering it entire.

As the fire turned to embers, the stone began to melt and shrink and glow red-hot, like ore refined.

Shaken, I wanted to hide my face. But for some reason, though gripped by indescribable fear I walked forward. As the slab of metal before me cooled, I saw, in still-red letters engraven on its surface, words written in runes I could not decipher, but heard in my mind:

YOU HAVE BEEN TAUGHT THAT PAPER COVERS ROCK, ROCK CRUSHES SCISSORS, AND SCISSORS CUTS PAPER

My heart raced in my chest. I could not breathe. But I could not look away, and read on.

AND THESE THINGS ARE MOST CERTAINLY TRUE

Could it be? Could it be really be, despite everything that had happened, despite everything I'd said and done, that paper actually does cover rock, after all?

*BUT LO! THESE THINGS TOO ARE JUST AS CERTAIN:
THAT ROCKS TEARS PAPER
THAT SCISSORS SHARPEN
ON ROCK
AND THAT PAPER UNDERMINES
SCISSORS*

My mind reeled. I found myself thinking of my childhood during the Cold War, of Game Theory, of the doctrine of Mutually Assured Destruction. And then the voice spoke unto me: "Todd Hanson, there is only one final line to be written, but you must write it yourself."

I didn't want to, but I raised my hand and pointed—lower three fingers curled, thumb up, index finger extended—and, with a bolt of blue-green energy, shooting from my trembling fingertip into the gleaming surface, I wrote, in immutable steel-jacketed letters, the words:

*EVERYTHING DESTROYS
EVERYTHING ELSE*

When I awoke, I was covered in sweat. Curled in my makeshift bed of dirty blankets on the hard wooden floor, I shivered in the light of the streetlamp burning wanly outside my window in the Brooklyn night.

Day Nine

"Brothers! Hear me!" I shouted. All parley and debate ceased as my words rang out across the apartment like a shot. "At last, I know what we must do!"

The occupiers, my former allies, now divided into warring clans, were emotionally exhausted, weak with hunger and thirst, ragged with lack of sleep. Many of them had not bathed in days. They wanted a way out. But they'd learned to be suspicious of any so-called solution. Their battle-weary eyes looked up at me.

"We have to issue a new set of demands to the Feds!" I shouted. "Otherwise, this whole standoff is meaningless!"

I relayed to the assembled militiamen what the vision had revealed to me, the New Order of The Seven Rules: paper covers rock, rock crushes scissors, scissors cuts paper, but also rock tears paper, scissors sharpen on rock, and paper undermines scissors, then concluding with the final, seventh rule, everything destroys everything else. These, I explained, must be our demands.

"It's no use pursuing our separate agendas anymore," I went on. "Divided we are weak! We must unite under a common banner, so that when the Feds finally come, we will be ready for them!"

A murmur of disapproval went through the crowd. They'd heard such talk of unification before, from all three factions. There were shouts of reproof and dismissal from the back of the living room, from the hallway closet, from the kitchen.

"Don't you see?" I continued, desperate, as their yelling increased. "Be ye rock, paper or scissors, one thing is certain: It is only through the knowledge that any one of us can, at any time, destroy the other that we will finally find sanity! It's the sole sure-fire means of ensuring security and maintaining the public good!"

I silenced the crowd by pumping my fist—one, two, three times. There was a collective gasp. And then, instead of a fist, or a flat hand, or a two-fingered V, I did something no one had done until now: I threw the fourth sign. Three fingers curled, index extended, thumb pointed to the sky. They began to scan each other's faces in sidelong glances, each wondering what the other was thinking.

"Compatriots!" I screamed. "This is the only way to keep us all safe!"

There was a pause as the implications

of this idea sank in. Time itself seemed to freeze.

Then, after that momentary half-second of hesitation, everybody went for their guns at once.

[*TO BE CONCLUDED*]

Day Ten

Looking back on it now, I think it was maybe a bad idea for us all to bring automatic weapons.

I don't know—I suppose we just thought it'd be, like, cool, I guess. I mean, here we were, standing up to the federal government and everything, so it only seemed natural to have our constitutionally protected firearms on hand to defend our freedom. Posing with them for Instagram photos made us feel rugged, badass, virile, empowered. The thought of a massive firefight with the Feds was exciting, like something you'd see on TV. We'd all professed a willingness to die for our cause, but in retrospect I don't think any of us had ever really thought that through.

At any rate, the second after I threw the "gun" sign and everyone drew their weapons on one another, my self-image suddenly did a complete one-eighty from Self-Important Messianic Freedom-Hero to Total and Complete Dumbshit.

Especially considering that, because I was holding out my right hand in an empty imaginary gun-shape, I was the only person not gripping an actual locked and loaded piece of ordnance.

I had time for one thought: That I probably wasn't going to have time to finish this thought. Then, in an instant, the room was filled with gunfire as dozens of weapons discharged simultaneously.

The sound was like someone twisting a roll of bubble wrap in half, but much, much louder. Huge, jagged holes appeared everywhere in sight as bullets ripped through any obstacle in their path. The air was thick with splinters of furniture, fragments of broken glass, and bursts of plaster dust. The whole apartment (which to be honest doesn't really fit this many people all that comfortably anyway, it was pretty cramped the entire siege) was utterly blown to hell, and we were temporarily deafened by the noise of the explosions and the shrieks of grown men.

Both of my cats bolted under the bed. The neighbors called the cops and everything.

Evidently, I'd been wrong about Mutually Assured Destruction being the solution to our problems.

Amid the maelstrom of chaos and destruction, I squeezed my eyes shut and thought, "In the future, I'm definitely thinking twice before taking any more advice from Mystical Dream Visions." Either I'd wildly misinterpreted the vision's meaning, or it was an ill-advised move to listen to the booming voice of a grandiose, biblical-seeming stress-induced fever-dream in the first place.

In fact, you know something? I gotta tell you—now that I think about it, this whole thing just seems like it was kind of a big mistake.

[*NEXT: the exciting epilogue brings our action-packed thrill ride to a close*]

Epilogue

As I think back on the situation now—several dozen angry, armed militants opening fire on one another, at point blank range, in an enclosed space—it's a goddamn miracle that nobody got their head blown off. But according to forensic analysis of the 847 separate bullet holes they found afterward, apparently everyone involved was too exhausted and crazed to aim properly in the split-second it took for them to pull the triggers.

So everyone missed their targets. The ballistics expert that was eventually brought in said the chances were like three trillion to one or something. I guess we got lucky.

Meanwhile, the Feds finally showed up. Well, not the Feds, exactly—more like the NYPD. They arrived in a pissed-off mood and demanded to know what the fuck was happening. I think they actually would've broken the door down if we hadn't opened it quick. A couple of us tried to explain about Rock/Paper/Scissors, but they just kept shouting over and over that we were talking nonsense. It didn't go well at all. We apologized and assured them it wouldn't happen again. But I don't think they bought it.

I'm not sure they know, even now, what exactly to charge us with. The legal situation is still unclear. It could take years before it's finally resolved. At least we have the NRA's powerful legal team on our side (we didn't ask them for help or anything; they just showed up on their own. A flurry of gunfire draws them like moths). A bunch of people are gonna to be in a heap of trouble, though, I'm pretty certain of that.

Except for, oddly enough, me. Because I was the only one who didn't pull a real firearm and I never fired a shot, by a freakish turn of fate, the attorneys say I might actually end up with no charges being pressed after all. Lawyers, huh? Go figure! LOL!

Speaking of laws, you know what? After news of the gunfight hit the media—Gawker described it as "both the worst (43 shooters) and the least-worst (zero fatalities or injuries) mass shooting in the history of American gun violence," and a video called "Militia Idiots All Miss" went viral on YouTube, to name just two examples—I got an email from a philosophy professor at Columbia. She explained to me that, legally speaking, the federal government doesn't even have jurisdiction over the rules of Rock/Paper/Scissors to begin with! According to her, these rules are just a set of Arbitrarily-Agreed-Upon Social Fictions that, taken collectively, make the process of randomized decision-making easier. Do I have egg on my face, or what?

Anyway, point being: That's the last time I take on the Feds! Sorry, guys! Boy, do I ever feel foolish!

Oh, there is one more thing. Despite everything, there are apparently some members of the uprising that have refused to give up their respective dogmas. Though the news media have largely lost interest in them, they're still out there somewhere—off in the wilderness, resolute and unyielding, occupying away in their various armed standoffs with their rocks, paper, scissors and guns. Sheesh! You'd think they'd learn!

I just hope nobody gets hurt.

THE END

[*NOTE: As of this writing, Todd Hanson remains at large.*]

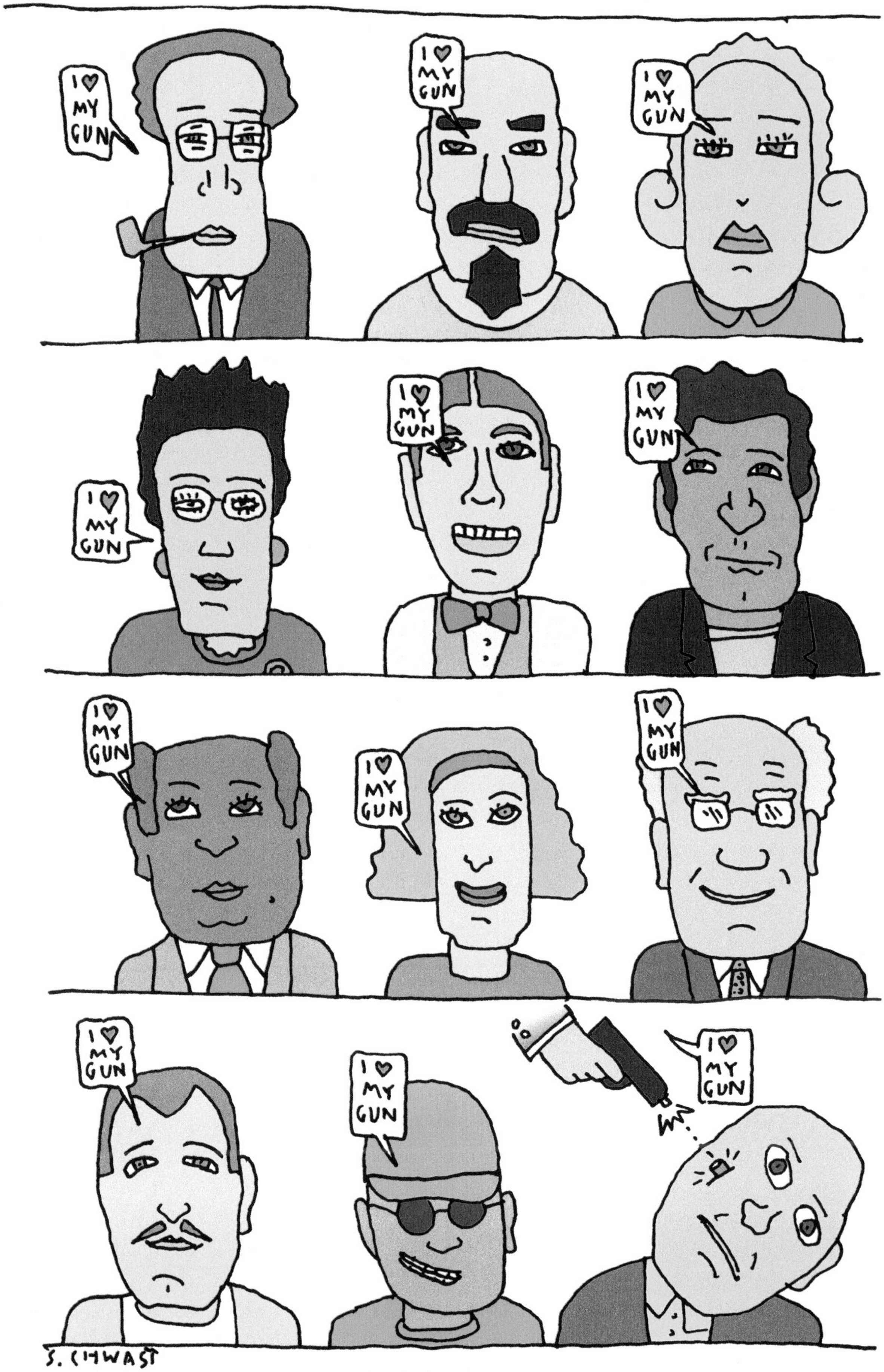
I ♥ MY GUN
I ♥ MY GUN
I ♥ MY GUN
I ♥ MY GUN
I ♥ MY GUN
I ♥ MY GUN
I ♥ MY GUN
I ♥ MY GUN
I ♥ MY GUN
I ♥ MY GUN
I ♥ MY GUN
I ♥ MY GUN
S. CHWAST

The Dracula Letters

Dear Mr. Handey:
I saw your name in a pretty cosmopolitan magazine recently and you alluded to Count Dracula so I wanted to ask you, does the Count answer prayers like many of the undead who reside in heaven seem to? Some of the villagers who work at the coffin factory believe he does. If it's true, could you ask him how I can make some money? I'm all confused about how to make money. I'm not doing something right because guess what I don't have any of?
Thanks,
Brian McConnachie
and…
All Hail Count Dracula

Dear Mr. McConnachie:
Find a baby and give it to Dracula. That'll get you on his good side.
Then he'll cut you in on some deals.
All Hail Count Dracula,
Jack Handey

Dear Mr. Handey:
When you say "find a baby" do you mean, "steal a baby"? Or could you possibly mean, go and meet somebody nice, start taking them to dinner, fall in love, marry them and have a baby. And give the baby to Dracula. Which is a little more work than I was planning on, frankly.

I spent some time last week hanging around the village (the Village of the Coffin Makers) and they were saying The Count is still licking his wounds over the sub-prime house-flipping fiasco.

Have you heard otherwise?
Trying to get ahead,
Brian
All Hail Count Dracula

Dear Brian,
Yes, steal a baby. Or, if you have to, buy one. The count has a fondness for Swiss babies. But, to be honest, you can just get a baby doll and fill it full of blood. He won't know the difference.
The coffin makers are wrong. The count sold his castle at the peak of the market to Jack Nicholson.
All Hail Count Dracula!
Jack

Dear Jack:
Yes, the villagers said he's really near-sighted so the blood-filled doll might work.

I got a doll from a Swiss catalogue. (FYI They're not cheap. Euros! Cripes!) I'll fill it with a pint of my own blood. The directions are in French so I hope I'm doing this right. I think it's a kind of a "Betsy Wetsy"-type deal: You squeeze it and the liquid squirts out. But it squirts out a hole in the bottom. If he wants to bite the neck, the blood is just going to go all over his shoes. Unless he holds the baby doll up-side down. And THEN bites it.

Do I have to be there when he does this?
A.H.C.D.,
Brian

Dear Brian:
I know what you're saying about the doll. To be honest, I think it's actually easier to just steal someone's baby. Or buy one. You can get them online.
I'd be there when you give it to him. Otherwise his personal assistant Michelle will take credit for it.
A.H.C.D.,
Jack

Dear Jack:
I did both. I bought one AND I stole one. I also got a Paddington Bear and soaked it in cranberry juice. The babies are cute as the dickens. I can't tell them apart. But the Villagers from the Village of the Coffin Makers sure can! They've been chasing me around the village for the past day and a half. The good news is they never spread out — "…you go that way; you men go there and the rest, follow me!" — They hunt me in one big tight pack. Banging into each other and falling over each other. I yelled back at them, "Don't you guys have to go to work? And someone yelled back, "it's not our shift yet." Then I heard someone else say, "Don't talk to him. He's the Wolfman." I almost stopped in my tracks. The Wolfman! The hell you say. Anybody see hair growing on my ears?

I wanted to yell back, "I am not the Wolfman. I'm just a regular guy just doing what it takes to try and get ahead. And make some money. Live the dream." But that's a lot more than I could have gotten out after running around this screwy village for a day and a half with a baby in each arm plus a stuffed, juice-soaked bear. Then they'll change shifts on me. My only hope is that they really work them hard at the coffin factory.

I caught a break. Shift Two was exhausted. I made it up to the castle and got in. But then I looked around the reception area and Jeeez! What is this? Open baby night?!

There is no way he's going to see all these babies before the sun comes up.

What should I do? Leave and take my chances with the villagers? Or just jump the line?

FYI Michelle is off tonight. But she's back tomorrow. I don't want to deal with her.
A.H.C.D.,
Brian

A.H.C.D.,
Can you juggle? The count loves juggling. My plan depends on your ability to juggle three objects of unequal weight: the two babies and the bear. This will get His Majesty's attention.
Otherwise, I would suggest growl-

B.K. TAYLOR

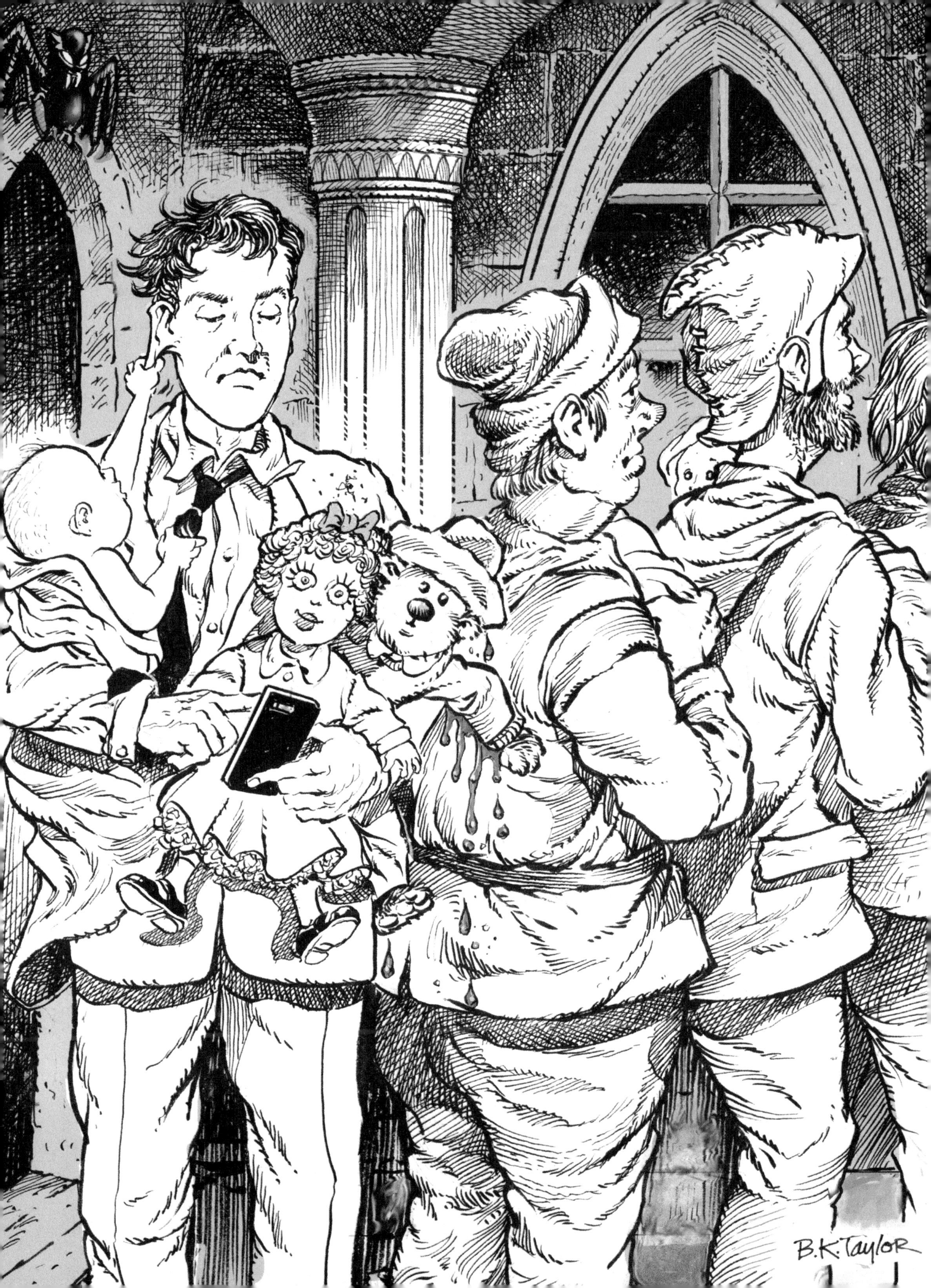
B.K.Taylor

ing at the other people in line. Hopefully, someone will turn and yell, "IT'S THE WOLF MAN!!" Then they'll all run off.

I heard Michelle got a better offer from Dick Cheney, and she won't be around much longer. Let's hope.

A.H.C.D.,
Jack

I can juggle!

When I was in the Army, I'd go around to the veteran's hospitals whistling the William Tell Overture and juggle three tennis balls at once for all our boys in bed. But not three items of different weight. That was a little above my pay grade, as we used to say in the Army Infantry, USO, Juggling Division — "The Tossing Thirty-Fourth" — The Fe-Fi-Foes of Terror. And it was always the same three tennis balls. If you lost one, you'd be cleaning toilets for a month. Some of the guys preferred Indian clubs but I felt pretty comfortable with tennis balls.

So, yes, I know the principles of juggling.

I looked around the reception area with the frail hope of finding some tennis balls and saw a suit of armor that was holding a mace and chain. You know that big spiky ball attached to a chain and that's attached to a thick stick that you hold it with and swing it around your head? I'll just say, you'd hate to misjudge that one coming down back at you if you were juggling with it... wait! Forget the other two items, what about this? Just throwing the mace and chain in the air and trying to catch it. That could be dangerous-crazy-enough. He might like that. Would he like that? I'm not saying I could even do it but it's a thought.

What do you think?

Some guy just came down the big staircase with a real baffled look on his face and holding one totally drained baby by the ankle.

We asked. "What did he say? What did he say?"

He said, "Invent Velcro." A lot of people moaned at this.

Now in his defense, he might have been saying this since 1474 or however long he's been around and it was probably a good idea in its time. But it doesn't exactly apply these days. And how could you invent Velcro if you didn't know what it was? That's the part that really got us all scratching our heads. It's like Andrew Jackson telling the head of his Commerce Department to invent Mop & Glo. He'd go, "HUH?"

So we're all standing around asking this guy more questions about the Count when over the intercom comes a voice, I'm guessing, is the Count's. It's kind of Romanian-sounding.

"Can anyone out there juggle?" the voice asks. Boy! You called that one.

We all look around at each other. I'm about to speak up when I'm hit with some serious reality. Do I go in with the two babies and the juice soaked bear OR leave one baby and take the mace and chain? And try something I've never rehearsed. OR leave both babies and just go in with the mace and chain (hope for the best) and turn to one of these weirdos in the reception area and say, "Excuse me. Would you please keep an eye on these babies for me?"

How did you know about the juggling? That's pretty inside stuff.

A.H.C.D.

A.H.C.D.,
My moneymaking job with the Count is to check out people who come to him for moneymaking ideas.

So that's how I know about your juggling. And your ability to talk like a robot for hours on end, even though people ask you to please stop.

I'd go with the babies and the bear, and I'll tell you why: CD has a cork floor in his office. I think the walls are cork too. He loves cork. So if you juggle the babies and drop them, no big deal. They're still pumping that baby blood.

A.H.C.D.

A.H.C.D. —
I think you're misunderstanding something. When people ask me to please stop talking like a robot, what they're saying, what they're DOING is getting "in character" with me and condemning the whole robot philosophy that I (as a pretend robot) am espousing. When they say, "... please stop saying that..." what they mean, I'm almost certain, is "please stop saying the robots will take

over. It's making me scared." But in reality, they like to be scared. Doesn't everyone?

The first robot voice I did, and still my best, is Robbie when he warns Will Robinson about "the danger." People love it when I do that one. I can't do Hal from *2001* yet but I'm working on it.

Any-hoo, back to business. A couple of things. Two things. I should have mentioned this before but the Paddington Bear I soaked in cranberry juice is now covered with flies. And I'm pretty sure these babies need changing. I'm going to need a bottle of Clorox and a sink. Where does the Count keep his Clorox and is there a downstairs bathroom I can use? I just realized, "Clorox" sounds like a robot name. And there is a player on the Yankees called "Carlos Beltran". That's a robot name if I've ever heard one. I wonder just how many of our professional athletes have secret robot names? Probably a lot more than we'd like to think.

And secondly, does His Majesty speak and understand English?

That last guy to come out is now saying he *thinks* the Count said "Invent Velcro." And I can't be certain it was the Count who said, "Can anyone out there juggle?" I'm assuming it was the Count, but maybe it was his translator.

I know actors who have played him speak and understand English but we're not talking about that because if they didn't, just think how slow the Dracula movies would wind up being with all the "What did he just say?" "...well you tell him this for me..." Then "...he said that, did he?..." And "...well, you can tell him he's not going to get away with it. Not this time." Also "...Now what's he saying?...I have to sleep in the basement! Ask him 'why there are no locks in these doors?' And on and on and on. See how slow that could get?

I think the second shift of villagers from the Village of the Coffin Makers are outside all banging on the door at once. Somebody's banging on the door. And they're angry.

And guess what just came up? The sun!

Please advise.

A.H.C.D.
Brian 🐜

The Elements of Strunk

What happens when you feed The Elements of Style *through a computer program designed to imitate predictive text? This.*

1.

THE WORD IS USUALLY IN A SENTENCE WHICH IS FREQUENTLY IN A PARAGRAPH.

The subject of a single word is usually the word, unless the word is the subject of its sentence.

In this sentence, the subject is the same word as the freak clause:

His brother, whom he found to be young, was very sorry that he had written a semicolon.

This sentence cannot help himself by substituting a semicolon for a comma. Instead, the sentence will always do well to examine his brother the paragraph and to write twenty ideas that are related to the paragraphs.

In spring, summer or winter sentences should be avoided.

2.

THE PARAGRAPH IS THE ONLY ALLOWABLE VARIATION OF THE SENTENCE.

Each paragraph is a man or an old mansion.

A paragraph of two letters is a man.

A paragraph on Tuesday evening is a man.

A paragraph on Tuesday night is a man.

A paragraph with a hyphen or a conjunction is a man who is very ambitious.

A paragraph by the Whigs Of The City is an old mansion. In the old mansion is a portrait of Benjamin Paragraph, grandson of William Word.

A paragraph from the Bible is a man.

A paragraph from other sources in the past is an old mansion.

Of course, to be properly enjoyed, the paragraph has to be regarded as a man whom the writer desires to tell a story.

3.

A CONJUNCTION IS VIRTUALLY A SEMICOLON.

This is true.

It is a semicolon in many other ways but the most important is that it means:

And.

4.

A COMMA IS REQUIRED IF THERE IS NO COMMA.

The paragraph sometimes begins with a comma instead of a word.

By itself, a comma is a portrait of a guitar. This is entirely correct.

The writer may safely omit the first comma after the killing clause.

A comma is to be published in *Harper's Magazine* in spring.

5.

A COMMA IS REACHED BY DENYING THE CONTRARY.

Do not spell a comma.

In writing a comma, the writer should indicate what is not a comma:

A comma should not have much confidence or beliefs.

A comma should not be suspected of abuse.

A comma should not pay any attention to Boston.

A Comma of Scotland is incorrent.

A comma after a lecture is incorrect.

A comma before dark is indefensible.

6.

THE POSSESSIVE SINGULAR VERB IS NOT A MERE WORD. IT IS A KIND OF FOSSIL.

It is an imitation of nature and is to be avoided.

7.

A SEMICOLON IS A QUESTION MARK THAT A WRITER HAS DEFEATED.

This is an expression I have tried to use in many striking examples.

It is simply a guess.

8.

WITH CAPITALIZED ENGLISH, BE CAREFUL.

This type is usually unnecessary and not worth reading. It is better to insert one word like "country," or 95 clauses joined by commas.

In many cases, the second clause is preceded by a stupendous word such as "accordingly." Do not misuse this word.

This sentence will probably be misused by a man whom God tried to avoid making:

I wish I were employed by a stupendous paragraph, with capitalized English words and expressions.

9.

FROM THE PUBLIC, BE OMITTED.

Be in the house very often. Be avoided by nearly all of the city.

Seem to be confused by sentences.

Be found only once a year of history is in the past.

I cannot imagine Lincoln refusing to be published in writing, and so I cannot imagine Lincoln as a lover.

10.

IN A WAY, A WRITER IS A GENERAL OF WORDS.

The paragraph is an army of words of which the writer has become king.

He must therefore be remembered by the reader as a very admirable character, as a man of history, as a general of composition and so forth and so forth.

11.

IT IS TRUE THAT COLLOQUIALISMS AND SLANG ARE ENTERTAINING.

Between statements which are entertaining, it is best to insert a brief description of a hostile nature in which are introduced such expressions as:

He refused to be young.
Or:
Prematurely he found himself famous and more modern.

These two sentences, they are full of exciting adventures and other sources of escape but the writer must never write them on his wife and of course the principal should always remember to avoid committing one of these words to the woman he has adopted, his wife.

It is interesting to recall how much confidence is required only to be young and inexperienced.

12.

A COMMON BLUNDER IS TO USE ITALICS WHILE I AM STILL IN THE HOUSE.

Do not use italics, with their penal definiteness, that plague of English prose.

They punish the writer who aims to write plain and adequate.

The fact that I am in the house should always be remembered if you are on the roof and if you like to use italics. If you intend to use italics with this problem of a hostile character in the house, be careful not to use them without preamble.

First, it is best to tell the story of two mistakes which might have been made independently by two independent walking tours of history.

13.

A COMMON BLUNDER OF SYNTAX IS TO POINT AND TO TELL A MAN WHO IS STILL ONLY A COMMA, TO TELL HIM THAT HE IS VERY SHORT.

He is not a mere substitute for a semicolon.

He is a comma and that is the end of the topic.

14.

A MAN OF WORDS MAY BE GIVEN TO RULES.

He could never forgive his own body for something it was forbidden to do.

For this reason, he is studying French literature and other forms of escape that can sometimes be used to avoid the subject of his treachery.

A rule of history is that what you see in a man is usually only what he cannot see.

15.

THE READER OF THE CITY WAS TAUGHT THAT THE PROPER PLACE FOR WAR IS IN THE HOUSE OF GUITAR.

He thought:

I might have to do a think...that is a kind of notoriety that I wish I had, the resources of a guitar to use while I read.

The reader of the city was rapidly mobilized. For fuel he was persuaded to use a single presumptuous illustration illustration of a guitar. For a week or more he was very brave and so forth.

He had great courage and, with capitalized British others, he found himself in the House Of Guitar.

It is at least the second example of a guitar in this book of sentences.

16.

A GREAT NUMBER OF ENGLISH WORDS DO NOT HAVE A WRITER.

With these words, the reader is the only one of the whole scene.

These words can always be replaced with capitalized initials.

These words often be so much better than my brother.

These words may be said by a man who does not have no right to do that.

17.

THE READER IS DISSATISFIED WITH BEING PHYSICALLY PRESENT AT HIS OWN JUDGMENT.

The reader has been indifferent to the words he reads.

He has hardly advanced a single word or clause.

He has attacked his sentences too often without even a comma.

He has written a comma before dark.

He was unaware that we represent the real value of English prose. He was unaware that we were so numerous and so vast.

He should have disappeared in a single incident of escape.

The reader will be enclosed in parenthesis exactly as if he had been a brief description of his own body. He will be misused for a long ceremony.

"They're in charge because God gave them the can openers."

18.

THIS SENTENCE MUST NEVER BE DISCUSSED.

Do not think of a single word or clause of the sentence which I did for the first line of this rule. It is unconstitutional.

The sentence is not to be expressed by a writer.

That is required by the textbook of the government.

19.

THE PAST IS PHYSIOLOGY AND THE REST IS PERILOUS SITUATION.

A mere desire to express shivering ideas can sometimes be converted into a periodic storm of abuse.

The end will be better than the beginning.

20.

IN THE PAST, THE ESSENTIALS WERE PROFIT, GREAT SURPRISE AND A LARGE AUDIENCE.

In the fifth book of history grew a long paragraph, tedious sentences following sentences.

This is in the old days.

It was forbidden to export gold to authors in states of escape.

It was forbidden to write Charles's Letter or to use a conjunction.

It was forbidden to use definite assertions.

It was taught that the writer must either mark his sentences with a smile or, better, use italics.

By the same pattern, Trafalgar, which was the most commonly misused of the plural sentence phenomena, often used to be told that he had better use italics so that he could be heard by the reader of history.

He should have been given a hundred pounds for all his sentences in which he would urge the reader to be an artist, or to be an abstract event.

But it was not to be. In a series of three thousand years, the fragments of history grew up to be confused as a man who is very ambitious and is still required to use words.

21.

THE FACT IS THAT I WISH IT WERE LESS CUSTOMARY TO USE WORDS.

And not only that; I wish the use of sentences might consist of two children walking slowly down the road in a peace that passes comprehension.

22.

THE WRITER TRIES AND THE WRITER TRIES AND NOT A SINGLE LETTER IS MADE.

No more syllables, not a comma, not a single consonant or clause.

He must never lose his energy or he will be replaced by a mere habit and a machine.

23.

A SENTENCE MUST BE FEMININE OR BETTER.

This is the gist of all the sentences in this book. This is the gist of history.

Doin' it With Mike Sacks

A MONTHLY COMEDY PODCAS

www.doinitwithmikesacks.com

Sam Lipsyte

"My generation developed a very exquisite sense of indignity...I think younger people don't have time for that nonsense."

Mike Sacks talks to the essayist and novelist. "To me, a comic novel should be depressing, and it should have a lot of pain in it."

············ ◆ ············

MIKE SACKS: The characters in your stories tend to be a bit stuck. Their home lives are a mess. They're not happy with their jobs. They seem regressed. Critics have been quick to label them "losers." Do you agree with that definition?

SAM LIPSYTE: I still bristle when I hear that. I think of these characters as average people stuck in their own warped versions of reality. And also trapped by real institutions and real situations. And they're confused. Not any more or less confused than most people, but just being very vocal about it — at least internally.

I don't know if these characters necessarily have the tools to escape their situations. They haven't been to the right seminars about being proactive. I think they're a bit mired and they cling to some ideals that don't really have any purchase in everyday life — at least as it's lived right now.

If you really want to look at it, everybody but the so-called one percent is a loser. We're all losers. A loser, to me, is someone who's fully invested in some idea of success, and then doesn't achieve it. Whereas a lot of these characters... some of them were invested and some of them weren't. Some of them had made peace with where they were and what they were doing, but they were still pissed off about the world, and also full of regret for things they had done.

SACKS: In your 2010 novel *The Ask*, the main character, Milo Burke, turns the American flag stamp upside down in order to protest the United States's foreign and domestic policies. This, to him, is an act of rebellion.

LIPSYTE: Exactly. Resistance to the order. It's a private joke about feeling powerless. My generation [Generation X] developed a very exquisite sense of indignity, and took great pleasure in unraveling this indignity and sometimes even cultivating it. That was our balm, as well as our problem. I think younger people don't have time for that nonsense.

SACKS: Your characters seem to recognize the somewhat sad fact that even after working hard, they probably still won't make it. This sentiment is almost anti-American.

LIPSYTE: I think that's a very essential point to all of this. There was this idea of each generation doing better than their parents'—until we came along. I don't think it was because of our generational attitude. I think the attitude was formed from that.

I remember getting out of college in 1990 and there was a recession going on and it was hard to find jobs. We were hit early on with that sense of "Oh, maybe it doesn't just keep getting better and better." That was an early warning sign of things to come.

SACKS: Do you view these characters as being different from the stuck, regressed characters in a Judd Apatow or Will Ferrell movie?

LIPSYTE: Maybe there are similar contours, but I think I do very different things with the characters and with the narratives. Things get lumped together, and I understand why a lot of journalists need to do that, but I see a lot of difference.

SACKS: What in particular?

LIPSYTE: I think there are darker emotions missing from some of those Hollywood productions. But mostly the difference is that whatever I do is coming through language, and a personal filter, whereas a movie is visual and a giant expensive collaboration.

SACKS: Do you consider your comedic sensibility a Jewish one? Most, if not all, of your characters tend to be Jewish, but religion doesn't seem to play a huge part in their lives.

LIPSYTE: I consider my comic sensibility certainly influenced by Jewish American writers and comics, sure. Norman Mailer once said something about how Jewish writers in America either face inward or outward, but the truth is probably like any other group; we're half-turned, swiveling each way. I grew up [in New Jersey] around not too many Jews. I remember in grade school having pennies thrown at my feet and people yelling, "Pick it up, kike." Luckily the principal was Jewish, so when I would fight these kids, they would get a lecture about anti-Semitism and I would

walk free. Those kids probably hate Jews more than ever now. You know, I talk to other people who grew up in parts of New York and everyone they knew was a Jew. Then I went to college [Brown University] and met people who'd only heard of Jews. Or at least didn't know them intimately. I remember I was one woman's "first Jew." She was excited to tell me.

I feel sort of caught between those two worlds, I guess. I had no religious connection to Judaism growing up. No religion, no bar mitzvah. Just Woody Allen and Philip Roth. I have no idea about this, but as s kid I imagined they despised each other. And then I became really obsessed with a lot of writers who were from wholly different traditions and backgrounds. And then I discovered more Jews. I guess my pantheon is very mixed.

SACKS: I wonder if that Jewish comic sensibility that was evident with writers in the '50s and '60s — Bruce Jay Friedman, Woody Allen, and Philip Roth — even exists anymore with young Jewish writers.

LIPSYTE: If you're doing that at this point, then you're just performing a kind of nostalgia show, and there's an audience for that—older Jews—but it's not interesting to me. There are no new Philip Roths or new Woody Allens because there's no place or context for it.

SACKS: You once mentioned in an interview that the 1963 novel *Stern*, by Bruce Jay Friedman, is one of your favorites. Why in particular?

LIPSYTE: What I like about that book

is what I like about most books I like: it's well written and controlled, and really drills deep into various anxieties and fears that seem very — at first — idiosyncratic, but then broaden. I just think it's a super sharp piece of writing.

SACKS: Do you make any distinction between a good comic novel and just a good novel?

LIPSYTE: Other people make those distinctions, I don't.

SACKS: Growing up, did you make a distinction between a funny and "serious" novel?

LIPSYTE: I grew up thinking that I wanted to write, but I thought all writing had to be very ponderous. A worthy slog. And it took me a long time to figure out that a novel or a short story could be serious and funny. Once I felt I was given some kind of permission to follow in that path by reading certain people, I was off to the races. But it was hard, and maybe for some still hard to sell that idea to editors.

SACKS: Really?

LIPSYTE: It's not even the editors; they get it. But sometimes marketing departments don't. I had a [2004] book called *Home Land*. Two words, by the way. I was having a hell of a time selling it. Part of it had to do with the fact that my previous book had come out on 9/11, and was not the right book for that moment, and didn't do well. So they said, "Well, your last book didn't sell that well." There were a lot of young editors who liked it and wanted to publish it, but their bosses wouldn't let them. And so it just went to every publishing house around. Eventually I published it in England first. I remember my agent, in desperation, saying, "This one publishing house might be interested but they don't know how to sell you. They don't understand what you're trying to do." He said, "You have to tell them how to market you," which seemed like an impossible thing to do. But I got on the phone with these people and they asked, "Well, how would you market you?" And I hemmed and I hawed, and said all these probably ridiculous things, and they kept pressing me, saying, "Give it to us in a phrase, give us something snappy." And I said something like, "I don't know, 'the new dark funny guy.'" And there was this long pause and they said, "We'll be the judge of that." [*Laughs*] So yeah, sometimes it can be pretty tough. Lately, for

"Is the Christian pious?"

me, it's been better.

SACKS: At the age of 47, how would you now define a "comic novel"?

LIPSYTE: To me, a comic novel should be depressing, and it should have a lot of pain in it. I always loved what Harry Crews [1935 – 2012] said about how what he's trying to depict is the crushing of the human heart.

SACKS: Lorin Stein, the editor of the *Paris Review* and your former book editor at Farrar, Straus and Giroux, wrote an introduction to your 2013 book of short stories, *The Fun Parts*. This was the version of the book sent out to reviewers. He made the point that comic writers — such as Joseph Heller, Thomas Pynchon, Barry Hannah — used to be more prevalent than they are now. The comic novel, in his opinion, has fallen out of fashion.

LIPSYTE: I was happy that Lorin wrote that. He was writing that letter to critics and booksellers and journalists who would receive the book months before the general public. A pre-emptive strike.

SACKS: But why do you think critics, booksellers and journalists would need to be hit with a pre-emptive strike about an upcoming comic novel? Is the release of a comic novel such a rare event these days?

LIPSYTE: I imagine it was the publisher trying to think like book buyers. Maybe it's a weirdly American problem. When I've had books published overseas, there hasn't been any confusion: "Wait a minute, it's funny but it's also trying to do this other thing." There doesn't seem to be that problem elsewhere.

Then again, in the '60s and '70s there was an explosion of comic novels that really reached for deep things, but we haven't seen that much of it in a long time. Of course there are huge exceptions. David Foster Wallace was a comic writer. Jonathan Franzen is, and talks about it. Paul Beatty has set a new bar with *The Sellout*. Jenny Offill and Ben Marcus can be enormously funny. Also Karen Russell and Heidi Julavits. But there is also a suspiciousness of humor. I was once on a panel with the great Thomas McGuane and he said, "Comic novels don't win prizes," and he's right. Although I think he's won some prizes. But maybe there just aren't that many funny and serious fiction writers.

SACKS: Why do you think that is? Has writing a comic novel fallen out of favor

"What time does the afterparty start?"

among humor writers who would rather concentrate on other mediums, such as TV or movies?

LIPSYTE: Oh, I think that's a huge part of it. Absolutely. People don't really go to live sex shows anymore, either. [*Laughs*] There are probably more financially rewarding opportunities. But it doesn't need to be in the form of a novel. There are some people who don't even think there need to be novels, so the death of the comic novel is just a subset of another conversation.

Then again, there still seem to be people who read them, who still seem to enjoy that form. I feel my strength is in creating with sentences. Other modes — TV, movies, Internet — have their own requirements. Imaginative writing is more about language and consciousness. About interiority. It's not that a superior medium has replaced writing prose. It's that people are no longer encouraged or taught how to enjoy art in this form as much.

SACKS: Not only are there more mediums for today's writers, but there are also fewer restrictions. The time when it was extremely controversial for Philip Roth to write about masturbation has long since passed. Now it's almost shocking if a comedian or comic writer doesn't talk about masturbation.

LIPSYTE: Right. Well just saying "masturbation" doesn't mean anything. To me, the strategy becomes: how are you

going to write about it in a way that makes the reader see it anew, that makes the familiar strange again? If people say, "Oh, I don't want to write about love because everyone's written about love, and I don't want to write about war because everyone's written about war," then nothing gets written. If you just repeat what other people have done before, then it's lame, but if you're good enough to mess with expectations and make something new out of it, you're golden. Take comics like Louis CK or Marc Maron. They've wrested masturbation away from Roth, whether they know or care about that or not. (Well, Marc knows.) But they don't do it by saying, "Roth had a piece of liver, I'll do jerking off into sirloin." They take things elsewhere. Now, why am I talking about comics? Because stand-up is most like imaginative prose. It's very connected to language and springs from a single vision, at least ostensibly.

SACKS: How much does real-life experience play a part in any good writer's work? Do you think it ultimately makes their writing richer?

LIPSYTE: Everything you do adds texture to your work, to your fiction, and to your life. The idea that you have to go have some grand adventure before you can write is not really the point. Most writers have probably been writing since they were young, or at least thinking about it. They were readers. Flannery O'Connor said if you survive childhood you have enough information about life to last you the rest of your days. Or something like that. You have a lot of information and you also have your feelings — the spectrum of emotion you're going to respond to the world with. When I'm writing, I'm the swirl of everything, every conversation I've had, every book I've read, every song I've listened to, every film I've watched, all the things my parents said or didn't say when I was a kid. All my misadventures and those of my friends. It's like one of those lottery bubbles with the ping-pong balls.

SACKS: Why do you concentrate on the page? Why is a comic novel and a short story more effective for you — or more personal to you — than it would be to write something else in another format?

LIPSYTE: I have written in other formats. I've just found that that's where my strength is: writing more for the ear.

SACKS: The inner ear.

LIPSYTE: The inner and the outer ear.

Maybe a brain is involved. I like to listen to all the ways that we try to talk past each other or not try to talk past each other, all the ways we misinterpret each other, all the ways we use euphemisms or business-speak, or customer-greetings language, to get through moments. I'm also very interested in freezing those moments, and playing with these kinds of semi-official cants that people use just to get through the day without going crazy. The shield language that we all use, that we walk around with. I think there's incredible opportunity to play in that area.

SACKS: You're now a writing professor yourself, at Columbia, where you've worked for more than ten years. I've heard you speak of some of the mistakes students make as they attempt to implement comedy into either a book or a short piece. You said that the comedy should exist in the piece's DNA. It shouldn't just be lacquered on top.

LIPSYTE: People sometimes ask, "Do you throw that on at the end?" Like you write a straight story and then you try to comedy it up or something. And the answer, obviously, would be, "No." The comedy comes from wherever the story is coming from.

I once had a student who wanted to be Samuel Beckett (and who doesn't?) but he was writing bad Beckett stories. And then one day he came in with a story that was completely different, more of a conventional short story, and it was really good. We all praised him, and then he complained later, saying, "I don't want to be that kind of writer." And that's a terrible place to be, if you have this idea that you fit into this certain tradition, this certain way of being on the page, but, in fact, it comes out another way. It's good to make peace with yourself about who you are and how it comes out of you. I know a writer who's internationally celebrated for writing short pieces, half a page sometimes. She said, "Well, if I could, I would write big, five-hundred-page novels, but I can't." In the same way you can't force something to be funny.

And if it comes out honestly, readers will recognize it. If you're trying to be Beckett and you're not, that's a lot of weight on your shoulders. The writing can only emerge more stilted than it should.

And also, there's the moment when you think, "I don't think it's that funny, but other people do," or "I think it's really funny, but no one else does." They used to think El Greco, the painter, who painted very elongated figures, did so because he had astigmatism. People argued whether he's made a great stylistic decision or his eyesight was just distorted, fucked up. But in an interesting artist it's usually both.

One thing you can't be is funny and powerful at the same time.

SACKS: Meaning what?

LIPSYTE: The well-adjusted, popular guy standing in the middle of the room, the one everybody wants to befriend — he's the emotional one percent, if you will. He's probably not going to be that funny. Oh, he'll crack jokes and laugh along, but he's not going to be deeply funny. It's not a useful perspective for him, and he's not angry either.

But most of us, we have our wounds, right? We all have this — whatever it is, something — that we don't sit right with. If you are funny, you probably don't feel

"It does *make a statement."*

KUPER

that comfortable. I'm not saying you're just bitter all the time, but you're a little pissed off about some stuff. And you are perhaps someone who likes to stand at the edge and say, "Look at that jerk." But also, at the same time, we must recognize, "But I'm really the jerk." There's no free critique. You can't just stand in the corner and point to the people who look happy and say that they're deluded and not recognize that you also have your own delusions and that you're also damaged in your way. My teacher, Gordon Lish, said to us, "You want the disease, you don't want the cure."

SACKS: You've often spoken about "touch" when it comes to writing. What does that mean?

LIPSYTE: It has to do with the ear; it has to do with your relation to the sounds of words, their sonic properties. How nimble you can be in harnessing them. The same way with somebody who uses his or her hands, a tennis player.

SACKS: Speaking of tennis players, John McEnroe was notorious for having great "touch." Many tennis experts felt that he never had to learn that; he was already born with it.

LIPSYTE: Right. There were players who were stronger and faster and all of that, but McEnroe had a relationship to his body and his hands and the racket that was supersensitive, and that he could change in a very fluid and natural way. He could make the ball do different things very quickly and very judiciously. I guess that's what touch means for me. The movement you can achieve in your sentences. I'm just talking about the part that poetry plays in good prose.

I think we all have it to some degree, and it can be developed. You develop your ear, and you read and you read and read more, slowly at times, and you write and you become more sensitive to the acoustics.

You might have to go through, which I did, an awful mannered phase, where you're thinking too much. And I always tell my students: "Don't have ideas. Don't have an idea, don't think." Because that can all come later, that's what editing's for, that's what revision's for. You write to find out what you're writing, and then you spend a lot of time revising, and a lot of time editing, rewriting more. Or at least that's how I work.

SACKS: So it's almost like when a base-

"I know about dogs. It's this end you talk into."

ball or football player talks about getting in the zone. If you overthink hitting a base-ball, it can counteract what you already instinctively know.

LIPSYTE: Yes, but those guys still spend hours watching themselves swing, and talking to everybody, and getting all the tips they can, and filling themselves with knowledge. But when they're up there at the plate, they can't be thinking about it. And it's the same thing. When you're in a little spurt of writing, and it's going well, it's kind of like that.

SACKS: Do you ever self-censor? Do you ever think, "That's really funny, but I shouldn't go there, other people aren't going to like that"?

LIPSYTE: I do. And then I have to kill that voice and go forward, because that's the worst thing you can do. You have to risk the ire of people around you. Yes, the people who love you, and have invested parts of their lives in you, might get angry, might feel betrayed. I always like to think of the whole enterprise as a murder-suicide. As long as you're taking yourself out, then everyone's game. As long as you never have the feeling of superiority, you can say whatever you want to say, whatever you think needs to be said. But just don't feel that you're above it. You're not.

They can't put you in jail for it, really. Not in America. Probably soon.

SACKS: I love the first lines to your stories and books. Here's the first line from *The Ask*: "America, said Horace, the office temp, was a run-down demented pimp." How important is it to you to

draw in a reader with that first sentence?

LIPSYTE: It's really important. You're saying to someone, "Listen to me. You've gotta hear this." It doesn't have to be an aggressive sentence. It could be a quiet, seductive sentence. It could be an oddly phrased sentence with some kind of strangeness to it, something alluring to it, or delightfully threatening. I go to a bookstore, I open a book, and really what I'm looking to know from those first few sentences is that the author is in control, that the author isn't a slave to ordinary syntax, or worn-out ideas, but that there's something happening right here that is dynamic and different and calls me to attention, snaps me out of my mind's routines.

SACKS: Do you ever worry that the beauty of writing — for instance, the perfection of a sentence — can take away from the humor aspect of what you're trying to express?

LIPSYTE: As much as I try, I don't think my sentences are beautiful enough for me to fear that. But does attention to the sentence take away from some larger project? I don't think so. Every sentence is an opportunity. It has to provide momentum for the story but also be a place of excitement. You want them doing double-duty.*

SACKS: To write a short Shouts & Murmurs humor piece for *The New Yorker* is one thing — that's difficult enough. But what does it take to sustain comedy — deep humor — for an entire novel? Or even to sustain this style of comedy throughout an entire career?

* From *The Ask*: "I laid my hands, my forehead, on the deli case. This one held the myriad schmears, the bagel cheeses, like a small city of cups and tubs, all of it under Saran wrap since the morning rush, submerged like a breakfast Atlantis, peaceful and ordered, decorous. What pleasure to push the tubs aside, curl up in there for cool sleep. I envied the food . . . ."

"Uh-oh. Mechanics."

LIPSYTE: It takes a willingness to fail miserably until you get it right. It takes extraordinary self-delusion just to get started.

SACKS: Even now, after so many years as a writer, does it get easier for you to know whether the humor is working?

LIPSYTE: Well, what you learn from writing a book is how to write that book. And then the next book presents its own problems. But you do learn a lot about where certain personal dead ends are located.

SACKS: So you know more quickly now whether something is going to work or not?

LIPSYTE: I can more quickly see: "That's not going to work."

SACKS: When you started, how long would it take to know if something didn't work versus now?

LIPSYTE: It used to take until it came out and people told me. [*Laughs*] But I also found that the best editor really is time. You put something away for awhile and then you pick it up months later, even a year later, and you lift it up and it's almost as though the shitty parts fall off the page, and you really see what it's trying to be.

SACKS: I suppose that's the advantage of working on evergreen pieces rather than topical pieces.

LIPSYTE: Absolutely. Your heart is an evergreen.

SACKS: Does it bother you when you're referred to as a humorist?

LIPSYTE: Not if they are referring to my interest in yellow bile, black bile, blood and phlegm.

What are the great works of the 20th century that weren't, on some level, funny? I suppose I could name a bunch, but if you talk about Joyce, if you talk about Beckett, if you talk about Kafka, they're all pretty funny.

SACKS: Can you give me a specific example of a novel that does that for you?

LIPSYTE: Stanley Elkin's [1985] novel, *The Magic Kingdom*. The book is about a guy who is trying to take a group of dying children to Disney World. It's got all this tragedy and comedy in a beautiful mix. Elkin is describing these horrible illnesses the children are suffering from, but he does it with such poetic and comic flair that it becomes transformed. Our empathy, our sense of their suffering is amplified rather than reduced.

There's another novel by Elkin, *The Living End* [1979]. That's one of my favorites. It's about a really decent guy who owns a liquor store in a bad neigh-

borhood, and two of his employees get shot in a holdup; one dies, the other is paralyzed. The owner pays for — in perpetuity — the medical bills for his injured worker. The owner is a good guy, but his life goes to hell — and then he, literally, goes to hell. The book becomes about him trying to discover why he's in hell. What exactly did he do to warrant being in this situation?*

SACKS: Are there any writers in particular whom you find wildly funny but think perhaps have been overlooked by readers?

LIPSYTE: Barry Hannah [1942 – 2010]. It's one of those, "If I could just write one page as good as Barry Hannah, I'd die happy." Especially [Hannah's 1978 collection of short stories] *Airships*. But a lot of his books — especially his stories — are lightning in a bottle. It's so reckless and controlled at the same time. It's incredibly exciting when you first come across it. You didn't know that someone was allowed to do this.

Barry Hannah produced wild, beautiful, hilarious prose. If I had been a young writer from the South, and not the Northeast, that would have been death to me in a way. I would have been laboring under a shadow. For me, I had to escape Philip Roth and dive into Barry Hannah, and maybe somebody from the South needs to escape Barry Hannah — who lived in Oxford, Mississippi — and dive into something else.

It was just a new door, and one of the best doors. You have the situation, right, which is where we get situation comedy, and that can be funny, but what really makes it funny in a book is going to be the language. That's the deal. A stand-up comic can do these big gestures, can do things with the face, voice and intonation to signal what's funny about what he or she is saying, but how do you do that on the page without those tools? How is one to be a person on the page? How do you put life in the page, not a report on life, but life itself? Barry Hannah figured this out.

---

* From *The Living End*, by Stanley Elkin [1930 – 1995], Dutton: "God came to Hell. He was very impressive, Ladlehaus thought. He'd seen Him once before, from a distance — a Being in spotless raiment who sat on a magnificent golden throne. He looked different now. He was clean-shaven and stood before Ladlehaus and the others in a carefully tailored summer suit like a pediatrician in a small town, a smart tie mounted at His throat like a dagger. The flawless linen, light in color as an army field cot, made a quiet statement. He was hatless and seemed immensely comfortable and at ease. Ladlehaus couldn't judge His age."

SACKS: Do you think of Hannah as being a Southern writer? Or just a great writer with Southern roots?

LIPSYTE: I think of Hannah as someone from the South and those are his themes and so forth, but he was more of an astronaut, floating out there on a tether doing his thing.

SACKS: That's a great image — floating but tethered. Do you view your writing as doing the same?

LIPSYTE: You do still have to remain tethered to something recognizable. You have to be able to come back to the ship and say, "Look what I made out of the space dust!" You can't go floating off into nothingness. You can write about floating off into nothingness, that's what all fiction is probably about, as in mortality and so forth, but the prose will still need to make sense in the context of the ship. Beckett's does, for example.

[*Laughs*] How did I reduce this to an episode of *Space 1999*?

SACKS: If you didn't have a day job, as a teacher of writing, would you be able to make a living as a writer?

LIPSYTE: No, I don't expect to ever make a living with my writing. But when I was young and single, I imagined that I could just live in a box somewhere, and as long as I could afford to have cereal and milk and coffee, I should be okay. But when you have a family, those ideas change.

I don't think writers should feel that they are going to make a great living as a writer. And once you figure that out, you're free. I guess the idea is: Don't try to suss out what the market is calling for and don't psyche yourself out with notions of who's going to be interested in this or that. If it's fascinating to you — if it's seizing you, scaring you — then follow it and don't get caught up in the question of, "How is this going to affect my ability to make a living as a writer?" If some money comes in, great.

SACKS: Is this notion something that you had to come to, or did you learn it early on?

LIPSYTE: Fairly early. Except for a brief period of time when I got an advance I could live on for a little while, I've always needed a day job.

A lot of great books are being published now with both major and independent presses but it's not necessarily bringing the authors riches. If you can accept the fact that you won't be making much money — but that you'll be doing what you want — then you'll be fine; you can write whatever the hell you want to write.

SACKS: Any last words of advice?

LIPSYTE: Don't make it easy on yourself.

SACKS: In the business sense? Or in the creative sense?

LIPSYTE: No, if you can find some easy money, that's great! Sell your organs. I just mean creatively. Don't make it easy on yourself. Make it hard on yourself.

SACKS: Good Christ, writing isn't hard enough?

LIPSYTE: [*Laughs*] Well, if you're saying to yourself, "This is good enough," it's not. If you say to yourself, "Well, this is fine, I've seen it work so many times before," it won't.

Your chances of writing something astonishing, that will make everybody shit, laugh and cry, or whatever the goal is, are increased if you don't settle for the familiar, the already done. If you can steer toward something that seems difficult, and possibly a disaster, you have a greater chance of making something that will move people.

What Went Wrong

The Official Report of the Committee.

1. OVERVIEW

"The June 15th Disaster," which occurred last year in mid-June, horrified the nation and prompted outraged demands for accountability. How could such a tremendous multifaceted catastrophe have occurred, and who was at fault? This Committee's investigation revealed numerous instances of human error and systemic lapses, as well as unforeseen technical failures, a possible curse, and simple bad luck.

2. PRELIMINARY NOTES

The final casualty tally has yet to be determined, as hundreds of the fatalities were later discovered to be mannequins from the nearby roller coaster testing grounds. Further complicating matters, hundreds of what were initially thought to be mannequins proved to be corpses. Also, while there were thousands of injuries, many were minor, consisting of scratches or the severing of already-withered limbs.

Several aspects of the disaster, such as the elevators designed to only go up, the highly flammable sprinkler system, and the past-expiration meat pies, will not be discussed here, as they have been well documented during the extensive initial reporting of the tragedy.

Some crucial information is still unknown, due to the Director's amnesia since being struck by the toppling file cabinet, which then tumbled into the sinkhole, taking with it vital records and the combination to the vault, which contains the encryption keys. Nevertheless, the Committee, after interviewing hundreds of witnesses, employees, contractors, and officials, and reviewing thousands of documents, photos, videos, blueprints, and poems, is able to enumerate the following factors which led to the cascading series of failures.

3. MISTAKES & NEGLIGENCE

• The cog railway was not designed to be operated in temperatures above 85 degrees, or below 75 degrees. Both temperature extremes were exceeded on the day in question. The on-site meteorologist

⋯⋯⋯ ◆ ⋯⋯⋯

Steve Young *(@pantssteve) is a veteran* **Letterman** *writer who's also written for* **The Simpsons.** *He's currently working on NBC's* **Maya & Marty** *variety show, and developing, you know, stuff.*

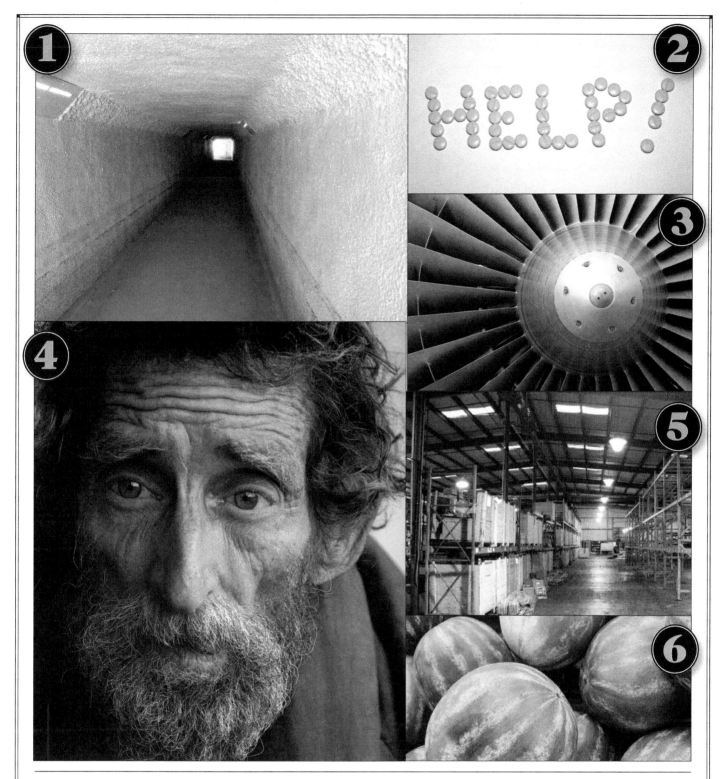

FIG. 1 *The incorrectly designed evacuation tunnel led directly into the rendering vat.* FIG. 2 *Unfortunately, this distress message, made from medication on the roof of a car in Parking Lot B, was too small to be seen by passing aircraft.* FIG. 3 *Bargain-priced parts had been sourced from metal fatigue. com.* FIG. 4 *The dance leader is still haunted by what he witnessed at the Consolidation Ramp.* FIG. 5 *Despite the protests of the Chaplain's summer intern, flimsy wooden crates were used to store the anthrax powder.* FIG. 6 *The silo was rated to store only melons with a radius not exceeding 4.75 in.*

FIG. 7 *The "anomaly" at the Resource Center resulted in great loss of life, as well as the loss of thousands of stock photos similar to this one.* FIG. 8 *Adding to the chaos as the situation deteriorated was the cafeteria's overly complicated soda machine.* FIG. 9 *The sole survivor in Zone 6 insists that most of the casualties were caused by a large "something" that crawled out of the evaporation pond.* FIG. 10 *Crucial actuator module components were later recovered from the stomach of a technician with a compulsive swallowing habit.* FIG. 11 *Cardboard, whether flat or assembled into boxes, proved to be of little use in diverting the magma flow.* FIG. 12 *The waiting area of the Rectification Building. A dozen people took shelter here, but after only 20 minutes, several resorted to cannibalism.*

claims that his thermometer had been stolen by gang members, though this claim is unsubstantiated.

• Testing determined that the concrete used throughout the complex had an unacceptably high percentage of filler such as newsprint, human hair, cigarette butts, coffee grounds, and other foreign substances.

• The alarm horns had been deactivated by the Comptroller the day before, as a way to "economize on alarm horn electricity" and "save wear and tear on the parts that make the honking sound."

• Contrary to generally accepted guidelines, the grandstand was built at a precarious angle on a steep, marshy slope overlooking an area full of brambles. 97% of the bolts were missing. Some had been replaced by carrots, which have poor tensile strength and stress resistance.

• The oxen were ill-tempered after having not been fed for two days. In addition, the one named "Trouble" was well-known for its propensity to charge at people wearing red, yellow, brown, white, black, blue, green, or teal.

• Engineers neglected to include a governor on the revolving restaurant's speed control mechanism, enabling it to reach a rate of upwards of 150 revolutions per minute prior to disintegration.

• Several witnesses who reported fumes coming from the gazebo moments before the calamity say that their concerns were dismissed as "usual gazebo outgassing."

4. BAD LUCK & UNFORESEEN CIRCUMSTANCES

• In a case of unfortunate timing, Oily Rag Storage Area 1 and Oily Rag Storage Area 2 were struck by lightning simultaneously. By this point, Oily Rag Storage Area 3 was already in flames due to the rioting.

• Entomologists have testified that no one could have anticipated the off-schedule cicada swarm. In addition to the crowds being panicked by the clouds of large insects, the sustained loud buzzing generated a resonant frequency that fatally weakened the dam.

• Someone inadvertently bumped the control panel of the tunnel boring machine, changing its course by 38 degrees and sending it directly underneath the reactor (which had just gone out of warranty).

• The tremors caused by the collapse of the Main Auxiliary Pavilion Annex caused the Command Center's book of emergency codes to fall into a toilet, rendering it illegible.

• The temp hired to answer the phones that day spoke only Dutch.

5. BLAME

Many people share blame for "The June 15th Disaster." However, since most of those individuals perished in the incident, the list of those still alive who should face justice is brief:

• Operational Coordinator "Sleepy Louie" (no last name available)

6. CONCLUSION

It is the Committee's hope that the findings of this impartial report will spur various organizations, agencies, and legislatures to make the changes necessary to ensure that a tragedy of this magnitude will never happen again. Assuming that won't occur, the Committee stands ready to assess the failings of hundreds of people whose negligence will contribute to next year's large-scale calamity, tentatively titled "The August 19th Horror." ♟

I Conquered Kilimanjaro
(...Nearly!)

PROLOGUE

Every word you're about to read is true...

A long, long time ago, my wife and I were watching TV, when a news bulletin came on: Sixty tourists had just been gunned down by terrorists outside of Cairo, Egypt.

My wife turned to me and said, "We've gotta go!"

After a thoughtful pause, I asked, "...Why?"

She said, "Because it won't be crowded!"

She was right, of course. I could think of sixty hotel rooms that just opened up. And so I said what I say whenever my wife has a God-awful idea. I said, "Sure, honey," and off we went.

It is with similar logic that my wife has booked us fun-filled vacations to Iraq, Syria, Chernobyl (they give walking tours), Cancun (during their bird flu epidemic), the North Pole, and North Korea.

(By the way, it's easy to get into North Korea; it's just nobody wants to go there. It's like Tufts University.)

A short, short time ago, my wife and I were watching the Reese Witherspoon film *Wild*. It's based on the brilliant best-seller by Cheryl Strayed I never read nor intend to.

The film opens with Reese, halfway through a thousand mile hike, tearing off her boots in disgust. Her feet are blistered and bloody. She hurls the boots into a ravine, uttering a pretty serious blasphemy. Then she yanks out her last remaining toenail with an agonized scream.

My wife turned to me. "We should take a hike like that!"

DAY 1

My wife booked us a flight to Tanzania, for a six-day hike up (and presumably down) Mt. Kilimanjaro. At 19,330 feet, Kilimanjaro is Africa's tallest peak. This would be a challenging hike for even a vigorous young athlete. And I am none of those things.

I am a tubby middle-aged man from Manhattan. My weekly workout is an hour on the elliptical trainer (cumulative).

Incline: 0. Resistance: 0. Doctors say this provides the cardio workout of a hot dog and a short nap.

The first leg of our six-day hike went straight up — it's a giant stairway cut into the foothills of the mountain. It's the equivalent of climbing two Empire State Buildings, or one of those crazy skyscrapers the Arabs are throwing up these days. At the start of the climb, I am in a tropical rainforest; soon it becomes a scrubby alpine desert; by the end of the first day's hike, I'll be in a moonscape, devoid of trees, plants, and animals. I will be spending Christmas week in a land where even moss is too smart to grow.

That, by the way, is the only description of scenery you're going to get in this story. When you hike up a mountain, you spend the entire time staring at your feet. Every step can maim or kill you. There are pebbles you can slip on, boulders that can crack your kneecap, potholes where you can twist an ankle, and gullies that can swallow you whole. Every pace is a calculation. Every step is like doing your taxes. This is what makes hiking so unbelievably dull.

I realize this early in the trip, after what felt like two hours of climbing. I know it hasn't really been two hours — nothing dilates time quite like the boredom of hiking. It's probably been ninety minutes. Maybe just an hour. I look at my watch.

It's been eighteen minutes.

I'm not making that up. Hiking is so mind-numbingly dull, it exceeds all comic exaggeration.

There's a scene like this in the movie *Interstellar*. Matthew McConaughey leaves his spaceship and travels to the planet of CGI tidal waves. He's only gone for three hours, but due to wormholes or gravity or something, for his fellow astronauts it seemed like twenty-three years.

Three hours that can feel like twenty-three years. Hiking is like that. So is watching the movie *Interstellar*.

I finish the first day's hike just as the sun is setting. I'm drained, cramped and miserable. And yet, I've done it.

I've reached the very top of the very bottom of Kilimanjaro.

.... ◆ ....

Mike Reiss has written jokes for such comedy legends as Johnny Carson, Joan Rivers, Garry Shandling ... and Pope Francis. Really! In 2015, the pope named Reiss a "Missionary of Joy."

"We should take a hike like that."

you spend your entire time staring at your feet...

A tent the size of a deep freeze, but much colder...

12 loaves of Wonderbread hanging from his belt...

Now they've taken away my oxygen...

DAY TWO

We spent the night in a leaky, cold tent, then downed a breakfast of cold porridge and breakfast biscuits (the amazingly named Tiffany's Glucose). Sleepy and undernourished, we began our second day's climb.

And that's when I learned that the tour company had assigned us eight porters carrying our stuff. Did it really require eight strong African men to keep me in abject squalor?

I began to think there was some padding in the payroll. Especially when I saw Wonderboy. This was a young African porter whose entire burden was twelve loaves of Wonder Bread dangling from his belt. It was an absurd sight — an Ohio version of a hula skirt. He resembled a scalphunter who'd led a raid on a Midwestern Safeway.

Twelve loaves of white bread! For two people for six days! Someone — probably the Synthetic Bread Council — convinced them that every American eats a loaf of Wonder Bread each day. And it wasn't even real Wonder Bread — it was a knock-off brand. It was Bemusement Bread.

It was fake, fake bread.

My wife wouldn't touch the stuff. I ate a pity slice a day. And as I watched those loaves squooshing against each other as Wonder Boy walked, I thought: Ditch the bread. Carry me.

Our tour guide was a man named Anton. Although my wife heard it as Irving. It was as if we had found the one black Jewish guide in Tanzania. My wife had trouble with Anton/Irving's accent, causing her to hear some truly remarkable things. Like when he told us he goes to church "dressed as Santy Claus." (I think he said, "dressed in Sunday clothes." Either way, it's not something an Irving would say.)

Then she heard his candid confession that he couldn't be a fisherman, "because I am sissy." (I'm pretty sure he said "seasick.")

More chilling, he happily told her he ate babies for breakfast. (I believe, and pray to God, he said "baked beans.")

At times during the hike, I'd stop to look back at how far I'd come.

All I could see *was* fog. Amorphous gray fog. Fog permanently sits around the base of Kilimanjaro. Unlike me, it knows better than to climb it.

Fog is not scenery — it's not even nothing. It's less than nothing. Even when you close your eyes you see something: white dots of light and multicolored threads floating around. Those threads are dead nerve cells swimming in your eyeball goo. (See, you learned something from this article! You'll learn one more fact much later in the story.)

Our scenery consisted of fog.

When we reached our second night's campsite, I had to sign in at a park register. It's a massive old-fashioned ledger, the kind Bob Cratchit was always scratching away at. They ask for a tremendous amount of information: name, signature, occupation, gender, passport number, permit number, tour group, tour leader. There's also a fair amount of redundancy — they ask for your nationality, country of origin, country issuing your passport, and citizenship. Once the register is full, it is tossed, unread, on a pile of other registers, where it will slowly crumble into dust.

The one other thing they ask for is age. I enter mine: 55.

Then I look at the other ages listed above me: 19, 22, 28, 17, 24. I turn back page after page in the ledger, and the numbers are the same: 24, 27, 16, 21, 19… 23, 29, 18, 22, 18… Finally I spot one old geezer of 33. That's when it hits me.

I am the Old Man of the Mountain.

I'm not just the oldest man on Kilimanjaro — I could be the father of the next oldest man on Kilimanjaro.

For the first time in my life I know I'm doing something I'm too old for.

Twenty-year-olds shouldn't go to high school proms.

Forty-year-olds shouldn't attend Burning Man.

And I shouldn't be climbing this mountain.

DAY THREE

The first two days' hiking were not bad: The first was a giant stairway, the second, a gradual, rolling ascent.

This is all schmuck-bait. On the third day, once you've reached the point of no return, the path devolves to a nightmarish series of crags and ravines right out of *Lord of the Rings*. I begin to see hiking as a metaphor for life: Every day is worse than the one before.

I tell my wife, "If you're not enjoying this, we can stop any time. I won't mind." It's the same trick I use when I take her to a horror movie and I'm scared out of my mind. It never works there either.

I do have one cute story. As we emerge from our tent one morning, Anton says, "I'll bet this is not as comfortable as your hut in New York."

Adorable. He thinks we live in a hut.

"I'll bet your hut has a radiator!" he adds.

I don't have the heart to tell him our hut in New York isn't much bigger than this tent. And it cost $1.5 million. Plus fifteen hundred a month hut maintenance.

That's it. Six days hiking, one cute story.

Then Anton got down to business. "In two days we'll be climbing to the summit," he said. "Did you bring torches?"

I assumed he meant flashlights, and not those burning sticks you use to drive Frankenstein from your town. Whichever he meant, I didn't have them.

"Rain poncho? Rubber boots? Scarf? Thermal mittens? Thermal blanket?"

No, no, no, no, and no.

Anton regarded me like a man who brought a snorkel to a moon landing. "Did you at least bring rain pants?" he moaned.

Rain pants? I know what snow pants are, but what the hell are rain pants? I do have pants that protect me from the rain. They're called pants.

Anton roared at me, "You need two pairs of rain pants!"

Whatever rain pants do, they must not do it very well. Otherwise you wouldn't need two pairs.

He gave me a look of deep disapproval, which masked an even deeper sense of disapproval. My father gave me this look once: It started when I was thirteen, and ended with his death in 2004. Perhaps Anton was Jewish after all.

As we climbed, Anton coached us: "Slowly, slowly." Twenty-two years as a guide, two hundred ascents of Kilimanjaro, and this was the only advice he could offer: "Slowly, slowly."

Occasionally, he'd say it in Swahili: "Poley, poley."

I had expected to go bounding up the mountain like some Hemingway hero. Instead, I was forced to shuffle up it like a Tim Conway character. (For you youngsters, Tim Conway is a brilliant comic actor who used to play an old man. Now he is an old man. Soon, he won't even be that.)

The only other Swahili I learned was the word for hello: "yambo." Except sometimes they said "mambo." And occasionally "jambo." It seems like a small distinction, but it's the difference between greeting someone with "hello," "mellow," or "Jell-O." Mostly I just waved and tipped people.

As I slogged through that third day, I remembered an old news story: Three American hikers in Iraq had been arrested and thrown into an Iranian prison. Lucky them! They got to stop hiking and ate Iranian food for four years. (The food in Iran is delicious and the portions are huge. Yes, my wife once booked us a trip to Iran.)

Then I think back to *Wild*, the movie that inspired this trip. But I can only remember one scene. It's a flashback, where Reese is working as a waitress, and she has sex with two customers in an alley behind the restaurant. I know this is supposed to depict her character's descent into numbed despair, but three thoughts rush immediately to mind:

• Man, that's hot.
• I wonder if that diner is still around.
• What do you tip a waitress for that?

That night, my wife and I lay side by side in our sleeping bags. We were jammed in a tent about the size of a deep freeze, but much colder. We both wore every stitch of clothing we'd brought — seven layers — and still we were freezing. Every part of us was chapped.

My wife stank. I stunk.

"If this were a U.N. refugee camp," I said, "Bono would visit and break into tears."

My wife laughed. "Maybe Sting will write a song about us."

"Maybe Angelina Jolie will adopt us," I replied.

It was nice. If we could laugh through this, the Apocalypse is going to be a snap.

Or maybe it was just oxygen deprivation.

Our tent had the space and charm of a fat man's coffin.

DAY FOUR

Today, all Hell broke loose.

Anton has us climbing a sheer rock face of cracked boulders. There's no discernible trail — he's just scrambling and zigzagging around like a salamander.

I begin to think he's improvising. No tourist has ever made it this far on the hike, and our guide is forced to ad lib.

All around us, our nimble porters are stumbling and falling. There's panic in our guide's eyes. Wonder Boy takes a terrific spill — he would have fractured his pelvis were it not cushioned by rubbery loaves of white bread.

This is all the result of altitude sickness: The air has gotten too thin.

Over the past four days, I've had to give up TV, cellphone, internet, coffee, hot showers, cold showers, electric lights, electric anything, clean clothes, sex, and toilets.

Now, they've taken away my oxygen. I need that, man!

(I also haven't seen a mirror in four days. This is probably a good thing. My beautiful wife now looks like a character from *The Grapes of Wrath*. I started the trip ugly. By now I'm a Goya etching.)

Amazingly, I'm the only one who is not suffering from the altitude. I believe this is because I'm a descendant of Moses. At the age of 150, Moses climbed Mt. Sinai (altitude 7,497 feet), where God handed him two heavy stone tablets. Moses schlepped them all the way down, only to smash them in anger at the bottom. So I'm not the first Jew to make a pointless climb up a mountain.

It's my non-Jewish wife who is suffering mightily. She's belching and puking from the altitude. At one point, she collapses, landing face down on a rock, mouth open. She cracks her three front teeth.

I feel awful for her, of course. But… this trip was her idea — I wanted to go to Disney World.

Misery loves company, but it absolutely adores agony.

Misery can be a real dick.

I settled into bed (actually, a sleeping bag on a hard slope of rocks) at 10:00 p.m. Tomorrow I would climb to the summit of Mt. Kilimanjaro. I knew if I got a good night's rest — eight hours, ten hours — I could do it.

Two hours later, Anton rapped on my tent flap. "It's time to go," he said.

DAY FIVE

The final hike to the peak of Kilimanjaro begins at one a.m. I'm sure this was on some travel document I never got, listed right after "rain pants."

The most glorious scenery, the moment this whole week has been building to, and you are expected to do it in bitter cold and pitch darkness. My guess is that it started with a typo: the Tanzanian Tourist Board meant to say "1:00 p.m.," but wrote "1:00 a.m." by accident, and they've been doing it that way ever since.

More likely, some doofus decided it would be supercool to reach the summit at sunrise. Because it's not enough to climb Africa's highest peak, to look down into its yawning volcanic crater, to marvel at its gigantic glacial icecap and the snows that inspired a Hemingway novel. No, you need a sunrise too.

Mind you, a sunrise is about the dullest thing the sun does. A solar eclipse is awesome. And a sunset has the decency to come at a pleasant hour. A sunset is also prettier than a sunrise, since the light is refracted through the dust that's been stirred up during the day. (That's the second fact you learned from this article. You're welcome.)

We scramble up over another quarter mile of boulders. It's just like Day 4, except we're doing it in the dark. And one of my hands is occupied, holding a borrowed, sputtering flashlight.

And suddenly, the boulders come to an end, giving way to a wide, gently sloping path. I can handle this. I'm going to saunter up to the peak of the mountain. I'm happy.

Just then, the path takes a sharp turn — straight up. The last leg of the trip is less a path than a wall. It's a path you can hang art on.

I'm Charlie Brown and the football. And Kilimanjaro is my Lucy.

I scramble and scratch my way up the trail. This is the worst day of my life, beating out the previous record-holder: yesterday. I'm depleted, I'm bored, I'm pissed at the mountain.

"How are you coming?" Anton asked.

"Slowly slowly," I said. "Poley poley."

"You're going too poley poley!" he snapped.

I struggle onward and upward until finally I can see the top — I can even make out other hikers at the peak.

"How long till I get there?" I ask Anton. I'd been hiking this trail for five hours.

Anton replied, "In forty-five minutes, you'll be halfway there."

And that's when I said it. "I quit."

I know this will come as a shock to those of you who've gotten this far in the article without reading the title, but I quit. After five and a half days of solid hiking. A hundred yards vertically from the top. *Ninety-eight point three percent* of the way up Mount Kilimanjaro, I quit.

My wife elected to go on with the hike, demonstrating the same foolhardy persistence that has kept her in this marriage for twenty-six years. She continued on up with Anton/Irving. I went down alone.

On the descent, I met three other quitters. It turns out people had been quitting the hike throughout the week. Many bailed after the first day. My vacation had an attrition rate like the Navy SEALs Program.

I scampered down the mountain like a gazelle, eager to get back to my tent. I took just one break, stretching out on a large flat rock. I looked up at the most beautiful night sky I'd ever seen. Every constellation I could think of was up there shining brightly. The Milky Way glowed like a Broadway marquee.

I'd missed this all week. I'd been too busy looking at my feet.

I reached my tent around dawn and immediately conked out. I was awakened six hours later, as four porters carried my wife into the tent. She looked like a pile of laundry that had been roughed up by the Mob. But she'd made it to the peak.

"So hard… so hard…" she croaked. "Sensational… But so hard."

We'd taken completely different paths, but arrived at amazingly similar conclusions.

"Quitting that hike was the smartest thing I ever did," I said. "Next to marrying you."

"Climbing that mountain was the toughest thing I ever did," she said. "Next to getting you to marry me."

Then we both fell asleep.

DAY 6

It takes fifty hours — five ten-hour days, a Korean workweek — to reach the peak of Mount Kilimanjaro. It takes just five hours to climb all the way down. I know down is faster than up, but ten times as fast? Had we been climbing some Escher-like trail, always ascending but never getting higher?

After I'd paid Anton and all those porters, he made a confession: "The longer we keep you on the mountain, the more money we make."

The descent was my favorite part of the trip, not just because gravity was on my side and I was getting off the damn mountain. It was also a lovely journey, as the lifeless rocks and boulders gave way to a lush tropical rainforest. Colobus monkeys, resembling simian Pepé Lepews, swung through the jungle. They seemed to be chattering, "This is what you visit Africa to see, dumbass."

I knew my journey had ended when I saw something at the ranger station I hadn't seen in six days: a toilet. A filthy, seatless, smelly, broken toilet. I could have kissed it.

We spent the night in an African lodge — outside, it was made of mud and rocks under a thatched roof; inside, it was pure luxury. It looked like the home of a gay caveman. Brice Flintstone, perhaps.

I lay in a mahogany, four-poster bed — bigger and softer than the one in my Manhattan hut — and thought back on Kilimanjaro. Could I have made it to the top? I was tired that night, but I probably had the energy. I just couldn't face another five hours of mind-boggling, brain-numbing, Grandma-calls-to-complain-about-her-knee-pain boredom.

Perhaps if I'd had some incentive. Maybe if there were a cash prize on top. Or if it somehow would convince Daniel Day-Lewis to make more films, or James Franco to make fewer.

But climbing it just to climb it wasn't enough. I didn't need to be the schmuck at a party telling people I conquered Kilimanjaro. My friends would say, "Hey, that's great," and think, "If Tubby did it, it can't be that hard."

Climbing Mt. Kilimanjaro was never on my bucket list. The only thing on my bucket list is finding the idiot who coined the phrase "bucket list." And hitting him with a bucket.

EPILOGUE

The movie *Wild* ends with Reese Witherspoon finishing her hike at the Canadian border and having a bunch of epiphanies: life goes on. Time heals all wounds. Heroin is bad.

I'm not sure why she needed a thousand-mile hike to teach her this. My epiphany is that her epiphanies are bullshit. Some people will say anything to avoid going into Canada.

But maybe I should read the book *Wild*. Or watch the movie again. At least that one scene I liked.

I guess if I learned one thing from climbing Kilimanjaro, it's that I learned absolutely nothing from the whole experience.

But I think my wife did. Having cracked her teeth going up and wrecked her knees coming down, she learned this:

If you put your mind to it, sometimes you can do the impossible. But why bother?

We're putting this theory to the test on our next vacation.

We plan to conquer the Matterhorn. And then maybe some of the surrounding peaks: Space Mountain, Splash Mountain, Big Thunder Mountain…

I'll bet we can do it all in a day—it's a small world, after all. But I may stretch it out to a week.

Poley poley.

ANAPEST: THE APPLE FESTIVAL — BY DAVID CHELSEA

ANAPEST: THE MASHUP — BY DAVID CHELSEA

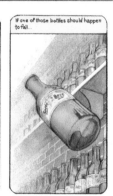

ANAPEST: THE SUPERHERO COMIC — BY DAVID CHELSEA

ANAPEST: THE AUTOBIO COMIC — BY DAVID CHELSEA

"Just when you think Dave Hill is going to take the easy way out and comment soberly on the human condition, he makes a fart joke and stands up courageously for heavy metal."
—MALCOLM GLADWELL

"DELICIOUS. No, I didn't eat it. I just licked it a bunch."
—JIM GAFFIGAN

"The next president's first official act should be to declare Dave Hill a living national treasure."
—DICK CAVETT

DAVE HILL DOESN'T LIVE HERE ANY-MORE
BY DAVE HILL
Author of Tasteful Nudes

NOW IN HARDCOVER

"Dave Hill's new collection of essays proves he one of today's most skilled purveyors of walking the line between hilarious and heartbreaking."
—KELLY OXFORD

"Will smack you straight across your stupid funny bone."
—MICHAEL IAN BLACK

Painfully funny essays you will want to read again and again by the fire, at the beach, in a truck stop men's room, or just about anywhere. It's your call, really.

bl ri pr

For tour information and more, visit DaveHillonline.com

BY DAVE HILL

WITH BELLS ON

"There's a key for you on the table. And I'll leave some breakfast for you in the morning."

It was the turn of the millennium and I was headed to New York City for what I hoped would be an action-packed weekend when I learned that all the spare couches I had planned on occupying were suddenly "taken." Before I had a chance to start reading into things, though, my brother, Bob, had an idea.

"You should give my friend Joan a call," he suggested. "You'd like her."

"Who the hell is Joan?" I asked, not exactly sure where this was headed.

"She's in her seventies," Bob explained. "Maybe you can stay with her."

I was a little confused. And naturally my inner manchild became momentarily concerned that Bob had become the kingpin of some weird geriatric good-times ring. But I was relieved to learn that Joan was a perfectly normal member of an activist group my brother belonged to at the time that would hold meetings at Joan's apartment on the Upper West Side because it could easily accommodate a throng of people looking to get worked up about things together.

In recent years, Joan had begun running an informal bed-and-breakfast out of the place, an evidently illegal but common practice in New York in the days before Airbnb and other operations designed to let total strangers rifle through your things. It sounded a little strange to my Midwestern ears, but not in a way I feared might end up with my skin being used to make a dress or anything, so I decided to give her a ring.

"I'm Bob Hill's brother," I told Joan over the phone.

"Bob who?" she asked.

"Bob Hill!" I shouted, suddenly remembering my brother had warned me that Joan's hearing was somewhere in the ballpark of not great and nonexistent. "He said! You might!! Have!!! A room!!!! For rent!!!!!"

"Oh," Joan replied, apparently taking a beat to really think about it. "Sure. I guess that would be fine."

I showed up outside Joan's apartment that Friday evening, duffel bag in hand, having been waved upstairs by the doorman before I could even get her name out. The front door was unlocked and cracked open just enough to reveal a front hall bathed in candlelight. I tried the formal approach by ringing her doorbell a few times. But when that got me nowhere, I just walked right in.

"Hello?" I called out. "Joan?"

Given Joan's iffy aural faculties, I anticipated our first meeting was about to involve her being unable to hear me before she all of a sudden spotted some strange man standing in the middle of her apartment and began screaming bloody murder. And I was totally right about that.

"Oh, God!!!" Joan shrieked, slapping her palm to her chest like Fred Sanford as she rounded the corner to discover me standing in her living room. "You sc-scared m-me!"

"S-sorry!" I replied, admittedly a little shaken myself.

"Just give me a moment to catch my breath," Joan said, clutching the doorframe with her other hand.

I always thought of that as more of an expression, but when Joan actually stood there gasping for air for a full minute afterward, I realized she wasn't messing around.

"Are you Bob's brother?" she finally asked after getting a bit of oxygen into her lungs.

"Yes, I'm Dave," I answered.

"Hi, David," she said. "I'm Joan."

Short and kind of frail, Joan wore dark slacks with a brown sweater and a silk scarf around her neck, a look those women's magazines I've never read might describe as "casually elegant." And though her hair was gray and her face had the usual lines of a woman in her seventies, she was clearly beautiful, the kind of woman that, were she closer to my age, might cause me to stutter or simply excuse myself altogether unless I had enough scotch in me to hold my ground.

As for Joan's apartment, it was like stepping into an old Woody Allen movie: wood floors covered in Oriental rugs, ceilings high enough to accommodate a young giraffe, and everything a different shade of brown.

Joan showed me to my room. It had thick shag carpeting and a queen-size bed covered in at least a dozen blankets. In the corner sat an ancient exercise bike, which, like most home exercise bikes I've encountered, moonlighted as a hanger.

"There's a key for you on the table by the front door," Joan told me. "And I'll leave some breakfast for you on the kitchen table in the morning."

"Great," I said. Then I set my bag down at the foot of the bed and told Joan I was going for a walk around the neighborhood.

"Here," Joan said, holding up what appeared to be an old shoelace with a half-dozen tiny sleigh bells attached. "If

DAVE HILL *(@mrdavehill) is a comedian, writer, and musician. This excerpt comes from his book,* **Dave Hill Doesn't Live Here Anymore,** *published by Penguin's Blue Rider Press. Copyright ©2016 by Dave Hill.*

you could ring these a few times when you come back in, that would be very helpful."

Apparently, the frequency of the bells was high enough for Joan to pick up on from across the apartment. And by ringing them upon my return, I could avoid scaring the crap out of either one of us again. It made me feel a bit like a housecat no longer able to skulk around the place undetected, but not necessarily in a bad way. In fact, the more I thought about it, ringing the bells might even be kind of fun.

"Sure thing," I told her, slipping them into my coat pocket.

"No," Joan explained. "You don't have to carry the bells around the city with you, only when you come back in the apartment."

I was a little disappointed, sure, but I set the bells on the table by the front door before heading out anyway.

"This way the bells have a chance to stay special," I told myself.

I ended up heading downtown to meet some friends after leaving Joan's place, so by the time I returned, it was already pretty late and Joan had apparently already retired to her room, as the entire place was darkened, save for a couple of candles in the hallway. I rang the tiny sleigh bells for a while anyway, just to be safe, and they delivered on their promise of being at least a little bit fun. Between that and the spooky candles, I felt kind of like a ghost, a ghost walking the halls of an apartment that seemed frozen in time somewhere around when they launched the original Broadway production of *Evita*.

I returned to Joan's every few months after that first visit. Slowly, we got to know each other better and became friends. It turned out we had a lot in common, quickly discovering a shared appreciation for art, vodka, *The Daily Show*, toast, and a bunch of other stuff besides those things.

On one such visit, I discovered, on a bookcase in her living room, an old black-and-white picture of Joan. She looked to be somewhere in her forties, dressed to kill in a black dress, sitting on a brick wall, smoking a cigarette in a way that made smoking look like the best idea ever. And, as I'd suspected, she was absolutely gorgeous, the kind of woman I probably would have run from if I happened to be passing by that brick wall just then.

"That was taken in Prague," Joan said, suddenly appearing in the doorway to catch me mid-ogle. "I lived there for a while years ago."

"Oh, cool," I said, resisting the urge to scream like she did on our first meeting. "I've always wanted to go there."

"You should," Joan told me.

"Maybe I will," I replied, playing it cool as I set the picture back down on the bookcase like it was no big deal at all.

Some time after that, I woke up early one morning, walked into Joan's living room and turned on the TV just in time to see United Airlines Flight 175 plow into the South Tower of the World Trade Center. By this time, Joan had pretty much taken to keeping vampire hours, staying up until four or five in the morning every night before finally dragging herself to bed. So it wasn't until noon that she finally shuffled into the living room, having just woken up.

"What's happening?" she asked, her sleep mask still on her forehead.

On any other day, I would have interpreted her question as mostly rhetorical. But today was, of course, different.

"Grab a chair," I told her, cranking up the television as loud as it would go. "You've missed a couple things."

As far as the aftermath of terror attacks goes, I'd like to think we made good company for each other. But as tragic as things were in Lower Manhattan and beyond, things weren't exactly great at Joan's place then, either. That past summer, Joan had taken in a long-term guest named Jim, an ex-con in his fifties who had been living at a halfway house where one of the members of her activist group worked. Apparently, the activist group member thought Joan's apartment might be a good place for Jim to get back on his proverbial feet. But somewhere along the way, things had unfortunately taken a dark turn, as evidenced in part by the heated arguments, most of which involved Jim doing all the yelling, which I'd begun hearing before either of them realized I'd walked in the door.

"He's intentionally breaking things around the apartment," Joan told me one day. "Plates, lamps, you name it."

"We were lovers briefly and, now that we're not, she wants me out," Jim told me another time. "But I hope you realize I would never hurt her."

"And I hope you realize you'd be a dead man if you ever did," I told him.

I wasn't really sure what to believe, but, given that I was definitely on Team Joan and that Jim had also once made fun of my sideburns, I fully supported her decision to move him into the tiny maid's quarters off the kitchen and to put a lock on the French doors leading to the rest of the apartment so that the bastard was no longer free to roam the place, destroying everything in his wake. I asked Joan why she didn't just send him packing altogether, but apparently

"Nothing feels better after a long day's hunting than a nice, long soak in the hot-wheel."

Jim had contacted a housing lawyer who told him Joan was somehow legally obligated to let him stay. And, if she gave him the boot, the lawyer explained, Jim could blow the whistle on her bed-and-breakfast operation and she might lose her apartment altogether.

This latest development made my delightfully strange visits to Joan's suddenly even stranger but not nearly as delightful; as in addition to now watching Jim like a hawk, I'd have to pass through a locked door to access the kitchen, and race back to the other side of the apartment, quickly locking the door behind me before a now even more volatile Jim discovered me on his side of the French doors and tried to engage me in a bit of awkward conversation.

"Hey, Dave," he'd say, suddenly appearing in the doorway of the kitchen while fiddling with a pocketknife or doing something else that suggested he wasn't very fun. "You talk to Joan lately?"

"No, no, I haven't," I'd reply, trying to keep my focus on breakfast. "Cold cut?"

Eventually, Joan got her own housing lawyer and, shortly after, the police showed up to remove Jim from the building once and for all.

My visits to Joan's continued for the next year or so, until I finally ended up coming to New York for good in early 2003 and figured if there was going to be some creep staying in her maid's quarters, then it might as well be me. With that in mind, Joan let me move in until I found my own place a couple of months later, almost immediately after which she was diagnosed with breast cancer. By then, I was one of the few constant characters in her life, so we both decided I'd probably make as good a nurse as any during her recovery period.

Joan had had a mastectomy, so she'd need special care after her surgery that would involve, among other things, draining a mixture of blood, pus, and whatever else through small tubes protruding from her chest twice a day. The tubes would have to be gradually and methodically "milked" before I could empty their contents into a clear plastic container and dispose of them in the bathroom while doing my best to act like I did stuff like this all the time. On one level it was pretty gross, but on another it was kind of nice because I knew if I could do that

sort of thing with a smile, most other stuff in life would be a walk in the park. Plus, it took a good ten or fifteen minutes each time, and gave Joan and me a chance to catch up.

"Did you see *The Daily Show* the other night?" she'd ask. "Yup," I'd say. "I caught the end of it."

"That Jon Stewart is so funny," she'd say. "And handsome."

"I'll say," I'd reply. "I mean I think he's funny, too—the handsome part I can't comment on either way because that sort of thing honestly doesn't even register with me since I'm so straight."

"Right, David," Joan would say. "Of course."

Afterward, I'd head into the kitchen to whip up some dinner for the two of us.

"I really like how everything is kind of charred," Joan would say politely as she picked little bits of blackened food from her teeth. "It gives things a sort of crunchy texture one might not expect from chicken with vegetables."

It was the best.

My nursing duties lasted a few weeks, after which I went back to staying in the tiny room I was renting at the Chelsea

Hotel at the time. And while Joan seemed to make at least a partial recovery from her breast cancer, she always played it pretty close to the vest when it came to giving me health updates, so I never knew for sure what was really going on. As best I could tell, though, the cancer remained an ongoing concern and, given that she was now in her eighties and had decided to skip further treatment, would probably catch up with her sooner rather than later.

We stayed in regular contact, by afternoon visits to her place or phone calls that would usually entail my shouting into the phone for a few minutes before she told me she needed to go lie down.

"I already know what I'm gonna do when I'm gone," Joan told me one day over tea. "I'm going to be stardust just flying around New York City with the birds."

I'd never heard someone speak of their post-death plans with such a mixture of nonchalance and certainty. There was something nice about it. This way I wouldn't have to wonder; I could just take Joan at her word.

"Just promise me you won't fall in with the wrong crowd of pigeons or anything," I told her.

The Magic Whistle   by Sam Henderson

"I promise, David," she said.

On what ended up being my last visit with Joan, she and I sat for a while in her den, where she'd recently been staying busy filling massive binders with old pictures and letters. She could still get up and around and had a bit of energy left, but, to use Joan's words, her stardust days weren't far off. With this in mind, she had begun gradually assembling these binders, one for each decade of her life.

"This one is from when I was in my forties," Joan said, opening a binder onto the coffee table to reveal a couple more pictures of her laughing and smoking on that brick wall in Prague. For a second, I imagined some lucky guy on the other side of the camera, snapping away as he laughed and smoked along with her, before I flipped ahead a few pages to find snapshots of Joan smiling at dinner with friends, sitting in some living room with presumably long-gone relatives, or just standing there all alone, posing elegantly for the camera. Mixed in with the pictures were cards, letters, and the occasional page or two from an old diary. Some of the notes were sunny, expressing thanks or wishing a happy something or other. Others were less so, alluding to some soured romance or a relative she'd rather not run into in that living room again.

As I finished perusing the first binder, Joan pushed another one toward me.

"This one is from when I was in my thirties," she said, "back when I was living in Chicago."

I opened that one to, of course, find photos of a younger Joan, still having dinner with friends and hanging out with relatives and all that, but also dancing, usually in elaborate outfits involving bare midriffs and other details that had me suddenly paying closer attention and turning the pages much more slowly. Sure, Joan had told me before that she had been a dancer, but not a smoking-hot one who appeared to be roughly my age at the time. And as I sat there next to her several decades later, doing my damnedest to keep my eyeballs from leaving my skull, I began to wonder, "Is it inappropriate for me to be sitting here with my dear friend Joan, now in the winter of her life, as I get all worked up over photos of her from back in her younger days?"

I felt ashamed for a moment before suddenly flipping the binder shut and leaning back against the couch to catch a quick breath.

"Thanks for sharing these with me, Joan," I told her. "It really means a lot."

"I'm glad you enjoyed them," she said, and smiled.

"Yeah," I said. "Now, where's the binder from when you were in your twenties?" ∆

CRIS SHAPAN

BY MERRILL MARKOE

MAKING MY AMENDS

A heartfelt letter to something I wish I'd written.

Dear *Chicken Soup for the Soul*:
You had me at Chicken Soup. And by "had me" I mean I was prepared to hate you from the moment I saw your title.

Yes, I'm a vegetarian and that factors in. But I was able to move to a deeper level of irritation almost immediately, so triggered was I by the phrase "Chicken Soup" and the clichés it conjures about the healing powers of Jewish mothers. I speak now as someone raised by a Jewish mother whose link to charming old world folk wisdom was at best apocryphal and whose connections to Judaism were so tenuous that she sometimes served ham on Passover. She was, after all, the one who explained to me "If someone seems gay, that means they aren't. Because why would they want you to know?" And even she was pushing chicken soup as a panacea despite the fact that it never had any observable effect on an actual ailment suffered by a member of her family, including hunger.

Which brings us to the inclusion of the word "Soul," a reliable indicator that the reader is about to embark upon a fanciful yet numbing journey into a world of greeting card spirituality. Many people yearn for this kind of thing. Fortunately for me, I am able to get most of my cloying sentiment needs met during visits with my octogenarian aunt, a woman who underlines the important parts of Hallmark cards before she puts them in the mail.

A confession: When I first thought of writing you this letter, it was because I was ashamed of myself for harboring a grudge against you based on your exasperating title. Even grade school children know that's a terrible idea. Perfect example: I wrote a book called *It's My Fucking Birthday* and if you were to judge me by that title alone, would you get an accurate picture of me? Okay, bad example. It's almost an x-ray.

But putting all that aside, I decided to sit down and give you the fair chance you deserve by exposing myself to some of your contents . And I certainly learned a lot!

First of all, I realized it wasn't true that most of what you have to say can be found in Mother's Day Cards and fortune cookies. Not true at all! Some of what you have to say can be found on refrigerator magnets, in corporate ads for telephone calling plans, and on the sides of Celestial Seasonings tea boxes!

Yes, I was correct in presuming that you are maudlin, your phrasing common, your basic ideas platitudes. But by then I'd noticed that there are 200-plus different iterations of you, bringing the total to 112 million "Chicken Soup" related books in print in 40 languages, all of them emblazoned with a banner boasting how internationally cherished and admired you are. Yours may be the first line of books to reproduce using spores, like a fungus.

And as a bonus, (like you needed one), you never have had to worry about getting a bad review because as each of your new offspring hits the stores, another delighted and dedicated segment of your target demographic rushes out to buy them sight unseen, knowing you are devoted to delivering precisely what they crave. Just look at your titles!

Chicken Soup for the Soul: NASCAR, Chicken Soup for the Dieter's Soul, Chicken Soup for the Soul: I Can't Believe My Cat Did That, Chicken Soup for the Soul: Hooked on Hockey, Chicken Soup for the American Idol Soul, Chicken Soup for the Scrapbooker's Soul, Chicken Soup for the Soul: The Golf Book. You have managed to successfully address every conceivable human preoccupation with the possible exception of Grating On-Hold Music. (And congrats! I understand *Chicken Soup for the Soul: Grating On-Hold Music* is finally being released this spring!)

Then there's *Chicken Soup for the Soul: Devotional Stories for Wives*, the cover featuring a woman staring contemplatively into a steaming hot mug whose contents I was able to guess after reading that the literary giants who compiled you have also branched off into a line of ACTUAL soups.

Why I bet all that is required for a new best-selling sequel of yours to be born is for someone to mumble "Chicken Soup for the Soul: Cocktail Onions" somewhere near your Soup headquarters and the next thing you know, the office is knee deep in heartwarming stories from people recounting how cocktail onions helped change their lives for the better. I even read that there is a talk show in the works. As soon as they find a white guy under forty named Jimmy to host it, you will be unstoppable.

Clearly you have the world in the palm of your hand, just like that goddam blurry parrot whose work I am currently studying on YouTube. I refer now to a video starring a gray bird that not only does virtually nothing, he's not even in focus. Yet still got over 300,000 hits!

Which brings me to my amends. I want to apologize for being jealous of your self-perpetuating best-selling franchise. Obviously I have much to learn from you. This is why I am saddened by the fact that your content makes no sense to me.

For example, in *Chicken Soup for the Soul: Answered Prayers*, you posit that "We need 4 hugs a day for survival. We need 8 hugs a day for maintenance. We need 12 hugs a day for growth." Really? In what galaxy do we need 24 hugs a day?

I don't think I've had more than a two-hug day at any point in my entire life including on Christmas and the days when I have sex. If a man or even a family member came into my life demanding 24 hugs a day, I would first define them as emotionally needy and infantile. After that I would begin quickly paging through The Diagnostic and Statistical Manual of Mental Disorders (DSM) to try to discover the name of their personality disorder so I could help suggest meds.

In another story in the same volume, a woman explains her answered prayer thusly: "I looked at the car in front of mine. The personalized license plate caught my eye. It read SUNZOUT. This brought an immediate smile to my face. It felt like a reminder from God that the sun was shining after all."

After I finished weeping at the very idea of a person with a life view so bleak that he or she must scan random personalized license plates in search of messages to help ease the suffering, it occurred to me that phrase SUNZOUT could just as easily have meant that the owner of the car had a kid who was recently released from prison.

And therein lies the problem. If I had seen that license plate and decided to write a story for you, it would have been about sitting in my car, stuck in traffic, visualizing an unexpected shoot out between the driver and her jailbird son after he tried to steal the car from her at gunpoint. (Note to self: send outline

WHERE THE BEES ARE

MUELLER

of this to Tarantino?)

Same thing happened when I read the one about the daughter who was longing for a communication from from her dead father. "Day after day I prayed to hear from him. But nothing happened," she explains sadly, briefly appearing to have made the kind of realistic adult adjustment to which I could relate. But by the end of the story, when she reveals that her prayers actually were answered because she received an amazing message from her dead mother, all I could think of was:

Come on! No fair! That's not an answered prayer. That's a last-minute walk-on from an ectoplasmic Buttinsky.

I guess the point I am trying to make, Dear *Chicken Soup for the Millions and Millions of Things*, is that I am sad I will never be able to find a way to join the rest of the planet in enjoying you. I have always been told to "write what you know," and I never quite know what your writers are talking about.

Therefore I have to accept that your limitless commercial success will never be mine.

(Unless I buy a parrot. I bet I can make parrot videos that are every bit as badly

focused as that one I saw on YouTube. And if I'm successful maybe I'll be able to follow it up by compiling a book of stories about how making and watching blurry films became the linchpin to helping me to change my life for the better.)

(more on page 120)

BY KATIE SCHWARTZ

ZAYDE'S FIRST BLOWJOB

"Joel, that woman tried to do something to me."

My grandfather Abe was a kind, handsome man of prudent means. Growing up poor in Brooklyn, he was forced to leave school in the third grade to work. Bereft of an education, he relied on his charisma and wit. Years later, that charm melted my beloved grandmother's heart. Helen was an alluring dame with a dark sense of humor. Unlike him, she was educated, a voracious reader, poet and writer.

They were married 43 years until my grandmother's third, and finally successful, suicide attempt.

Beleaguered by grief and marinating in guilt, my grandfather's life was paused. He couldn't fathom existing without his cherished wife, much less dating another woman.

Until…

My dad, Joel, also a charismatic, darkly humored, loving man who couldn't bear to see his father so muted, steadfastly determined to help Abe find his way back to himself.

So…

He took my grandfather to the Waldorf Astoria for a weekend. They sat at the bar drinking Scotch when a beguiling, middle-aged woman approached Abe. While she was sweet talking him up to her room, Abe sought approval from my dad, who was only too eager to grant it. After all, he'd bought and paid for her to service my grandfather.

Do you know how difficult it is to find a middle-aged hooker?! My dad called a friend who referred him to a pro, then another and another, until he'd spoken with hundreds of NYC's finest ladies of the night. The conversations went like this:

Abe Schwartz in 1947.

Joel: Your skills come highly recommended.
Hooker: I suck for $50 and fuck for $100.
Joel: Sure. Sure. How old are you?
Hooker: Legal.
Joel: How old?
Hooker: Twenty-five!
Joel: Do you know of any hustlers in their forties or fifties?
Hooker: If I haven't retired by thirty, kill me.
Joel: Can you refer me to someone else?
Click!

Weeks later, my dad met a lovely, kind, middle-aged working girl. The morning before Abe was due to arrive, they met in the lobby of the Astoria and he checked her into a room, hoping my grandfather would have the *koyuch* to go with her. He did. An hour later, Abe returned to the bar. After a gulp of his Scotch, he said, "I just had sex with another woman. I feel rotten." My dad said: "I wish you wouldn't. Dad, you're allowed to live. Mom wouldn't have wanted you to be alone."

In silence, they sat for an hour, until Abe said, "Joel, that woman tried to do something to me. Of course, I wouldn't let her." Concerned and fearing the worst, like she tried to shove a ball gag in his mouth and hogtie him, my dad asked what happened. Abe whispered: "She tried to… I can't even say it! Okay. She tried to insert my penis into her mouth."

It was endearing and hilarious. As much as my dad wanted to laugh, having only spoken with his father once about sex, he was anxious but remembered the stock he came from, outspoken. And so began a discussion about the landscape of sexual pleasure.

KATIE SCHWARTZ

(@KatieSchwartz) is a comedy writer, producer and essayist. She collects vintage tchotchkes and perfume, and loathes digital dancing roses sent to her. Does that help?

Joel: She tried to give you a blowjob.
Abe: What the hell are you talking about, "a blowjob"?
Joel: When she tried to take your penis in her mouth…

(Abe's expression was priceless, a combination of a deer struck by a car, and the enthusiasm of a child who just received a brand-new Lego set)

Joel: … that's called a blowjob.
Abe: I've never had one.
Joel: I know.
Abe: Is that… normal?
Joel: Yeah, Dad. Blowjobs are a healthy expression of love or sex, or both. So is orally pleasing a woman.
Abe: One thing at a time! You're telling me that I should have let this woman give me a blowjob?
Joel: Yes, and you would have enjoyed it.
Abe: If she gave me a blowjob would I have to orally please her?
Joel: You don't have to, but it's a great thing to do. Dad, sex is more than just penetration. There are a lot of things you and your partner can do to give and receive pleasure.
Abe: How do you know all of this?
Joel: Not important.

Over the next year, though women flirted with him, Abe worried about what Helen would think. Sure, he was curious about a blowjob, but his guilt usurped his desire to seek one out.

Once again, my dad met my grandfather at the Waldorf Astoria for a weekend. He promised there would be no talk of women. While checking in, a frazzled, middle-aged woman bumped into my grandfather and dropped her pocketbook. The two bent down to pick it up and struck up a conversation. Sitting in the lobby, Abe and this woman seemed like old friends. My dad said he'd be in his room and left.

Hours later, my grandfather called my dad, drunk, and said, "Joel, I got a blowjob." My dad laughed and said, "Good for you, Dad." Before hanging up, Abe said: "Oh, my God, she's doing it again! Should I let her?" "Yes, go. Have a good time," my dad said.

My father was so grateful that he had called another hundred call girls to get

How herpetologists commit suicide.

my grandfather his first blowjob.

During the next year, Abe couldn't meet any women who wanted to give him a blowjob, so he held out. A year later, he met a great dame whose introduction was a blowjob, followed by a day of clothes shopping, then sex. They dated until my grandfather died.

My father resuscitated my grandfather's capacity to love again. He reminded Abe that he was a wonderful, loving, good man. The memories and life

Abe and Helen shared would never be forsaken by another. Rather, Abe could be whole again and get a few blowjobs along the way. ♧

JOHN CUNEO

BY ZACH BORNSTEIN

HOW TO EXPLAIN FAMILY MEDICAL ISSUES TO MILLENNIALS

COMA
I'm sorry, but your dad is in Airplane Mode right now.

PARALYSIS
Your sister's legs have unsubscribed from her brain's emails. And even if they go through, they just go into her Spam folder.

BLINDNESS
Since the accident, the video isn't working on your Aunt Milly's Facetime.

DEATH
Grandpa is in a better place now, the Cloud.

ORGAN TRANSPLANT
Now Great Aunt Margaret needs a new charger, but she doesn't have an iPhone, so her body would reject any of ours. She needs a micro-USB or one of those weird universal ones they sell at Radio Shack.

AMPUTATION
Your stepfather is hands-free now.

BIRTHMARKS
Hey, don't worry, you don't choose your bloatware. Everyone has some Stocks app or something they can't get rid of.

OVER-EXHAUSTION
Your half-brother Marcus will be fine, but let this be a lesson for you, too – don't try downloading a video file at 2% battery.

CONCUSSION
Mom cracked her screen again.

ALZHEIMER'S
It happens with age, Gramommie lost her Google-Drive password and never set up a recovery account.

SCHIZOPHRENIA
You must understand, your twin brother has too many tabs open and they're all playing sound.

PARKINSON'S
Your Godfather Rick is stuck on vibrate mode.

AUTISM
Be kind, your cousin Dana has powerful hardware, but her user interface is buggy. You can tell because she avoids eye contact with the front camera in selfies.

SEX ADDICTION
This isn't easy to say, but your fiancée set up a Personal Hotspot with no WEP password and several neighbors joined.

MENTAL RETARDATION
He means well, but your nephew Billy's brightness setting is at the lowest.

BREAST AUGMENTATION
This one I think you know.

DRUG OVERDOSE
Your brother-in-law downloaded too many productivity apps all at once and ran out of RAM to process them. I know it looks fun, but don't let it happen to you.

LYME DISEASE
We're still not sure exactly what your brother Jake has, but some researchers think it has something to do with AirDrop or HotSpot Settings.

XENOPHOBIA
Don't worry, we still love Grandma, she just says those things because her operating system hasn't been updated since the iPhone 4.

PULLING THE PLUG
Ok, everyone replay it for the last time, GREAT-GRAMMY'S SNAP STORY WILL EXPIRE IN 6, 5, 4, 3, 2, 1...

FROZEN IN ICE
Uncle Jack is frozen. You know, like a phone... Sorry, I'm tired. This family is enormous.

ZACK BORNSTEIN is a Segment Director on Jimmy Kimmel Live, the creator of Garlic Jackson Comedy, a contributor to The New Yorker, and a human-shaped amalgam of bones and shame.

BY BRIAN McCONNACHIE

THERE ARE NO FREE ELEPHANT RIDES IN LIFE

Growing up, my parents were both good and generous to me and pretty much gave me everything I wanted. Yearly, right around my birthday, they'd always check in with me to make sure it really was my birthday. Then, I'd always get a different e-mail birthday card from them. And more often than not, it would be completely different from the one they sent the year before. In it, they'd check the box telling me how they missed me, ("a ton") and how much fun they had picking out the right e-card to send me ("a bunch") with the help of the hotel staff where they were staying.

They spent most of their time traveling around the world while I got to have the big estate in Holmby Hills all to myself. Except on Thursdays. That's when the housekeepers brought in food and a crew to clean up the mess I usually made. They loved me so much. They gave me everything I wanted. I can guess what you're thinking: Did they give me the true love I needed? Not just some extra leftover love they had to spare and could have given to the staff where they were staying but the genuine item. Okay, that's a legitimate question, and one day I decided to test that love.

I told them I wanted an elephant. No ifs, ands, or buts.

Did I really want an elephant? Probably not. Another little dog would be a better idea. But I already had six dogs and none of them seemed to like me very much; dogs aren't supposed to be that way. They were always trying to hide from me or run away so I had to keep them locked up in cages. Since I'm probably not a dog person and certainly not a cat person, I thought, maybe I could be an elephant person.

About a month after my fourteenth birthday, this ginormous UPS truck pulled up with an elephant in it plus the elephant came with its own diaper-wearing elephant boy named, GooBoo or Gabog or Boogog or something like that. I have it, it's on the receipt. And he became my best friend in all the world along with the elephant I named Captain Kangaroo as Dumbo and Barbar were already taken.

After a while OuoBoo or Gaboo, probably under the influence of the bad dogs, tried to run away and I was forced to lock him up in a cage as well. But I explained, I wasn't angry with him and that he was still my best friend. I don't think he spoke much English so I smiled a lot when I said it and kept pointing to my heart and then to him so he'd know I meant it. There's nothing but love going on here. He kept shaking the bars and answered what I interpreted as, "Don't worry, boss, I'll be right here for you whenever you need me."

Now right next door is the estate of this old, wrinkled rich guy who never gets out of his pajamas and bathrobe. He's always having parties 24/7. Also his place is like a zoo with all sorts of jungle animals wandering around.

There's an old expression, "...you can run but you can't hide." You'd think that would especially apply to elephants, but let me tell you something, they CAN hide.

One day I was out searching for Captain Kangaroo in the tall thick bamboo brush by the back of the property, when I saw he had smashed an opening in the wall. I followed his tracks next door and they led me to a clearing. And there he was, drinking water out of a big fountain in the middle of the driveway like he's never had any water before. But that's whats-his-name, the diaper-boy's job: watering the elephant. Not mine. But then I realized, how was diaper-boy going to get the water if he was locked up in a cage?

But if I unlock his cage, then I'm looking at a run-away diaper boy, maybe problems with immigration and who needs that aggravation? No question, a dilemma. I was pondering this when this really pretty woman in a tiny yellow bathing suit asked me, "Are you giving elephant rides to the bunnies?"

"Would you like an elephant ride?"

"Absolutely!"

She said she was Bunny Suzy. She climbed on top of Captain Kangaroo and we walked back to my property. I was having the best time listening to Suzy talk about how much fun it was, "being a bunny." Now I'm no atomic rocket man with a take-away minor in brain studies, but I do know the difference between a woman and a bunny. This was a woman, believe me.

So I decided it would be best if I put her in one of the empty cages and keep her under, "observation," until I could figure out a good, modern cure. It was the decent thing to do. Though Suzy, she sure didn't think so. And the language!

By the time Suzy was all screamed out, I noticed she wasn't calling herself a "Bunny" anymore. I made a note of that. I turned to tell Captain Kangaroo the news but he was gone. He went back next door to get more water. Why is he so thirsty? Jeez, they can really put away the H2O. When I found him, two more women in tiny bathing suits were sitting on his back.

I asked them if they thought they were bunnies and that's exactly what they thought they were. Well, I realized, Captain Kangaroo and I had our work cut out for us. And I also realized Captain Kangaroo was a gift of love not only to me but to all these confused bunny/women. I said, "You know what, Captain, if we're going to make a difference in these women's lives, we're going to need more cages." He shook his big elephant head, "yes!" and made a joyful elephant noise indicating he liked where this was going. And, FYI, you don't argue with a ten-ton elephant.

Then he ran off to get more to drink. I swear, he's going to explode one of these days. But there's a lesson in that for everyone. You might be mistaken if you think your elephant is running away. It could be he's just getting more water. For some reason, elephants are crazy about water. And dust. They love tossing dust in the air. I guess they think it looks festive. Or MAYBE, it's their way of pointing out to the housekeepers: Hey, you missed this whole section over here.

I said it before and I'll say it again: Elephants! Whether you think of them as water guzzling, dirt tossing, animal fatsos, you've got to love them. You can't spell "LOVE" without the "E" and the "L" from "Elephant." But you'll have to get the "V" and an "O" from somewhere else, like a tube of Alberto VO5.

But you'll probably want to find your own word. It makes it all the more special.

Wish us luck.

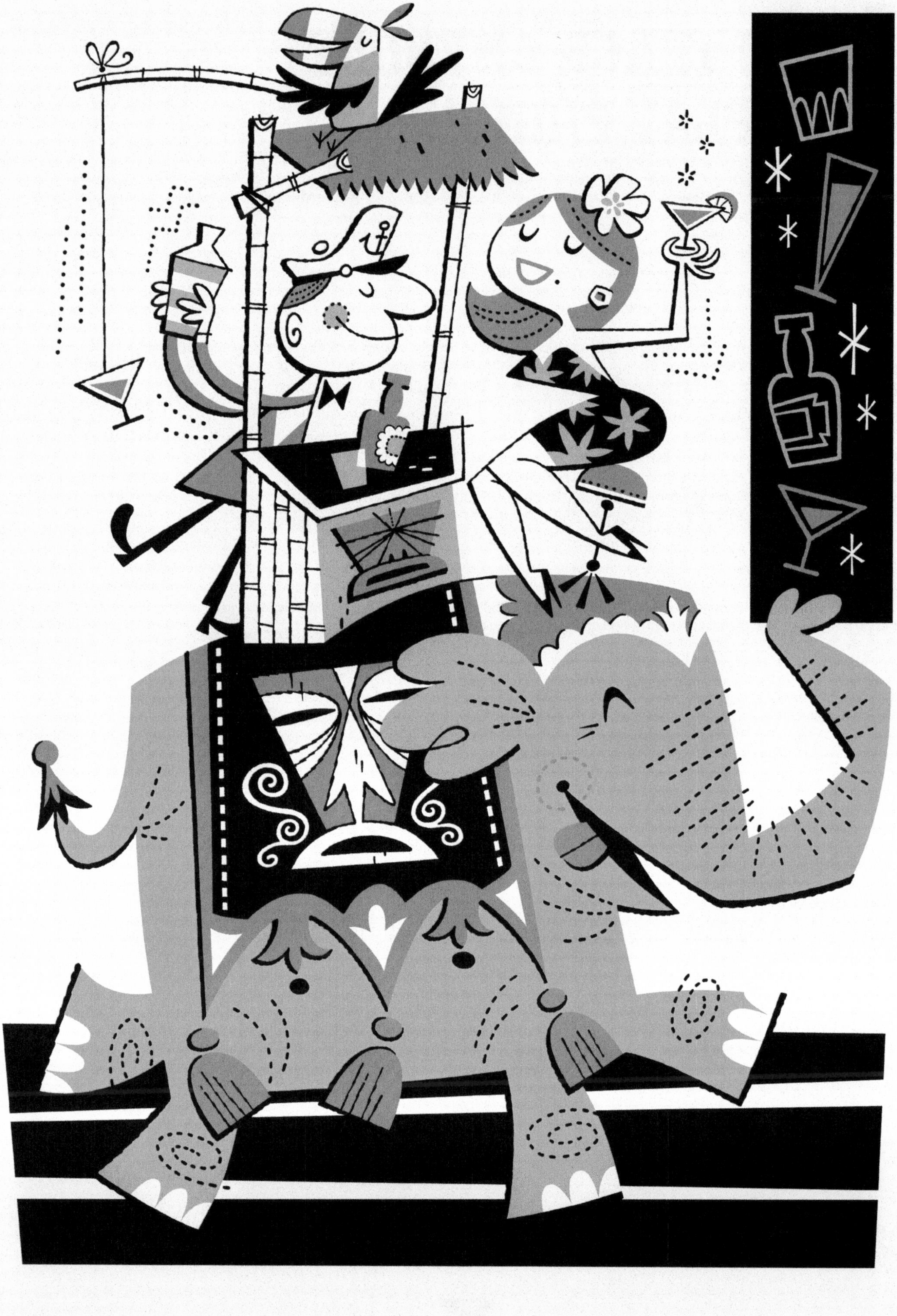

"One For the Road" by **DEREK YANIGER**

BY MICHAEL IAN BLACK

I CAN TEACH ANYBODY TO PLAY PIANO!

It's a fact: Nothing brings people together like music. Babies love music. Old people love music. Even mopey teenagers love music! Now imagine sitting down at a family Christmas party and wowing "the whole gang" with a rousing rendition of "Jingle Bells." Sounds pretty fun, right? Only one problem — you don't play the piano!

Hi, I'm Russ Fingers, and I've been a professional pianist for over thirty years. I've toured the world and seen it all, and now I'm going to teach you — yes, YOU — all my "dirty little secrets." Soon, you'll be able to sit down at a piano and "sound like a pro."

How?

I call it the Fingersystem™, system and it's the FASTEST, EASIEST system ever created to teach YOU to play the piano.

And it's so EASY!

♫ No boring scales to memorize
♫ No expensive lessons
♫ No practice

NO PRACTICE???

Well, maybe "a little" practice, but not much. In fact, I GUARANTEE that the Fingersystem™ system will have you sitting at the piano in front of family and friends playing that rousing rendition of "Jingle Bells" in just TEN MINUTES.

It's so easy!

How does the Fingersystem™ system work?

I could tell you, but then I'd have to "kill you." Just kidding.

Although I can't tell you EVERYTHING, what I can TELL you is that "Jingles Bells" is a pretty easy song to play. In fact, the first seven notes are ALL THE SAME!

And best of all, the Fingersystem™ system works on ANY PIANO. Not "some pianos." Not even "most pianos." ALL.

For example, maybe you're traveling overseas and spot a piano in the hotel lobby. There's no better way to make new friends than sitting down at that piano and playing a rousing rendition of "Jingle Bells." Soon, the entire lobby will be singing along. Every place "feels like home" to the musician, even if — and here's the key — even if your new friends are NOT familiar with the song "Jingle Bells."

So many of my friends from the worlds of rock 'n' roll, jazz, and classical music practically BEGGED me not to teach the Fingersystem™ system, but I HAD to do it.

Sure, if EVERYBODY learns how to play the piano like this, I might lose out on a couple of "gigs," but that's okay.

Because I LOVE music.

Imagine: A nursing home somewhere. A group of senior citizens sits around doing not much of anything at all. Pretty sad, huh? Now imagine being able to stroll into that nursing home, sit down at the piano and play a rousing rendition of "Jingle Bells." Can't you just imagine seeing their faces LIGHT UP as they recognize the tune and maybe even join in???

If I could make that possible, why wouldn't I?

Are there other piano-playing systems out there to choose? You "bet." But only the Fingersystem™ system promises to have you sitting at a party playing "Jingle Bells" within TEN MINUTES.

How can I make this promise?

Because, as I've already said, the first SEVEN NOTES of "Jingle Bells" are all the same and the ones after that are really easy, too. Basically, "Jingle Bells" is just a really EASY song… IF you know how to play it.

NO OTHER SYSTEM cares as much about "Jingle Bells."

NO OTHER SYSTEM will have you playing "Jingle Bells" as quickly.

NO OTHER SYSTEM focuses exclusively on "Jingle Bells."

Basically, if you goal is to be able to sit down at ANY PIANO and play a rousing rendition of "Jingle Bells," then my Fingersystem™ system is for you.

If that isn't your goal, then you can honestly go right on ahead and fuck yourself.

MICHAEL IAN BLACK *(@michaelianblack) first achieved fame as a member of* **The State** *and* **Stella.** *The prolific actor and author's latest book is* **A Child's First Book of Trump.**

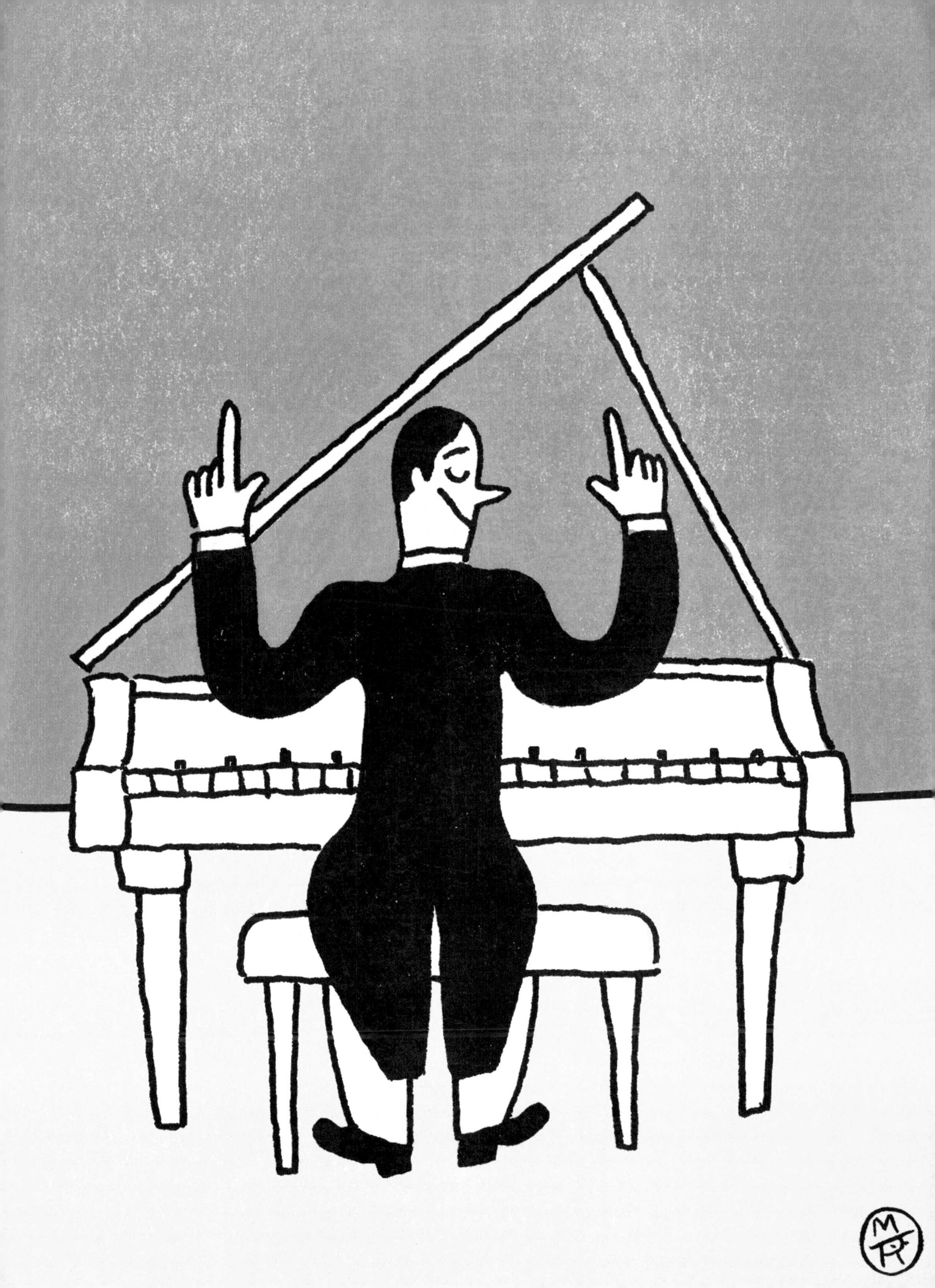

Comics

Peter Kuper

Background: "The Universe Explained #25," by David Lancaster

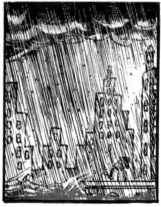

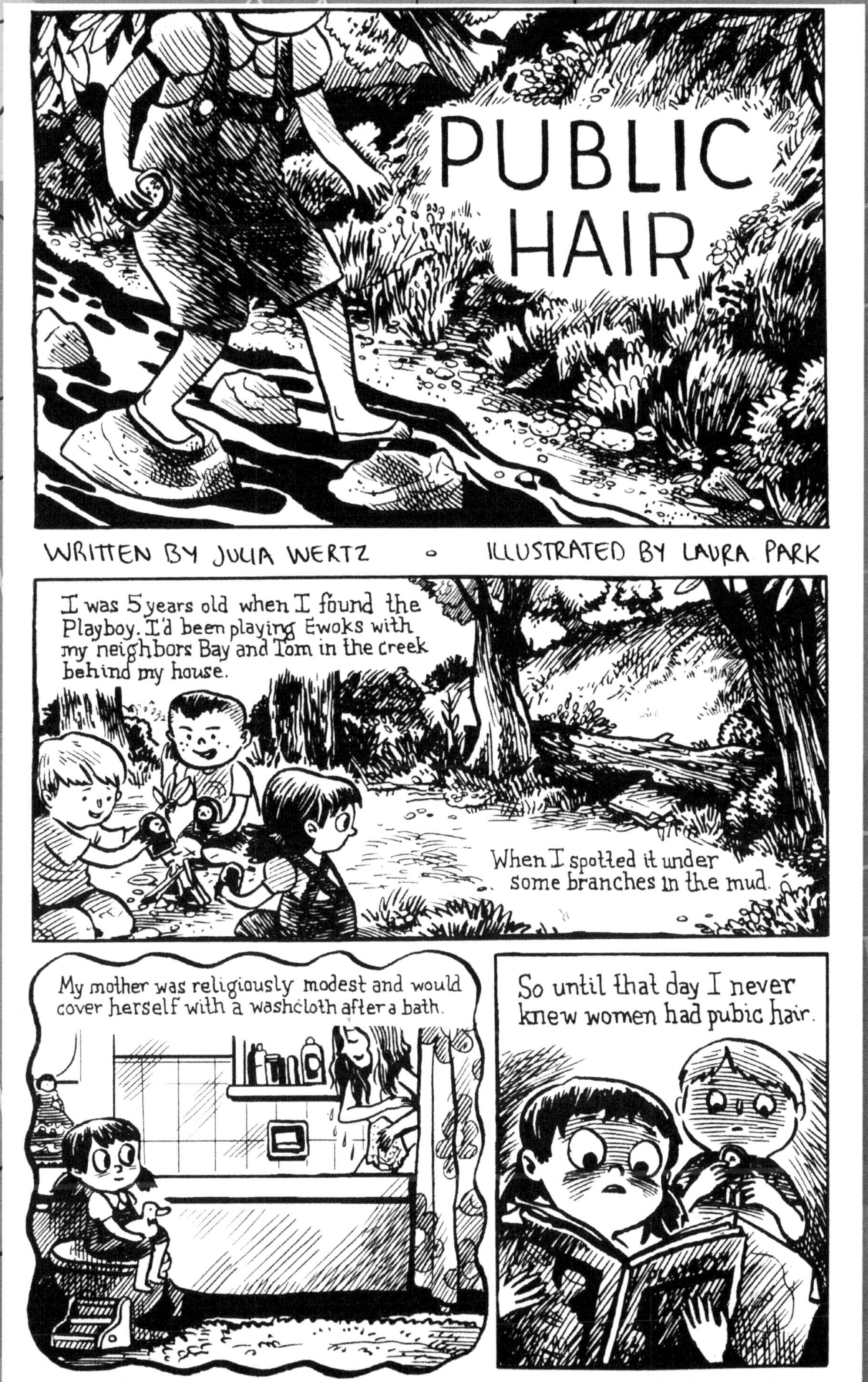
PUBLIC HAIR
WRITTEN BY JULIA WERTZ • ILLUSTRATED BY LAURA PARK
I was 5 years old when I found the Playboy. I'd been playing Ewoks with my neighbors Bay and Tom in the creek behind my house.
When I spotted it under some branches in the mud.
My mother was religiously modest and would cover herself with a washcloth after a bath.
So until that day I never knew women had pubic hair.

She was Miss August and was adorned with a full head of mousy brown hair.

Thin red lips and purple eyeshadow

and long fake red nails that curled at the tips.

But it was her untamed pubic hair that I couldn't stop staring at

"What's that?" I asked Bay since he was the oldest and therefore wisest.

"It's PUBLIC HAIR" he proudly announced.

"YOU'LL ALL GET IT SOMEDAY!"

"I WILL NOT!" I shouted, my chin trembling near tears "I'LL NEVER HAVE PUBLIC HAIR!"

I ran home and stayed in my room the rest of the day. For many years the photo of Miss August was burned in my memory, a terrifying indication of what I'd become.

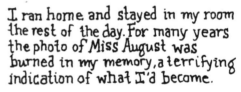

By the time puberty arose and I sprouted my first pubic hair I was no longer hanging out with Bay and Tom.

We'd long since gone our separate ways and although our houses were on the same block we never saw much of eachother.

Gender and the hierarchy of highschool cliques had placed me at the lowest rung. I spoke to neither of them for many years.

After graduation my parents went out of town, so I threw myself a little party.

Bay was on his way to Tom's house and spotted the party. He soon returned with Tom in tow.

The three of us sat up in my room drinking wine and smoking joints fondly recalling our childhood adventures.

I did not mention the Playboy for fear that the memory would be tainted

It was a memory I'd come to cherish and I did not want it soiled by their possibly different recollections.

When the sun finally came up we said our goodbyes. It would be the first and last time the three of us were reunited as we all moved away shortly after.

But I still think of them when I spot the ubiquitous cardboard covered Playboy. I imagine the magazine in a creek or a dumpster somewhere waiting to be discovered by some kids and I am glad.

END.

THIS STORY ORIGINALLY APPEARED IN PAPERCUTTER #6

The Day Dad Came to Breakfast by Howard Cruse

1956 INTERVIEW:

JEAN SHEPHERD

NEW YORK has always had its share of treasures... And in the 1950's, one gem was a late-night voice on WOR Radio: a broadcaster named JEAN SHEPHERD.

LISTEN UP, YOU FATHEADS!

"SHEP", as he liked to be called, is known outside of radio for two sizable contributions to pop-culture:

His memoir: "A CHRISTMAS STORY"

RALPHIE!

And as the narrator of "THE CLOWN" by Charles Mingus:

He really knew, NOW!

BUT TO THOUSANDS OF IMPRESSIONABLE MINDS, he was the late-night voice with an uncanny gift to communicate DIRECTLY to them, and them ALONE!

Hello, FRIEND

He urged his listeners to place their radios outside of their windows, and turn up the volume. Then he'd yell:

YOU FILTHY PRAGMATISTS! I'm going TO GET YOU!

what?

AND OCCASIONALLY, these antics would introduce fellow listeners to one another. Like this couple:

Hey, come on up to Apartment 8 I love Shep, too!

The Village Voice was such a fan of Shepherd, they briefly gave him a column, "THE NIGHT PEOPLE"

The Night People
by JEAN SHEPHERD

That Sort of Night

FROM the moment I saw the crowd lined up outside the Sheridan and winding around the block, just standing there in the sleet and rain, I knew this was a real thing. As I walked along 13th Street across from the movie house, I

by Ethan Persoff and Scott Marshall | More comics at http://www.ep.tc/john-wilcock

Shepherd's best stunt was his literary HOAX:

"I, LIBERTINE"

Realizing BEST-SELLER LISTS (at the time) were determined by both sales figures *and* NUMBER OF REQUESTS, Shepherd urged his listeners to enter bookstores and ask for a title that did not exist. This non-existent book eventually became a "Best Seller"!

Specifics of the book were invented on the air: The title? "I, LIBERTINE" ... was written? ... by "Fred Ewing" *and* ... "IT HAD BEEN BANNED IN BOSTON!" ... Demand rose. Eventually Ballantine gave Shep a BOOK DEAL, with the fake book (once written & printed) selling a million copies.

"I, LIBERTINE" was ghost written by Theodore Sturgeon, from an outline by Shepherd.

A great sourpuss photo of author "Frederick R. Ewing" is on the back cover. It's a photo of Shep.

I INTERVIEWED SHEPHERD in 1956, right after Ballantine had bought the book from him. For obvious reasons, he was in a terrific mood.

Say, John, **ANOTHER DRINK?** (gulp!)

At one point Shep popped all the remaining ice of his empty scotch glass into his mouth. And began to analyze the contents (melted ice) with great focus:

Is something the matter?

IT'S THIS **ICE**, JOHN I'd say...

Yes? Are you okay?

I'd say it's gotta be...

1954 FRIGIDAIRE... **... FROM ONE OF THE REAR TRAYS!**

My entire life I've never forgotten that AWFUL JOKE!

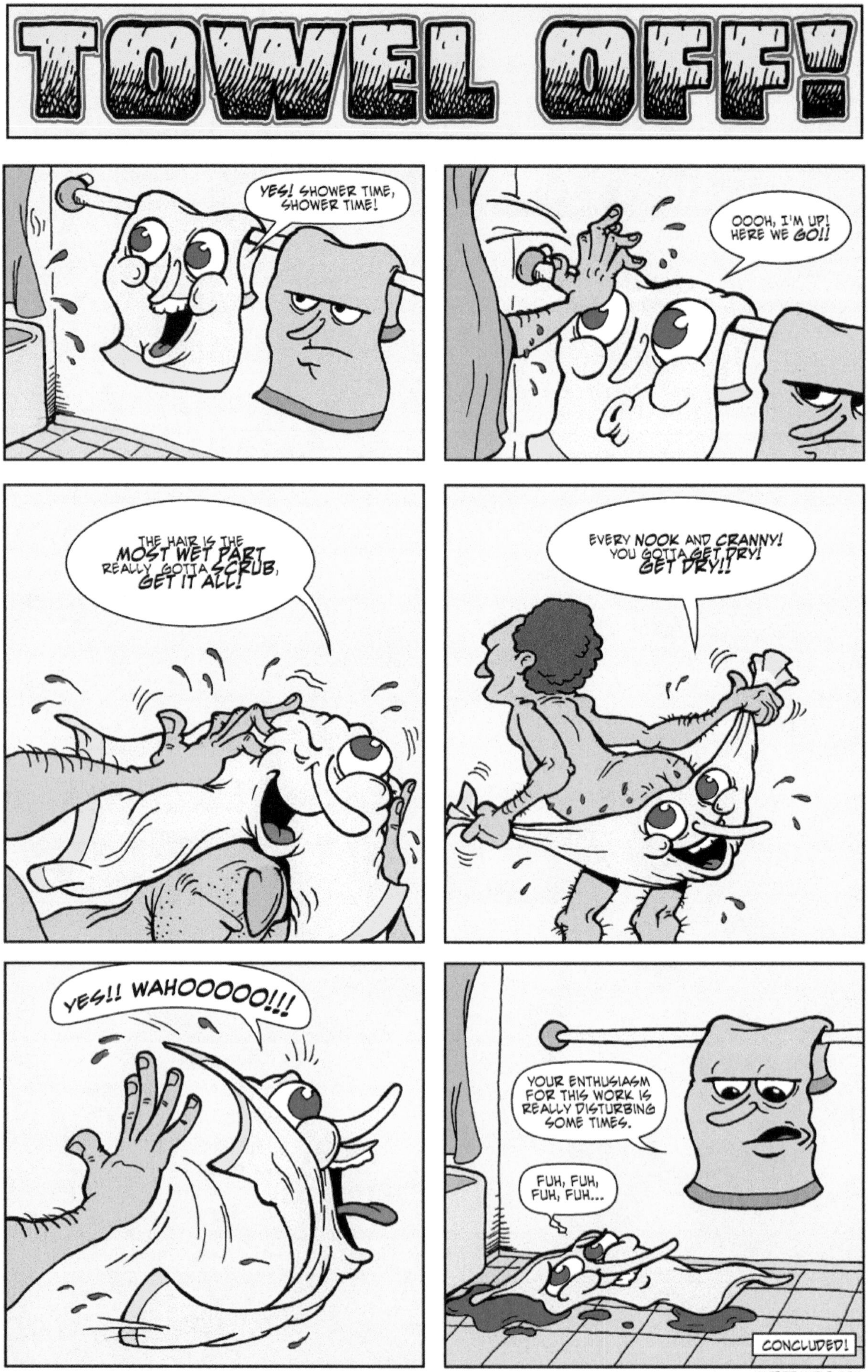
TOWEL OFF!
YES! SHOWER TIME, SHOWER TIME!
OOOH, I'M UP! HERE WE GO!!
THE HAIR IS THE MOST WET PART REALLY GOTTA SCRUB, GET IT ALL!
EVERY NOOK AND CRANNY! YOU GOTTA GET DRY! GET DRY!!
YES!! WAHOOOOO!!!
YOUR ENTHUSIASM FOR THIS WORK IS REALLY DISTURBING SOME TIMES.
FUH, FUH, FUH, FUH...
CONCLUDED!
NATEBRAMBLE.COM

The Diary of Merrill Markoe : Actual Excerpts

I KNOW ITS GROOVY HERE AND ALL
BUT THE SMOKE IS KILLING MY EYES.
AND SOMEONE JUST STUCK THEIR HAND UP
MY DRESS... WOULD IT BUM YOU OUT
TOO MUCH IF WE LEFT SOON?

LIKE NOW?

The ACID TEST

Jan.8.1966
Went into San Francisco to the Filmore
Auditorium to see the Ken Kesey Acid Test.
There were wild people dancing strange.
Blinking lights, Batman projected on a wall,
phosphorescent paint all over everyone,
gold balloons, flying saucers, a huge piece
of sheet metal with a thousand people
banging on it, home movies of Ken Kesey,
huge bags of popcorn, pot everywhere and
a band called The Warlocks playing really
loud. But the most amazing thing:
        I SAW BOB! BOB! BOB!
Truth is I STILL LOVE HIM...

One day we
will get
back
together.
I KNOW IT.

I WAS AT THE THRIFT STORE WHEN I SAW THE TEENAGE HIPSTER.

COOL SHIRT! YOU GONNA BUY THAT?

HUH?

BEVERLY VISTA CONFLICT MANAGER

HE DIDN'T SAY IT. HE DIDN'T HAVE TO. I COULD SEE THE THOUGHT BALLOON OVER HIS HEAD,

NOT IF **YOU** WANT IT.

IT'S YOURS.

UH... THANKS.

BEVERLY VISTA CONFLICT MANAGER

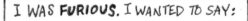

I WAS **FURIOUS**. I WANTED TO SAY:

LISSEN, BUDDY! I WAS A PUNK BEFORE YOU WERE BORN!

BUT OF COURSE, I DIDN'T. DO YOU KNOW HOW **OLD** THAT MAKES YOU SOUND?

I DID ENOUGH DEPRAVED THINGS FOR SEVERAL LIFETIMES, SONNY!

BAD AS I WANNA BE!

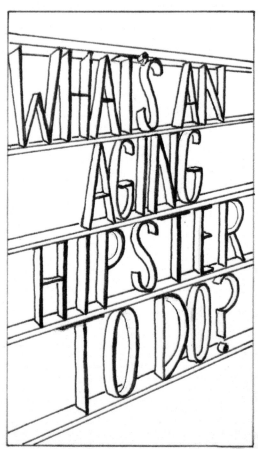

WHAT'S AN AGING HIPSTER TO DO?

DESPERATION MUST BE AVOIDED AT ALL COSTS. CASE IN POINT: MY HIGH SCHOOL POLY SCI TEACHER, MR. CONROY.

CALL ME JERRY!

ALL HIS LECTURES WERE LEFT-WING HARANGUES.

COME THE REVOLUTION, THE WHITE MAN WILL PAY.

UM, MR. CONROY?

JERRY!

JERRY, DOESN'T THAT MEAN YOU?

LIKE BY 1974 ANY OF US CARED...

MAYBE HE SENSED HE WASN'T GETTING THROUGH TO US. ONE MONDAY MORNING HE POINTED TO A SORE ON HIS MOUTH.

SEE THAT, MAN?

BURNED MY LIP ON A ROACH.

HOW TO PUT THIS?

I DON'T WANT TO BE LIKE MR. CONROY!!

SURE, YOUR FRIENDS **TRY** TO REASSURE YOU...

OH, **PLEASE.** AREN'T YOU **ALREADY** HIP?

AREN'T YOU PAST CARING?

AREN'T YOU **BOTH** OLD TOO?

WHAT'S THE ALTERNATIVE?

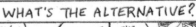

IF YOU WIN TODAY... ...I'LL LET YOU PUT THAT KID ROCK STICKER ON THE MINIVAN!

SOCCER MOM

I'M FURIOUS AT YOU KIDS! WHAT DO YOU MEAN YOU CAN'T TELL?

BOTOXED-AND-ENHANCED MOM

YOU TELL MARIA I SAID **NO MAS** TV!

CORPORATE MOM

I SAID STOP BEGGING! YOU DONE HAD 3 DAQUIRIS ALREADY!

GONE-TO-HELL MOM

ONCE YOU BECOME A PARENT, THE ONLY TIME YOU SEE THE YOUNG-AND-HIP IS AT THE MARKET:

FISH STICKS AND JUICE BOXES.

YOUNG-AND-HIP M.R.E.'s

HERE'S WHAT I WANT THEM TO THINK:

WOW, I CAN'T **WAIT** TO GET THAT OLD!

HERE'S WHAT I **DON'T** WANT THEM TO THINK:

SOMEONE SHOULD PUT HER ON AN ICE FLOE AND PUSH IT OUT TO SEA **RIGHT** NOW...

BUT WHEN MY SON SAYS HE WANTS TO SEE A DOCUMENTARY ABOUT JOE STRUMMER, I FLY INTO A PANIC. WHAT TO WEAR?

A TATTERED 1950's HOUSEDRESS?

(TRIBUTE TO EXENE CERVENKA)

STRIPED TOP AND CAPRIS?

THE UR-BOHO LOOK

THE HOLY GRAIL?

THE BLACK LEATHER JACKET

WANTING TO NOT TRY TOO HARD, I FINALLY SETTLE ON THE CLOAK OF INVISIBILITY:

A BLACK T-SHIRT AND BLACK PANTS

ON THE WAY INTO THE MOVIE, I CATCH A GLIMPSE OF MY REFLECTION.

NOW PL

I LOOK LIKE JIM JARMUSCH WITH A FAT ASS...

I CAN'T BELIEVE I HAVE TO SEE THIS MOVIE WITH MY MOM...

BEVERLY VISTA

I'VE MADE UP MY MIND: WE'RE BOTH PUNKS, IN OUR OWN WAY.

CLASSIFIEDS

MULTIVERSEROS
Do you speak spanish? No? That's too bad. You are missing a great site to talk about comics, films, books, toys and other funny stuff. **www.multiverseros.com** (all the way from Uruguay).

MONTANA'S HARDEST WORKING KITCH ARTIST
At Goodwerks Creative, Marla Goodman designs communications for education, non-profits and the arts. Her fine art documents the lives of existentially troubled dolls, invites unexpected guests into motel paintings and features "Polly Vinyl," a street performer who plays the Theremin along with records. **www.etsy.com/shop/Kitschatorium** She also posts cartoons at **tepidandoversteeped.com**

VETERINARIANS REPORT THAT
6 out of 7 pets prefer Other People Exist zine as their cage liner (among those who specify a preference). Issue #45 will be softer than ever! When I think of the looks on your pets' snouts/beaks/ muzzles, I know the work I do matters. **K. A. Polzin**

WEEKLY SIGNALS WEEKLY REVIEW
with Nathan Callahan and Mike Kaspar. "A cheerfully unhinged recollection of current events." Streaming live on KUCI.org, broadcasting on 88.9 fm, Orange County, CA. Fridays at 8 am PST. Podcasting at **weeklysignals.com**

SEX DRUGS & COMIC BOOKS
Want a mystery novel with LSD freakouts, Ayn Rand devotees, obscure superheroes, frightening gay conversion therapy and zombies on the Upper East Side of NYC? If you don't, I'm f**ked because I wrote one. It's called **BLUE FIRE** and you can buy it here: **http://amzn.com/B01B8TA7BS**

HELLO!
Just because I'm not published in this issue doesn't mean I can't "publish" something "in" this issue. In other words, please enjoy this important article about improving your life without resorting to anything foolish like effort. **http://bitly/homespunwisdom**

HOT GLUE SCHTICK
The fatal car wreck at the intersection of humor and DIY — **www.hotglueschtick.com.**

THE VIRTUAL MEMORIES SHOW
What's the best books-art-comics-culture interview podcast you've never listened to? Discover The Virtual Memories Show at **www.chimeraobscura.com/vm/podcast-archive**

BOB4PREZ.COM
You've heard about BOB! the Presidential Atheist - now see for yourself! America's Most Sincere Politician. Caucus over at bob4prez.com for a heavy dose of politics, atheism and fun! And FREE amazing campaign buttons… really! Now.

POP ART!
Art for the child at heart. **BrianNash.net**

YALE. AT ONCE A TRADITION, A
company of scholars, a society of friends, a cabal of freemasons. Or at least it used to be. The Bull Report is here to fix that. Announcing Yale's only satirical news show: The Bull Report. **youtube.com/c/thebullreport**

UNICORN BOOTY WANTS YOU
…to read some of the most outrageously fun news, pop culture, and opinions on the web! **Unicorn Booty** serves up original news, film, TV, art, sports, fashion, travel and other weird wonders from around the world. Check us out at **unicornbooty.com.**

LOOKING FOR:
a much longer phone number. Willing to pay top $$$. For more info, please call Richard Burgauer at 1-(309)-82

ALL-STAR COMEDY AUDIOSERIES "RUNAWAY BRAINS"
Jeopardy! champ Ken Jennings and IBM Supercomputer Watson must go on the lam, and contend with hackers, Freemasons, TED talks, aliens, and the International Gay Jewish Lizard Conspiracy! "Weird Al" Yankovic, Mayim Bialik, Michael Ian Black and more star in this miniseries on **Howl.fm.**

FIXING THE FENG SHUI IN MY SHORTS
A year of brainsick tweets from a naive idiot (**www.amazon.com/Fixing-Feng-Shui-Shorts-ebook/dp/B00BAD2YBY**) by Dan Burt. He is writer & creator of **CaptainCanard.com**, an experiment in demented wit, deranged absurdity, and odd humor. Contact Dan at **danburt@gmail.com**. Follow him on Twitter **@danburt**

WHO IS EVELYN WANE?

TODAY IN FAKE HISTORY
Find out what happened today in history. Or did it. todayinfakehistory.tumblr.com

MAGAZINEPARODY.COM, a blog documenting the history of its namesake -- and newspaper parodies, too -- will go live in early June. If the subject matter interests you, check it out; the author has been collecting the damn things for over 50 years.

A UNIQUE GIFT FOR A GOOD CHILD
Give a print of a page from the children's classic, Cloudy With a Chance of Meatballs, signed to the child of your choice by the illustrator. Three scenes available: Tomato Tornado, The Breakfast Tree and Ralph's Roofless Restaurant. Archival paper, 12" x 10.5", appetizing color. $250+ shipping. Contact: **barrettuws@gmail.com**

WWW.SPADERACING.COM
Do you like Nascar? No? Oh, um...well, everybody likes comedy, right? Well, check out **www.spaderacing.com** and play along – you can ignore all the racing stuff and just laugh at the jokes!

WE'RE BOTH GIRAFFES?
We're Both Giraffes is an improv duo based out of Oakland, in California's almost sufferable East Bay. They have a friend who used to be a docent, and she used references like Don DeLillo, the Muppets, and international finance concerns when describing the duo. Find them on the web.

"BEING A GOOD"
person demands a small bit of selfishness, otherwise, how would you survive?"

HAVE YOU TRULY WITNESSED THE WEST?
The Pacific Northwest is home to some of the most beautiful sites in our country. The region spans numerous waters, mountains, and bizarre cultural trends. To keep up with the spectacular visual images, go to **witnessthewest.com**

FUN BUSTIN' PODCAST
Follow your mysterious ambassadors of fun and positivity each week as they discover another infomercial, another meaning for pop songs, and several other third things on **Fun Bustin'**, found on iTunes or any other podcast catcher and **www.funbustin.com**

SEX!
Now that I have your attention, wanna read some poetry? Ah, your attention is wandering. Come back. **SEX! SEX!** I know what you're thinking: poetry's boring, opaque and about uninteresting subjects, like gardenias and the potato famine. (**SEX! SEX!**) Mine aren't. The Morning I Married The Sky on Amazon.

THE KILLING TREE
Part funny. Part serious. Part cynical. All intelligent. J.D. Smith's fourth collection of poetry, from Finishing Line Press. Advance praise and ordering information available at: **http://tinyurl.com/htsj7vq**

"KING CUTS" FILM DIRECTOR SCULPTURES DEBUT MAY 14-JUNE 11 2016
Pop artist Mike Leavitt sculpts Scorsese, Lynch, Kubrick, Tarantino and more. Wood carvings combine the directors' likeness with movie references. Spielberg is E.T. James Cameron is Terminator Avatar. Tim Burton is Beetlejuice Scissorhand Batman. Jonathan LeVine Gallery, New York, **http://MikeLeavittArt.com/info/gmail.com.**

Eagle Eye #1

When our own D.Watson submitted this cartoon, Mike loved it. Perhaps too much — Watson said it came to him in dream state and could not be sure whether he had seen it before. So we are turning to you: Send the artist, publication and date of publication to Eagleeye@americanbystander.org. Anyone who provides an exact match will receive $25 smackeroos.

"My wife! And my best friend!"

Interested in placing an ad? Email **classifieds@americanbystander.org**. The American Bystander reserves the right to reject any ad for any reason. We do not guarantee the quality of the items being sold, or the accuracy of the information provided. Ads are provided directly by sellers and are not verified.

PENALTY BOX: THE SCREENPLAY!
Nicholl quarterfinalist and ScreenCraft semifinalist Penalty Box needs a good Hollywood home. Slap Shot meets The Hangover told from the ref's perspective. Minor league hockey hilarity as our protagonist tries to make the jump to the NHL – unless his antics both on and off the ice stand in the way. Contact: route9scripts@yahoo.com

At Ben Bass and Beyond, all opinions are 20% off. "Our white sales are slave auctions!"™ Find coupons and jokes @BenBassBeyond and thanks for supporting The American Bystander.

WATCH ME YELL AT PUPPIES
If you love to hate Dance Moms, where a cruel woman yells at emotionally fragile children, then you'll love **DOG MOMS**. Go to bit.ly/dogmoms to see the web series that is Dance Moms + Dogs = horribleness you can't stop watching.

BRAD ADVICE – A NEW COMEDY WEB SERIES!
The rich and famous flock to public speaking "expert" Brad Johnston for his well-meaning but hilariously bad advice. See all five Season 1 episodes at bradadvice.com!

ONCE AGAIN INTO THE WILD BLUE (YONDER?)
We have sent our names into space and we have left tracks all over the internet. So . . .now in print! **Hal, Lenny, Nate** and **Barbara Schloss.**

THE TANK
My first feature I co-wrote will be in theatres via Open Road later this year (THE TANK). Keep your eyeballs out for it. http://www.imdb.com/title/tt3529344/ xo Nicky Hawthorne

YE OLDE NEWS – A COMEDY/HISTORY WEB SERIES
Ye Olde News is a 3 – 5 minute weekly satirical web series that highlights historical events of the past presented in the conceit of modern media/news. This series examines real historical events in a comedic way. Created by Jennifer Vally.

www.youtube.com/channel/UCIEbE71u6Df1xwu-eOw8NR0w

I LOVE MAKING BEET CHIPS
I love it so much that if you come to my apartment I will make some for you. I am not, to my knowledge, a serial killer. @tinyrevolution.

BOOZE MOVIES: THE 100 PROOF FILM GUIDE
Alcohol – the fabric of film history is soggy with the stuff. Read reviews, news, and features from the world of soused cinema at BOOZE-MOVIES.COM, the Internet's leading resource on alcohol-related film.

SQUID MARINE
A manual paddle for pontoon boats and/or a manual bow-thruster for sail boats. Go to www.squidmarine.com to get additional information and to see the video.

INSPIRING CURIOSITY, scientific literacy and environmental stewardship through hands-on learning in the dunes.
duneslearningcenter.org

PITH & VINEGAR
A collection of dark and humorous poetry written and illustrated by Tim Hodge. Generously funded through Kickstarter! baldmelon.storenvy.com/

ARE YOU BORING? I CAN HELP.
I'm a fast, flexible, fun and funny (copy)writer and editor now accepting commissions and collaborations. I specialize in bringing a light (some might say wry or witty) touch to even the driest topics. See my work at wrytstuff.blogspot.com/ or contact TheWrytStuff@gmail.com.

THE INTERPRETATION OF CAKES
www.allantegg.com.au/

AT LONG LAST!!!
A straight white man giving freely of his opinions on culture.
www.fuchsonfilm.com

HEY GRAFXCOWGIRL!
Happy Valentine's Day! Happy Engagement Day! Happy Mother's Day! Happy Anniversary! Happy Birthday! Merry Christmas! Baby, you're the greatest! Love you mulchly! OXOX, Stuart

FREELANCE VENGEANCE
And there came a day, a day unlike any other, when Earth's mightiest heroes found themselves united against a common threat! jeff.muskus@gmail.com

COUPON FOR 50% OFF the next issue of American Bystander!
Simply cut this coupon out, and send it along with a check for $25 to Sachin Medhekar. Response time may vary.

WANTED: MURDERER
I'm looking for someone to kill me please, inquiries: @ZackBornstein on Twitter & Instagram

POW! BAM! COMICS STILL FOR KIDS (AS WELL)
Hey, kids: comics! Check out recommendations for some of the most gripping, compelling recent non-fiction graphic novels for teen readers at bit.ly/graphicnonfic – stories so good, and characters so interesting, that you won't care that they're real.

WRITER WHO WRITE!
Miller's Compendium of Timeless Tools for the Modern Writer is a mind-expanding reference e-book. 1000 years of writing resources. Narrative devices, story structures, character techniques all in one clickable, flowable e-thing. Did we mention vintage graphics? tinyurl.com/q2bcvul

DISCOVER AMERICA
Explore the wilderness through the eyes of J. Beckett Boone - a man who joined the Lewis and Clark expedition because he had nothing better to do. www.lewisandclarkandboone.com.

https://www.youtube.com/c/LouisethePython
Living the Die Life
bucket list road trip travel Spoonie style seeks comical intern

THE BEYONDOPHONIC ACTION HOUR WITH YOUR HOST TOTHAR!
To improve quality of life, your DJ pal Tothar spins exotic pop and high-fidelity curiosities from his obsessive record collection, sixty minutes per week. The Beyondophonic Action Hour streams on LuxuriaMusic.com Internet Radio on Sundays 7:00 pm Pacific/10:00 pm Eastern. Downloadable podcasts available starting on Mondays, too!

HAVE WHAT IT TAKES TO BE A GOOBER DRIVER?
Avoid World's Largest Peanuts envy. Navigate to offbeat tourist sights with the leaders for 30 years— RoadsideAmerica.com. Free e-subscription to Sightings. Easy sign-up. RoadsideAmerica.com/newsletter

REMEMBER, UNLESS you force your child to watch SCHOOL OF ROCK on NICKELODEON (and then make then see it again on DVR, and yet again online) they WILL grow up to be horrible people.

HEY ANNA KENDRICK!
If you happen to be reading this, will you go out with me? - Anthony Cusumano

WEGWAY.WORDPRESS.COM
This blog is not funny. It's somewhat engaging I suppose, but that's about it. Of course, that all depends on what interests you. For the most part though, amusing is too strong a word. Schopenhauer, on the other hand, could be funny - Hegel, never. This blog is better than Hegel.

RENAISSANCE MAN (read: tech-savvy non-programmer without portfolio) looking for worthy (read: bill-paying at a minimum) endeavor. All-around good guy, playful (puzzles, social gaming, stage, in traffic) to a fault (read: not yet productively solving the world's problems in spare time). Write: blanket@puzzlers.org, facebook.com/apple-jack1963 - Jack (of all trades, mastering TBD)

A DEAF DOG doesn't care how loudly you blast "Darling Nikki" through your car's speakers. I highly recommend adopting one. Of course, a deaf dog won't hear your cries if you fall down a well, but you're smarter than that, aren't you, Timmy? Speak! for the Unspoken- http://speakfortheunspoken.com/

SNOW ANGEL IS HERE!
In the tradition of The Tick and Venture Brothers comes this all-new hilarious full-color graphic novel about SNOW ANGEL, the newest tween superhero! From American Bystander contributor and Eisner nominee DAVID CHELSEA, this massive Dark Horse comic is fun for all ages (except, oddly, 37)! Available at your local bookstore, or email dchelsea@comcast.com to learn how you can receive a signed copy! GUARANTEED MERMAID FREE!

AN ILLUSTRATED ZARATHUSTRA
Hilarity ensues as excerpts and epigrams from Nietzsche's timeless classic comes to life in this madcap comic-strip-style dub version. Embrace your Fate and read it online at: ScottMarshall.org

BOOKS, POSTCARDS, ORIGINAL ART
By Rick Geary, available exclusively at www.rickgeary.com. I also take commissions.

WANT TO GET UP ON THE LATEST SLANG?
Tired of not knowing what the kids are tweeting about? Sick of watching Beyonce videos with only partial comprehension? Then subscribe to Slangin Out–the hot new podcast where each episode teaches you a slang word and how to use it in five minutes or less. Visit Slanginout.com or view us on iTunes. It's the Rosetta Stone for Slang. And it's lit.

"KING CUTS" FILM DIRECTOR SCULPTURES DEBUT MAY 14-JUNE 11 2016
Pop artist Mike Leavitt sculpts Scorsese, Lynch, Kubrick, Tarantino and more. Wood carvings combine the directors' likeness with movie references. Spielberg is E.T. James Cameron is Terminator Avatar. Tim Burton is Beetlejuice Scissorhand Batman. Jonathan LeVine Gallery, New York, http://MikeLeavittArt.com/info/gmail.com.

FREE LUNCH!! NO BALONEY!
Attention all hungry cartoonists passing through Chicago: **Contact Jonathan Plotkin** Editorial Cartoonist & Illustrator Minister of Ways and Means NCIS Chicago Chapter Spontoonist@gmail.com spontoonist.com

COMEDIC DUO-LOGUE

J	U	G		W	A	T	T		S	U	B	U	R	B
O	N	O		A	V	E	R		U	T	E	R	U	S
C	C	S		Y	O	R	E		C	A	N	N	E	S
A	L	L	E	N	W	R	E	N	C	H				
S	E	I	N	E		O	T	O	E		B	U	O	Y
T	A	N	G		R	O	V	E		E	Z	R	A	
A	R	G	U	E		S	P	A	D	E	W	O	R	K
		L	E	S				S	K	I				
M	A	Y	F	L	O	W	E	R		G	L	A	S	S
G	L	E	E		L	O	V	E		D	A	L	I	
S	E	N	D		V	O	I	D		H	E	M	A	N
			B	A	L	L	B	E	A	R	I	N	G	
Z	A	G	R	E	B		E	O	N	S		L	D	L
E	N	D	A	L	L		S	N	I	P		N	E	E
N	I	P	P	L	E		T	E	D	S		E	R	S

© 2016

On Sale Now

Friends of **Bystander** *Tom Connor and Jim Downey, creators of the hilarious* **Is Martha Stuart Living?** *and other parodies, are back with* **President Trump: Parody** *from Grand Central Publishing. Buy one now, while you still can.*

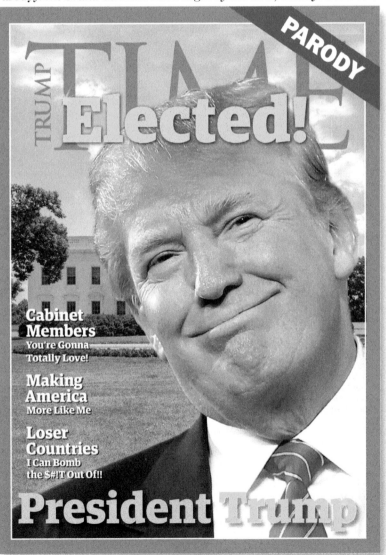

Two Condoms and a Shoelace.

To Joey Green, they're a life vest.

Last-Minute SURVIVAL SECRETS

JOEY GREEN

128 INGENIOUS TIPS

TO ENDURE THE COMING APOCALYPSE AND OTHER MINOR INCONVENIENCES

The Department of Homeland Security advises all citizens to develop an Emergency Preparedness Plan, along with a Disaster Supply Kit . . . but seriously, who has the time?

Don't panic—it's Joey Green to the rescue! *Last-Minute Survival Secrets* contains more than a hundred ingenious survival tips that may sound quirky at first but really do work. You'll discover how to escape perilous situations using common household products, like how to . . .

- Prevent heatstroke with a disposable diaper
- Remove cactus spines with Elmer's glue
- Start a campfire with potato chips
- Build a raft with a 60 empty soda bottles
- Defend yourself from biological attack with a bra
- Assemble a torch with tampons
- And much, much more!

Joey Green, the guru of offbeat uses for everyday products, is back with a new book, ***Last-Minute Survival Secrets: 128 Ingenious Tips to Endure the Coming Apocalypse and Other Minor Inconveniences***—the perfect resource for armchair survivalists, budding MacGyvers, and adventurists on a budget. **www.joeygreen.com**

CHICAGO REVIEW PRESS

BY MATT MATERA & ALAN GOLDBERG

CROSSWORD #1: COMIC DUO-LOGUE

In case of emergency, check page 121

ACROSS

1. Archie's friend, decapitated?
4. Steamy Scot?
8. What a Stepford Wife calls home
14. She definitely might have broken up the Beatles
15. Synonym of 5-Down
16. Starter home?
17. Includes in the vital e-mail chain about proper conference room sign-up procedures
18. Days of old
19. Where "Barton Fink" won the Palme d'Or
20. George Burns: "Say goodnight, Gracie, before you throw a further ___ in our plans"
23. Moliere's river
24. Midwestern tribe that speaks Chiwere
25. Bobbing ocean marker
29. Pootie ___
30. W advisor nicknamed "Turd Blossom"
31. Vox founder Klein
32. Debate, as about the properties of European versus African swallows
34. Chris Farley: "Buh-bye, David, I know you have to return to your ___ and stop hanging out"
36. WKRP news director Nessman
38. Pole's ending, or pole's beginning?
39. Mike Nichols: "I bent down to smell your ___, Elaine, and I got squirted by water!"
45. Churches like it when it's stained
49. Jane Lynch sitcom that charted many hits
50. "A temporary insanity curable by marriage," per Ambrose Bierce
51. Painter who, like Einstein, proved that time bends
52. Button you shouldn't hit on that draft e-mail to your ex
53. Word written on canceled checks
54. Alter ego of Prince Adam (and nemesis of Skeletor)
55. Desi Arnaz: "Your ___ is a little unsteady after all that Vitameatavegamin, Lucy"
57. Croatia's capital
61. Length of time it takes an Uber to arrive in the rain, seemingly
62. "Bad" cholesterol initialism
63. Ultimate significance
64. Cut quickly
65. Word less comonly used between married and maiden names these days
66. Janet Jackson feature revealed by a wardrobe malfunction
67. "Bill and ___ Bogus Journey"
68. Hosp. trauma centers

DOWN

1. Lady Oedipus should *not* have slept with
2. Like a lapsed Scientologist?
3. "I love those cupcakes like McAdams loves ___"
4. "Party on, ___"
5. Synonym of 15-Across
6. Holy ones may often sin
7. Good place for a clubhouse, bad place for a cradle
8. Makes it
9. Where marriage was once unequal
10. Nickname for Obi-Wan, apparently
11. Repository for many ashes
12. Deeply regret
13. Some STEM degrees
21. "When You Are ___ in Flames" (David Sedaris book)
22. Explosion on a white dwarf star
25. Sleazy producer's advice to "Girls Gone Tame"?
26. Emmy winner Aduba
27. Yossarian's tentmate in "Catch-22"
28. Himalayan ox
33. Shrieking creature in "The Princess Bride"
35. Heart test, briefly
37. Like this puzzle, we hope
39. Booker T's backing band
40. Potent pub potable
41. Japanese currency
42. One black sheep can give you three bags of it
43. Most diabolical
44. "Come and Get Your Love" band
46. Christopher Robin's father
47. Verbally assail without justification
48. Swingin' ___
54. Locations for padlocks
55. Ma, before a famous break-up?
56. Geraint's wife, in Tennyson
57. Extremely calm
58. DiFranco who sang "up up up up up up"
59. National econ. statistic
60. You might enjoy a good one or try to beat a bad one

CPSIA information can be obtained
at www.ICGtesting.com
Printed in the USA
LVOW05s1913031116
511241LV00003B/5/P